SECONDHAND SMOKE

SECONDHAND

PATTY FRIEDMANN

smoke

A NOVEL

COUNTERPOINT
WASHINGTON, D.C.
NEW YORK, N.Y.

A cataloging-in-publication record for this book is available from the
Library of Congress.

ISBN 1-58243-217-1

FIRST PRINTING

Text design by Trish Wilkinson

COUNTERPOINT
387 Park Avenue South
New York, NY 10016-8810

Counterpoint is a member of the Perseus Books Group

10 9 8 7 6 5 4 3 2 1

For Rabbi Thomas J. Friedmann,
also known as my little brother Tommy
and
In Memoriam
Andrew Christopher McInrale, Ph. D.
1974–2002

You are, all of you in this community, brothers. But when god fashioned you, he added gold in the composition of those of you who are qualified to be Rulers (which is why their prestige is greatest); he put silver in the Auxiliaries, and iron and bronze in the farmers and other workers. Now since you are all of the same stock, though your children will commonly resemble their parents, occasionally a silver child will be born of golden parents, or a golden child of silver parents, and so on.

Plato, The Republic

1

Jerusha

I'M GOING TO HOSE DOWN THAT ANGELA. I'VE WANTED TO DO IT since the day her mama brought her home from the hospital forty-two years ago. I was expecting then myself, slept on my back in ninety degrees and no breeze, and my baby was going to come out looking like that little frog next door with the poker-straight Orlon Woolworth's-doll hair and flat black eyes if I had to listen to it scream one more night. Now I'm up all night thinking about Woodrow dying, and if I hear *Girl you a fine motherfucker won't you back that azz up*, with all that boom bass and colored men hollering and Angela's Styrofoam-squeak voice come from her house one more time, I'll lose patience. I don't know why a white woman would listen to that, but I didn't understand Elvis, either.

I used to try to lose my temper only when Woodrow was out the house. Now he's never out the house unless I'm with him. I don't wish him dead, but there's a limit to how long I can hold my breath like this.

I stand on the front porch and holler out her name, but she doesn't hear me. She has the cheap hair and dead-looking frog eyes that she came with at birth, but she's lost a lot of that fuzz in her ears that picks up sound, with all the racket she's made for forty-two years. "Angela Puglia! There is a man dying in here," I call out, so everybody else in the neighborhood will know what's going on even if she doesn't. But we live across from the Valence Street Cemetery, and we don't have as many living neighbors within earshot as your regular household. The only person who hears me is Woodrow, who's known for ten hours that he is not going to get any better.

"Oh. That's. A good one," Woodrow says, coming up slowly behind me, clutching at the low furniture, sofa arms and my writing desk, ready to pitch forward. He ought to stay put, but this is not the day to tell him that. He looks me in the face, and he has a good smile. Then he cries like a baby. The doctor said he was going to be *friable*—that was his word—and I nodded my head though it sounded disgusting, like something I'd say about a slab of bologna, but when I got home I called Wilson, who knows everything, and he said it means crumbly, and feelings can be crumbly. I told Wilson, "Don't talk down to me." Woodrow is friable, all right, he's been laughing and crying all evening. He put *Gone with the Wind* in the VCR, and when Scarlett held up that turnip anybody with nothing but pure clean brain in his skull would've dropped his jaw and held his breath, but Woodrow laughed so hard he almost flipped over in his chair.

I tell him come on, and he leans on me with what might be gratefulness, and I lower him onto the settee in the den we made from the dining room after the children moved out. I look up Angela's phone number in the book, because I do not make a habit of calling Angela. She is so bad that I would be calling her every day if I didn't keep myself from doing it, but tonight is different; Woodrow deserves peace, in case he wants any. She is listed under her daddy's name. Her daddy died first, and her mama kept his name in the book, like somebody was going to go through the white pages and find the name Hazel and think it would be fun to call her and scare her. Now she's dead, too, and it is the same number that's been ringing in that house for forty-four years. I dial, and I get a recording that says, "The number you have reached is not in service at this time," which everybody in all the United States knows means *The fool you are trying to reach is not paying her bill at this time.*

I head for the kitchen door, and Woodrow tries to talk. I haven't been able to make out most of what he says for weeks now. That's why I was sure this was nothing but a stroke. He got so numb on the left side of his face that he chewed up his cheek when he ate: you could look inside his mouth with a flashlight and see tatters of flesh, like what floats in the pickled-pigs'-feet jar and makes me sad to look at it in the corner grocery. I have to put all his food in the Osterizer now, take it all the way through chop-grate-grind-stir-puree, first five gears of a truck going downhill, and quit there, at least for the time being. He may have to put me through whip-mix-blend-frappe-liquefy before it's all over, and I'll do it, but turning the back end of a cow into something a man can drink through a straw is sickening.

I get up close to him. He puts out a couple of sentences with no vowels, and I tell him, "Sorry, you got to say that again," and now he bawls. I don't know why he wants to ramble on. Woodrow is a man of few words, everybody says that. "Just little words, slow, come on Woodrow," I say.

"Don't. Tell."

"Angela bothering you?" The sound from her cheap speakers is shaking the house harder than an RTA bus. He nods his head, and he's wobbly at it, the way an uncooked egg is when you spin it. "Then I *got* to tell, you know you can't shake up Angela with anything less than death and destruction."

"Tell her. 'Struction," he says, pleased with himself. I wish he would start losing his sense.

"Look, Angela's never remembered anything for more than the time it takes for her to fall asleep." It's true. That girl tried doing her studies for a few weeks when she was in tenth grade, and she'd come over here the night before a test and memorize all her geometry proofs, and damned if she didn't forget it all before first period over at McMain High School. "Mama says I got a brain like a sieve," she'd tell us, proud as she could be, and soon she was shooting hookey twice a week again. Woodrow shrugs, a good shrug on his right side.

"You want to close the windows?" I say. I say this because Woodrow will say no. Woodrow only closes the windows in this house in December, January, and February, like it's 1940 when there was no air-conditioning and no colored boys fearless enough to climb into a person's house and leave him for dead. He shakes his head no, the yolk sloshing around in its shell again.

"You do what you want. Ru." Clear as a bell, like a call from across the ocean for that split second when the static dies down. Woodrow called me from Subic Bay twice.

I head out into the backyard, and the noise is louder. Angela lives in a shotgun house, and she uses the last room before her kitchen as her bedroom. The screen door that opens onto her little steps is stuck open, and the wood door must be open, too, because music and light pour out onto her grass. It is April, and she has nothing but knee-high crabgrass and yellow dandelions and the biggest clover flowers from fence to fence. Rats are going to be dancing around over there before June if she doesn't sweet-talk some man into hacking through there with a machete soon.

Her boy sits on the steps, blowing bubbles. It is two o'clock in the morning on a weekday, and he is out there blowing bubbles like there's some kind of sunshine that they're going to float up into. He keeps aiming in my direction, and the bubbles keep popping in my pittosporum, which has been filling up my yard with its honeysuckly smell for a week or so now. The pittosporum grows along the property line, and it knows better than to cross over into Angela's yard, where it will wither and die. On my side it is getting full enough to need beating back, and I am going to have to get out Woodrow's pruning shears and learn some new things soon. I like letting him be important. I expect I will feel pretty bad the first time I'm the one out here making that *chunk-chunk* sound.

"You know what time of night it is?" I say to the boy. He nods up and down, blows and misses and hits the bubble ring so two little streams of bubbles come out in a row. Then, like he knows what I'm going to say next, he turns to face me. "Where's Angela?" I say.

"She gots company." This boy must be in about third grade now, and I bet he weighs a hundred pounds, full of bad food as his mama keeps him. *Gots.* I tell him there's a man dying in my house, to get his mama out here. Please. In case Woodrow is listening. His eyes get big with interest. Dead people will get a child's interest. And dying people run a close second. "Angela don't know much about CPR," he says. He's already hefted his blubbery little body up toward the top step, imagining himself on *Trauma,* I guess.

"The man's not dying fast, he's dying slow. Though that music is speeding things up considerably."

"I like the Beatles," he says, and stops now that there is no emergency. "Angela and me fight about it all the time. Well, *discuss,*" he says, catching himself with what is probably one of only two lessons his mama has given him in his life. "We're in this elevator downtown, see, and they're playing 'Long and

Winding Road,' and Angela says, 'You just watch, you're going to be riding in an elevator twenty years from now, and you're going to be hearing Master P, I mean it.'"

"Get her out here," I say. "Please." I'm glad I have low blood pressure.

He trudges back into the house, bowlegged and leading with his messy blond head like some cowboy sidekick. He's out in less time than it could take to reason with a normal person. "She says give her twenty minutes."

"And not twenty-one, either, I mean it," I tell him. I want to say something *else*, and I stomp back into my house, check the clock over the stove, and then I pace, front to back, checking the stove clock on each pass. In this house no two clocks have agreed ever since Coca-Cola quit sponsoring that number you could call for the exact time and temperature. Cox Cable has its own time on the converter box, another time on the Channel Four schedule, and neither one agrees with the stopwatch on *60 Minutes*. I pick a clock and go by it; I could never bake otherwise. Nineteen minutes, and I holler out my bedroom window into the alley, "One more minute, Angela." Twenty-one minutes, and I still hear jungle drums.

I head for the back door again, and poor Woodrow follows me, shuffles and doesn't say a word. I turn and look at him propping himself on the jamb and looking hopeful, like I'm going to save him from something worse than Angela.

The boy is still on the steps, trying to blow bubbles, but he's low on soap the way he's dipping so deep and frantically into his little bottle. "Tell Angela to get out here," I say, and I pick up the hosepipe, turn on the water as far as it'll go, so the thing is full and ready, put my finger on the nozzle trigger, and point it at him. He moves as fast as a fat boy can, and I want to holler, "Hey, I'm not after *you*."

He pops his head out the door, like a cowboy hat on a stick, winces, waits for a hit. "Angela says she told you twenty minutes." The music gets louder. "*Angela* says that," he says like he's apologizing. He pulls his head back in fast.

I drag the hosepipe down the alley. I think I hear Woodrow say, "No, Ru," but this is a big effort, with the hose having sat out all winter tangling up on itself, so I pay no attention. I don't want kinks, and I have to flip and jerk, but I get it down the alley as far as Angela's room. I can't see in. Shotgun houses sit on brick pilings like little legs running down the side, so all the pipes are exposed under the floorboards and can burst in a freeze; half the things about shotgun houses make no sense. I want to see what I'm doing. I may be sixty-seven years old, but I'm nimble as hell when I put my mind to it, and I scale the side fence holding that nozzle like I'm as good as a young boy, and now I can see right into Angela's room. She is buck naked, her skin as yellow as a dead woman's, her titties droopy and brown the way they get if you don't suckle your babies, and a greasy little man is standing by her with his pecker pointed at the ceiling, and everything is covered with dirty clothes and Domino's pizza boxes, and I let that water rip. Wide open, full throttle, soaking everything in about five seconds. I keep away from whatever is plugged in. Not because I've read about people peeing on the subway tracks and getting electrocuted in New York City, but because I don't want to be mean. Whatever Angela did to get herself a twenty-one-inch television and a CD player and a portable telephone, she's not going to want to have to go through all that again. Though what Angela does to get fancy things involves lying on her back for the right man with the right money. I figure Angela doesn't like sex any better than I do. She's not picky enough about her boyfriends to like it.

Angela jumps up and down, screams like she's being flayed with a switch off the bamboo clump like her mama used to use. Some water dribbles down my arm; it is good and cold, the way it comes out of the pipes all the way into June. The man's pecker has shrunk to the size of a kumquat. "You fucking old bitch," Angela screams at me. I ease up on the nozzle, and she looks at me expecting something, and I squeeze that trigger until the water is coming out like a laser that'll cut through anything, and I aim right at her navel, give her one long blast, then lower myself down on the chain-link fence nice as you please. The volume on the music goes up, and I hear the man holler, "You're going to electrocute yourself, you stupid cunt," and then he and Angela laugh like there's no tomorrow. The music cuts off, and their laughs come down to little giggles, in turns, and just before I get back to the end of the alley I hear Angela holler out her window, "You think you got even, Mizz Bailey, but you did me one big favor." The window slams shut, and I can hear that man laughing, all muffled, and I wish I could go back with that laser of water and sting her all over, guggle to zatch, but for Woodrow's sake I won't try to do it tonight. It'll be worth waiting to get even with her after Woodrow dies. I'll need to then. I wind up the hosepipe, and it's easy now that it's full as a tick.

Woodrow is standing in the middle of the yard, not holding on to anything, his arms out at his sides like he's walking a tightrope. The boy is at the fence, and his arms, too, are out at his sides, like he's wishing with his whole body that Woodrow will be able to keep on standing up. "I'm watching him," the boy says to me. "I'm watching him."

2

Wilson

ALL I KNOW ABOUT MY FATHER COMES FROM MY MOTHER'S anecdotes in which he was a bit player. She was so preoccupied with pretending that she comes from refined people that her stories about the Bailey line focused heavily on meanness and lightly on struggles. My mother's litany never changed by more than a word or two. "Your Uncle George," she would say—usually in public, in crowds; her specialty was Carnival parades, because my father's brother George lived within a block of the parade route but never let us park in his driveway—"he never left his mama's house except to go to maybe fifth grade, though he was sitting in the back row of the fifth grade when he was six-two and shaving. So what's your Grandma Bailey do? She fixes pork chops for your Uncle George when your daddy's picking collard greens off the neutral ground like a nigger, and your Uncle George sits on her front porch farting and smoking her cigarettes right up until she dies."

She would look around at the crowd, which was layered black and white like geologic strata, daring anyone to look back with anything but fascination. The marching-band drums would be too far off in the distance to drown her out; she had an audience three-deep in every direction. "She leaves him all her money," she would say to whatever nearby person matched her most closely demographically. "And that poor Woodrow, he lies and goes into the Marines when he's sixteen, sends home half his pay, soon as he's out drops in on that woman every Sunday. With flowers every time, you believe it? Woodrow's tripping over that retarded brother of his, bringing his mama fresh flowers when I'm pregnant and I never even got a half-dead daisy in my life, and one day the old woman keels over with a stroke, and damned if George doesn't stand over her until she quits breathing, like she's some goldfish jumped out the bowl. She leaves every penny to George, twelve thousand dollars and that house on Carondelet Street, and Woodrow's still putting flowers on her grave. That's trashy behavior. Louisiana's got laws so you don't mess over your own children, got to be a good reason for that, and what's Mrs. Bailey do but make up her own laws. Serves George right, one day that porch is going to fall off that house, and that old bastard'll be sitting in the yard in a pile of rubble looking surprised."

"Father went into the Marines?" I would ask, as if that were the only salient fact. I did not know what it meant when the clusters of Tulane boys, no more than five years older than myself, soon would be screaming "cannon fodder" as each military formation passed in the parade. I imagined my father in a smart uniform. He had a uniform when he worked as the security guard at the vault of the Whitney Bank downtown on St. Charles Avenue for twenty years, too, but that sort of uniform is more serious, less romantic. "What was he supposed to do?" my mother would say to no one in particular. "The old woman didn't feed him. Sixteen years old; it was that or jail. And don't go calling him *Father*. Father, sheesh."

When the hospice worker tells my mother that my father will not live more than a few weeks, I arrange for a teaching assistant to cover my classes and prepare to fly down to New Orleans. Barbara is annoyed that I am leaving on an open-ended ticket. "You went to Kenya, and I could stand over the sink and say, 'Well, I only have to wash the dinner dishes eight more times, and then he'll be back,' that I could stand, but *this*, Jesus, Wilson, maybe I should come along." Barbara sometimes forgets that she no longer *needs* my presence to be able to take care of herself.

"Have you considered paper plates?" I say, and I cock my head to the side to show that I am trying to mollify her; Barbara often cannot tell when I am joking.

She scowls anyway. "Please don't come back with that crazy woman in tow."

"Listen, my father is dying."

"That's what I'm afraid of," she says without looking me in the eye.

The queer thing about brain-stem tumor is that it eats away at all functions, but it leaves fear and knowledge completely intact. The only distortion comes from pain and humiliation. My father used to be a happy-bellied little man, half a head shorter than his brother George, whom Mother compares to a dinosaur, "shaking the ground, with a brain the size of a raisin. Not that your daddy has any particular brain, either, at least not when it comes to fighting back." My father never has smoked. He rarely talks, as if he sees all emissions into the

air as foul and tainting, and he holds back any puffs and eructa-
tions he can. He has mostly gray hair, but he always slicked it
up with brilliantine so it seemed darker.

Now he lies in the bed, hair dry and blowzy like a lonely
Barbary macaque's, spindly arms and a sunken chest hoisted
up out of the bedclothes, the rest of him almost flattened into
the mattress. "Help me, Wilson," he says when I walk in for the
first time.

"What you need?" Auxiliary verbs are to be avoided con-
sciously in my father's presence. It drives Barbara crazy, hearing
my side of phone conversations, dropped final consonants,
double negatives, even an occasional ain't. "You're condescend-
ing to your father," she says.

"You think my father is trash," I say.

"I take it back," she says. "Given the way you talk to your
mother."

"Got to help me. Son." He whimpers, then wails piteously
and, put off by his weakness, I push the disappointment down
deep inside myself for another time.

I look around for an easy solution, a glass of water. "You
thirsty?" His eyes open wide, as if saying, *Don't you know nothing?* It seems he has slipped down too far to be comfortable,
and I take his shoulders gently, try to tug him up a bit, and he
howls, "No, no, no, no, *no.*" I want this to be as if I have walked
in on someone else's newborn baby. For a newborn baby, failing to find a solution, I would back out of the room, wait for
another person to come along. But my father will have memory, judgment, for a few more days, or perhaps for eternity,
though I doubt it. "Okay, okay, sorry," I say. He never has fussed
at me before. I want to close my eyes, be a small child again,
start having a father who has some benevolent scolding in him.
I would like to have learned something from him, even if it is

nothing more than whether he has had anything on his mind, ever, yes or no. As far as I know, he is going to forget everything in a few days, and in so doing forgive everything, but I am going to remember the smells and failures of the next week or two, and I want to go back to Chicago having given a fine performance, with no mistakes, no moments to explode in the middle of quiet dreams, waking me with regret.

"You got to help. They're going. To kill me. I was fine." He inhales as deeply as he can, his chest rattling as if he has been crying for hours. "She takes me to the. Hospital. I'm going to die. If you. Don't do something. You got to make them. Stop. I got too much. To do." By now he is screaming, sending out powerful noise from a body that does not have an ounce of fat or muscle left on it. I find the strength reassuring somehow.

My mother appears in the doorway. "Don't pay him any attention, he's been talking like that for days. Doctor says he thinks he's hurting and he's not, his brain's pulling tricks on him." I ask her what she is giving him for pain, talking over him but catching his eye; I think I see only the vaguest interest in his expression. "I told you, he only *thinks* he's in pain."

"Well, if you *thought* you were in pain, wouldn't you want somebody to do something about it?" I am trying to be gentle, not to attack her with what I know about psychogenic suffering; it only would make her furious.

"If the doctor told me it was only my imagination, I'd *believe* him, Wilson," she says, walking out of the room, convinced as always that having a Ph.D. makes me a limited, foolish man.

I bring him a Tylenol No. 4 that I find in the bathroom; my mother has a full bottle, a prescription given to her by her dentist. I imagine she had a root canal, that the dentist told her to expect ghost pains, and she filled the prescription because she was obedient to real doctors; she went home to unbearable nerve twinges in her jaw, laughing because they weren't real. I hand him the tablet, proffer a glass of water, and both fall from his hands onto the bed. "Don't call her," he whispers, and I mop up the mess with a bath towel, tapping at his bones under the covers. "Got to powder it," he says. "Can't swallow nothing." At that he lets half of what I put into his mouth dribble down his chin, and I crush him another pill.

The analgesic effect is almost immediate, perhaps in his head after all; he loosens the knots in his poor muscles, lets out a trembling sigh, and falls asleep. Only his shallow breathing assures me that I have not put him out of his misery like an old dog.

I sit at his bedside, holding his hand, figuring that as long as he is silent my mother and her bitterness and her killing cloud of smoke will stay on the other side of the door. His hand is covered with bruises the color of dark plums, and the skin is soft, even around the thick arthritic knuckles, as if he were a wealthy, idle old woman, rather than a frightened little man who, before he became sick, spent all his days in the shed attached to the back of the house fashioning crude wood trucks and diminutive cradles for my children, coming inside to face Mother and her hissing friend Gloretta only long enough to eat and wash the dishes in a sink full of warm, soothing water. I suppose that I have not held his hand since I was four, when my mother told me that now I was a man, that I did not kiss or cry unless I was still a little baby. Night has not fallen when he wakens, but only because the days are becoming longer, approaching the summer solstice that he is not going to see anyway.

"Longest day of the year," he said to me when I was seven. We were sitting on the front stoop, looking out at the cemetery, not sure where exactly the setting sun was—there is no east or west in New Orleans, only uptown and downtown, lake side and river side—but satisfied to see a screaming orange sky somewhere out toward the lake. "Longest day of the year was three weeks ago," Mother said. She was standing over us, waiting for an opening.

"No, Ru, longest day of the year's June twenty-first."

"Longest day of the year's the one after school lets out," she crowed triumphantly, then turned on her heel and went back into the house.

"Father," I say, forgetting myself, when his eyes come half open. I see refusal in his expression. "Hey, Pop," I say.

"Knew you were here," he says. "Going to be all right. Now you're here." His words are slurred and soft, but I can understand what he is saying.

"I will stay long as I have to," I tell him, letting myself believe for a moment that perhaps that promise will stretch out over years, a small sacrifice for saving him.

"She wants this over with."

"Aw, no," I say, though I know it is true. Since I was told that he is not going to improve, I have kept a private countdown of the days he probably has left, wanting to reach the end and find out whether I am going to survive that sort of loss at all. My mother, of course, already has learned that her mother and father can die and she will keep on living, a little bit angrier, a little more put-upon; she even has reached the passage in life when her friends can die off and she can get past the funeral with no more than "I told that old fool she should've gone to the doctor." I have a quiet, terrible fascination with the possibility that my father will die and I never will eat or sleep again. I want to arrive at the day after, to eat a sandwich and fall into a well-earned sleep and know that all is going to be all right. Everyone dies, and with that reassurance I almost am accustomed to the concept of my own death, but knowing that everyone experiences another's death, too, does me no good.

"Was getting better. Was walking, you know." I did not know that. "Yeh. Takes me over. To Baptist. They give me this. Radiation. I get better. It was fine." He takes in a ragged breath as if gauging whether he can get out a few dozen syllables with enough air. "Didn't feel nothing. Say it's going to burn hell out me. But it's fine. So what's she do? Tells them stop. Going to give me." He runs out of breath, inhales so quickly that he coughs, takes in another raspy supply of air. I never have seen him so determined. "Going to give me cancer or something. What you think I already got, I want to know?"

"Mother!" I call out.

She comes running, and her collection of plates from the Bradford Exchange on the bedroom wall clatters in the feeble wire hangers. She walks in carrying the chihuahua she bought when my father first was diagnosed. Its eyes are even larger than usual. Mother sees my father sitting halfway up with his eyes open, and she says, "Jesus, Wilson, you make me think somebody's died in here."

"See?" my father says.

"Why did they stop the radiation treatments?" I say.

She motions me out into the hall, as if she has been wanting such a dramatic moment for the entire duration of her marriage. "They couldn't do any more," she whispers. I ask her why not. "Because a human can take just so much, and then his brain fries or something," she says.

"His brain is not doing particularly well *without* it."

"Look, Mr. Ph.D., you can sit up in Chicago and call me up once a week and act like you know what's going on, but you haven't been here, and you don't know, and you can't come marching into town and think just because you're supposed to be some kind of expert that you're going to fix something that can't be fixed."

I am beginning to be a little hopeful. I know I should have come down weeks ago. I should have come down at Christmas, when my father was getting flimsy and disoriented and Mother blithely diagnosed him as having had a mild stroke and put him to bed until his headaches were so terrible that he sobbed at night and kept her awake. Then two months ago she took him to Baptist, and it was too late. "Take him to New York," I said calmly over the phone, having learned long ago that most problems can be solved by leaving the Deep South. "You are too conceited for words," my mother said, and I called the doctors at Baptist, who assured me that they knew everything that was going on in New York, and that they were going to give him exactly the same treatment as he would get in New York, and that I had better get ready for him to die. Only then did I come down, and only for two days at that, just long enough to look at him sitting up in a chair and to fool myself because he was fat and intact.

"Sometimes it helps to have a fresh point of view," I say.

"Yeah, you're fresh, all right," my mother says. "You're so fresh I'd paddle your backside if you weren't bigger than me." She gives me a playful swat on my rump, and I feel terribly sad for her.

"Tell me something," I say to my father when I go back to sit with him.

He shrugs, and I can see his collarbone make a *grand jeté* under his pajama top. "What you want. To know. You don't already know?"

"No, I mean talk to me." I am imagining a huge store-house of rich tales and well-earned aphorisms that he has been hoarding since before I was born; all along he has been waiting for the right question. "What is on your mind?"

"Your sister's on my mind."

"Well, that is a major surprise," I say, smiling. I have not been jealous of Zib in her entire life. She was born before I had a sense of what was happening to me; we are fourteen months apart, a startling fact when I think of how vocal my mother has been about my father's heavy-handed ways in the bedroom. Father always has favored Zib, but he has been awkward about loving, and I have been content to let her get most of it.

"Don't make fun. Wilson."

"Christ, Pop, she is coming. Zib has a stressful job, and she does not have a whole lot of maneuverability this time of year; you know how those things go." Zib is an assistant manager at a Winn-Dixie, and my mother does not respect her title any more than she does mine, but my father talks to Zib as if she is a corporate executive. He used to pull words like *personnel* and *profits* out of some odd whorl of his undamaged brain. I plan to become a consummate liar over the coming days—to him, to myself, to my mother, perhaps even to my sister. My father never has known stress in his life, as far as I know. He had the world's most soporific job, sitting in a quiet antechamber with only the sounds of downtown air-conditioning and boxes full of secret treasures. He came home at night, beat and fussy from the silence, turned off the only window unit in the house, even in dead summer, and sat in front of the television until he fell asleep, pausing only to fetch himself a plate from the dinner table. He could not be interrupted, busy and important, straining for the nuances of *Hogan's Heroes*. He found Colonel Klink and

Sergeant Schultz sympathetic, and sometimes I thought there were things about him that I did not want to know.

I ache for time, not regretting all the stretches squandered in his silence over the years but wanting excellent fragments of time now. He and I have hundreds of thousands of fractions of seconds left, and it is possible to find meaning in a moment. I have to believe that, or I never could lecture students, going on and on for fifty minutes at a time, telling them that the female human is more evolved than the male, with the danger of never making sense to even one of them, not for a second. "I don't got. Enough time," my father says, and I think he is reading my mind for the first time. "Too much. I need to do."

"There stuff you want me to do for you?" I say. I still am holding his hand, and not feeling uncomfortable, not sensing that it is another man's hand.

He pulls his hand away and begins pounding his loose, arthritic fists on his hipbones. He is sobbing. "Where's your sister?" he says. I tell him I do not know. And I do not: Mother phoned Zib at the same time she called me. "Caught her on the first try, too," she said. "She goes completely crazy on the phone, telling me she can't cope with this. I tell her think about her daddy, and she says, 'Hey, nobody's thinking about me.' The man spoiled her so bad she stunk, and now he's not going to be slipping her five-dollar bills every time she turns around, she can't cope. Shit, truth is, it'd be a lot better if she never showed up."

I tell him I am sure Zib is on her way, that she has to get off work, remember, that she has to drive to New Orleans, that a lot can go wrong. Especially with Zib, but I refrain from saying that.

"*She'd* know what I'm talking about," he wails.

"Sorry," I say.

We sit in silence for a while, long enough for me to take in the size of the room, the tenuous hold it seems to me he always has had on survival. Mother never worked; Father paid off the mortgage ten years early by sending all he saved on utilities each month directly to Fidelity Homestead. Never mind that a 4 percent interest rate and a Schedule A deduction would have given me and Zib a few frills to take for granted, a few chances to be like the others at school; Father had to be locked into ownership. My mother has kept her rage in check all these years as her end of the bargain, believing him after a while that they should take no risks, letting his frugality rule her because she is convinced he knows what he is doing. I am certain he has made plans for her future, but I want to hear specifics. Account balances, insurance-policy premiums, maintenance contracts. I will not ask, but I want to know that Mother is not coming up on the Panama Limited in a cloud of smoke to choke all the joy out of my family.

"You want to know something, Wilson?" he says softly, perfectly. Tears are streaming down his cheeks, diffused by sparse silver stubble. Mother shaves him only every three days now, and she says, "I don't know why I bother at that."

"Sure," I say, willing to take whatever he says next as extremely important, keeper words.

I lean over, and he speaks in a stage whisper, his breath full of the sweet rot of death. "Never trust nobody," he says.

"I know that," I say, relieved for some queer reason.

Mother walks in. "I could've told him *that*."

"The family motto, *numquam pone fidem in ullum*, put it on the coat of arms," I say, wanting them to laugh, but both give me a hard look, and for a second I am nine years old again, four and a half feet tall, a skinny, sincere boy who has asked his parents why all the music they listen to has words.

I detach, like a poor patch of wallpaper that hangs loyally over its spot, loose and covering nothing. I float away, as I once did, a boy happily swimming on strains of classical music, funny polysyllables, and fully realized analyses. "A far way from *semper fi,* huh?" I say quietly to my father. He rolls as far as he can to his side, which is not far, just enough to moan with pain and avoid looking at me. "I don't know what you're talking about," my mother says. "But that's usually what you want, anyway."

"'Always faithful'; 'Never trust anyone': there is a big difference," I say.

At that my father rolls back, grimacing, but with a half-smile in his eyes. "I married Ru. She taught me. Lot more than a drill sergeant," he says. "Huh, Ru."

"Sure, Woodrow," she says.

Each day now, the tumor takes another small hill: comprehensibility and then all speech, single vision and then all sight, awareness of where he is and then who anyone is. It is almost comforting to watch, the day-by-day loss, at such great speed, my father disappearing from himself before he disappears from us. If he were not so terribly afraid, like a dog that has been hit once in the road and waits to be hit again, I think I would be able to go away without nightmares.

With me in the house, Mother stays out of Father's room, moving around noisily to be sure I notice that she continues her routines, dusting furniture on a deathwatch. She offers to do my laundry, and I smile, let her do it. Usually on visits, she launders and packs for me the day I leave, and when I am home, I open my suitcase and out comes the heady barroom smell of stale cigarette smoke, and I ache the way a schoolboy, away from home for the first time, might ache, walking through a department store and catching an evanescent breath of his mother's Chanel No. 5. Barbara used to offer to run everything through the wash, but I would tell her, "No, I can hang them up; they air out after a while. No one ever said I smelled bad when I was a kid." "That's because everyone smelled the same way," she would say, smiling a little tentatively; I suppose I fell in love with her because she once was a woman who never could quite give forth with a feeling until she had checked it out. Her parents, with all their generations of money, also began smoking when each was fourteen, but they quit after they finished raising asthmatic, gray children and decided that they wanted to spend the rest of their lives jetting off to beaches where there are no cigarette butts in the sand.

Mother puts my clothes through the machine, my undershirts, my shorts, socks, the shirts that I ordinarily send to the laundry. The washer and dryer are in her kitchen, and she sits at the old Formica table with the pattern that, when I was a child, reminded me of undercooked scrambled eggs; I pointed that out when Zib was eight, and she made herself vomit on the spot. A cigarette dangles from my mother's mouth, and she coughs constantly and folds my clothes, expertly, never dropping an ash. Her lips are pursed to hold the cigarette, with just the tiniest air hole from which the rage can slip. "You know what he said the week before you came?" she says. "There he was, watching *Gone with the Wind* for the third time in one day—the man is dying, mind you—and I say, 'Jesus, Woodrow, how about giving it a break?' And he says, 'Christ, Ru, I'll be dead inside a week, you can watch anything you goddamn want.' I don't think in all the years we've been married the man's understood one thing I ever said to him."

When I first arrived in New Orleans, I phoned Barbara every night at 8:45, when the children were asleep. After a week she asked each time when I was coming home, as if my father were a research project never reaching completion because I was distracted. "Tell you what, give it another week, I will come home regardless," I said, and she said, "You're not under any pressure here, for Chrissakes, but we do need you here, too," and I called every other day that week, and now it has been four days between calls, two short conversations full of sodden silences. "I want you," I say; "I need you," she says.

For the past two days my father has screamed with the vigor of a very healthy man, deluding me if not the hospice worker, and Mother refuses the morphine. "One more day, one more day," she says, and over the din I scream at her, "For Chrissakes, *now*," and she says, "Tomorrow, I swear; now lay off." I go to bed early, sensing I will be able to sleep through the constant rhythm of the cries, the distant bass of Angela's anger next door. I am grateful for Angela's immutability. Mother has turned on the air-conditioning, closed the windows, now that my father no longer can think about Entergy bills, and she is doubly pleased with herself. As I go to my room, she is standing outside my father's door, tears in her eyes, saying, "Angela thinks she's getting even, and she's not," and then she lets out a sob before she catches herself and tries to smile.

At some moment in the early morning I come out of a doze, and in the house all I can hear is Mother's phlegmy snores in the living-room recliner and a steady, sad, "Sib, Sib," from my father, and I am satisfied that after all Mother is right, that if we wait one more day he will be better; I go back to sleep, and around six my mother comes in, shakes my shoulder, and says as gently as I ever have heard her speak, "It's over. Get up, it's over."

3

Zib

THERE'S ONE MAIN DIFFERENCE BETWEEN MY BROTHER AND me. Wilson's got his name on more kids than I can keep track of. I still can't even get used to the *idea* of a cat. Half the time Mama thinks he's a saint, half the time an asshole. He hops into bed every time a wife of his says, "Wow, Wilson, I'd really like a baby." So he's a saint. And there must be something wrong with *me,* never settling down. She says I'm always trying to be different. Says I used to rent old Katharine Hepburn black-and-white movies to prove something. Mama loves the comics. Wilson's an asshole, though, whenever Mama gets word that one of his kids is getting too much out of life. "He lets them get off with murder; you talked to me like that, I'd've broken your leg off, wrapped it around your neck and choked you to death with it." I say, "Oh, Mama, I can't wait to have kids." She gives me back this look. The "this time I *will* break it off" look.

Lately my current sister-in-law has generally quit trying to be in touch. With my parents *or* me. So Mama gets less ammunition. Barbara used to write prideful letters. One time Connor came tearing through the room hollering, "You are no match for my dark warrior penis!" And Barbara wrote how

Morgan said back, "When you grow up it dries up and falls off, look how wrinkly it is already." Barbara was thrilled. Their daddy was teaching Organic Evolution, and they were acting it out. All Mama heard was that these two kids who were not yet six were talking about penises like they were ingrown hairs. And not with much originality, I wanted to add.

Mama favors Wilson because it's so easy to be furious at him. I figure that's why she has him at the house right now. I could tell when she called with all that business about the hospice worker. She was just being dramatic. She knows when she acts like that Wilson'll come running. And I'll stay as far away as possible.

The phone rings at 6:12 in the morning. I have a digital clock next to my bed with one-inch numbers. I'm nearsighted, and when things happen in the night I want to know when. Gunshots in the night blew out half the glass in my car. I told the police: 12:02 A.M. Mr. Scamardo at the store called at 3:48 A.M. to ask me to open at seven. When he walked in at noon I could say, "You call me at 3:48 in the morning again, I quit."

"Elizabeth?" Mama says. I expect to be hit by a two-by-four. "He's gone, your father's gone."

I don't want to, but I scream. "You can't do this to me. I never got to say good-bye. You've got to be lying. Tell me you're lying. Is Wilson there? Why's Wilson there?"

"You said you couldn't come," Mama says. I think I actually hear sadness in her voice. She has no right. She's there. She could say good-bye.

"You didn't tell me it was a goddamn emergency."

"I told you the hospice worker said it was a matter of days."

No one believes that sort of thing. "You didn't tell Pop that, did you? People have a way of making bad stuff like that come true."

I can tell I just did Mama a favor. I didn't mean to. She's happiest when she's angry. "Listen, you empty-headed twit. These people may be nothing more than a bunch of niggers with a high-school education, but watching people die is their *job*. They tell you: he's stopped eating, it's a matter of days; his heart's slowed down, it's a matter of hours. They don't make that up. You don't have to be a Ph.D. like your brother to tell somebody's not going to get up and tap-dance; even I knew that, for God's sake. You couldn't get off from that thing you call a job before, don't bother now. I just figured you ought to know." Then she hangs up.

I dial her back. "I'm on my way home," I say. Then I hang up on her.

That's another thing different between me and Wilson. I won't go so far as to say Mama has *complete* respect for him. But something like it. He's got a Ph.D. He publishes papers and takes trips to Africa. For her, Africa is not the cradle of civilization. It's the place where black people had no business leaving. Never mind how they got here to begin with. And writing papers for a handful of other Ph.D.s is the square root of shit to Mama. It has to be on television, and high in the Nielsen ratings, to make its mark on the world. Mama respects Wilson's job because it pays him eighty thousand a year. "They want to pay him a young fortune for running his mouth off about stuff that makes no sense at all, let them," she'll say. Especially in front of people like Gloretta Higgins.

Mrs. Higgins has lived down the street forever. She's as good at passing judgment as Mama herself. Or at least Mama thinks she is. My being assistant manager at Winn-Dixie isn't worth mentioning to Gloretta. Except maybe to say, "We give that girl everything she wants, and here she is, over forty years old, and she's a checkout girl in a grocery store, same as I was when I was sixteen." I'll be in the room, and I'll say, "Hey, I'm an assistant manager. I haven't laid my hands on a cantaloupe except to eat one in four years." Mama will roll her eyes toward Gloretta and say, "Her boss is this wop, hires only girls with big titties, Lord knows how Zib got to be a manager— excuse me, *assistant* manager—guess he gets tired of watching her lean over those fruits and vegetables and seeing nothing down her shirt. Huh, Zib?" "Look," I'll say, "I'm not working at the Winn-Dixie as a *career.*"

I call the store at seven. Mr. Scamardo isn't in the office. I tell the bag boy who answers that it's an emergency. It's the beginning of summer. The store is starting to staff up with seventeen-year-olds. All their parents have houses at the beach. They want to make cash for beer. On top of that, Winn-Dixie never cards anyone. So every summer we get a dozen or so green kids who think they can hold a job a few hours a week. They collect a paycheck, cash it. Then they run through one another's lines with twelve-packs of Heineken. The girls don't know any produce but bananas and kiwis. The boys don't know they're supposed to wring out a mop before they splash black soapy water on the floor. Mr. Scamardo likes white children with clean faces and fresh haircuts in the store for the summer crowds. Somehow I manage not to fire any through sheer hatred.

The boy who answers isn't sure he's supposed to go paging the manager. So I get loud and try to breathe. "This is a matter of life and death. I'm the assistant manager. If I don't have Mr. Scamardo on the line in *two* minutes. I will personally come over there. And fire you. Before you ever touch your first paycheck." Mr. Scamardo comes on, out of breath. A fat man who is always red in the face. Though he isn't much older than I am. "My father died," I say.

"Who's this?" he says. Like he'll kill me if I'm not his sister saying *his* father died. I tell him Zib. "What kind of emergency is somebody dying, for God's sake?" he says. "I mean, somebody already being dead. What's my running to the phone going to do to fix that?"

I could cry and make him feel bad. But I can't bring up tears. And I don't want to fake it. "I'll tell you what kind of emergency this is. I'm supposed to close tonight. And every night this week. And I'm leaving town as soon as I hang up this phone." I let it sink in. "You want somebody to cover for me? You've got about eight hours to find her."

I hear nothing. Then, "Didn't your father die once before?"

I laugh so hard I don't think I'm going to stop. "Oh, God, you must think I have one hell of a hangover," I say. I'm still laughing. I replay his words, his deadpan delivery. I choke with more laughter. Punchy laughter, full of good pain.

"If I find out you're lying, you're in serious trouble," he says.

"This isn't something I'd lie about. I'm too superstitious." I tell him I'll bring him a copy of the obituary. He says he thinks that's a good idea. "And by then it'll be too late to send flowers," I say.

"Hey, if your father really did die, I'm sorry."

My eyes fill up with tears. I wish he hadn't said that.

My car is a 1976 Mercedes. I've had it for fifteen years. I'm in New Orleans by noon. I try my key in the front door. It no longer works. Mama has finally put in a deadbolt. I pound on the screen door, and Mama answers. I reach out and put my arms around her. I can feel her freeze up. That doesn't mean she's still angry. Mama always freezes up like that. I have a photo of me with her when I'm about six months old. She's sitting in an armchair. I'm on the tips of her knees. She's holding me around the middle like a trophy she *has* to display to the crowd. She's gritting her teeth. I seem to have just figured out how to sit up straight. Not knowing how displeased Mama looks behind my back, I'm grinning with toothless pride. Mama's never kissed me.

"I told you don't come," she says. "There's nothing for you to do. He's not having a funeral or nothing."

I brush past her. The smell of him is still in the house. The air's thick with cigarette smoke. But Pop started putting Vaseline Intensive Care lotion all over himself months ago. It was when he had nothing to do all day but scratch. The clean, gentle nursery smell is still there. "It took me four and a half hours. Any time, I could've been here in four and a half hours." I speak low, in case there's a ghost.

"For what? To sit over that old man and holler like you're being killed? You want to tell me who needs something like that?"

It's true I didn't hold up well in April. Pop went into the hospital right after they told Mama what was wrong. I stood in the hallway outside his room and cried noisily. The nurses lost their patience. The doctor walked away embarrassed. Mama said she'd slap me if I didn't shut up. Wilson took me out. He bought me a smoothie. I guess he hoped I'd keep my mouth busy with it. But I couldn't swallow. We were sitting at one of those outdoor-café sorts of tables. The umbrella kept off the sun, but not the late-spring heat. I watched the people coming into the smoothie shop, daring them to stare.

"You won't believe what happened," I told him. "Last week I went to a psychic."

He gave me a completely neutral look. I suppose he was getting used to his father dying, too. But I figured men took that kind of news like finding a pet turtle dead. Fascinating, nothing more.

"She said there was only one man in my life. And he was going to die soon. I told her I wasn't dating anybody. You know I'm not dating anybody?"

Wilson shook his head no.

"Anyway, I'm not dating anybody. But she says, 'Well, what I see is that this is the most important man in your life, and you are going to be devastated.' I'm sitting in Florida. Not thinking about Pop. I'm thinking about every man I've ever gone out with. You know, wondering which one was so goddamn special that he's going to come back just in time to fucking die. I can't think of anybody. So I figure she's a big fake. Now we're standing up there at the hospital. And that doctor keeps saying, 'Get ready for him to die.' What a bastard. I feel like throwing up."

He nodded. He took my smoothie. He sipped at it. I knew men weren't affected by death. "Psychics are mutations, Zib. Or maybe we are on the verge of all evolving into psychics, I do not know. But you ought to take some comfort in her having predicted this," he said.

I wanted to dump the smoothie in his purely male intellectual lap. "I don't know what you're talking about. I'm not sure I care, either."

He ignored me. Like a scientist. "Look, all the great religious leaders were physical mutations. Jesus, Mohammed, Zoroaster, Buddha. They already had reached a level to which we all eventually will evolve, unless we self-destruct first. The next stage of evolution is mental, not physical; that is why those people did not fit in. That is why your psychic probably is sitting in some storefront in a strip mall, right?" I nodded. I had an urge to get all wide-eyed and say, "God, Wilson, *you're* psychic." But I didn't. He kept it up. "Our brain chemistry is evolving; one day we will know what is going to happen. Do you like the idea of inevitability?"

"Not today," I said. He didn't get it. "Pop's lying up in that bed. His head's about to explode. *Inevitably*. It's not time for Darwin 101."

"You are not thinking about him, either," he said, pushing my smoothie toward me. "You are thinking that now you are going to pick up the phone and ask for someone to bail you out, and no one is going to answer."

My hand closed into a fist. In front of my face. We both knew I wouldn't hit. I haven't hit him in thirty years. Not since it quit being fun. I broke his nose when he was ten. Mama blamed *him*. Now he grabbed my wrist. Forgetting our rules, I guess. He lowered my arm onto the table. With a lot more ease than I'd've expected in a brainy man.

He walked away. Probably to the bathroom. When Wilson's upset his fussy little spastic colon gets out of control. That's a fact I'd rather not carry around. I'm sure he got the problem the first time Mama turned the garden hose on him.

She said she was going to knock some sense into us. Chasing us like a riot policeman. No expression on her face. She used a wide spray on Wilson and me. But for friends who picked on us, a narrow stinging power-stream. I figured she loved us. She never sprayed Angela. Said that hearing Angela shriek from her mama's bamboo switch at night was almost good enough.

Wilson checked into a hotel that afternoon. Mama kept us away from each other the rest of the two days we were there. Probably it was good for her. Nothing cheers my mother like having a chance to complain about Wilson and me.

"Sorry, Mama," I say. Her hair is mussed. Her eyes are puffy. She's still in her hot-pink housecoat. For the first time she looks to me like somebody's grandmother. As a child I was shy of people's grandmothers. They were going to die any day. I probably was afraid of their brittleness and sadness. Like it was contagious.

"No matter. It's all over anyway," Mama says. "He asked for you right up to the end. He asked for you and I told him you were coming. Truth of the matter, I didn't believe this was the end myself, or I'd never have gone to sleep, and I *would've* called you in a day or so. I mean, he was hollering so loud I figured he was going to outlive *me*."

"You were asleep when he died?"

I had a little finch named Samuel when I was twelve. A Jew-bird, Mama called him. He'd been hanging around the bottom of the cage. Mama said that meant nothing. Only fish went to the bottom when they were sick. I put a lamp next to his cage.

He huddled close to it. Hanging strong on a low perch. I went off to bed. Next morning he was feet-in-the-air. I told my mother I should've sat up with him. She said, "What for, to give him mouth-to-mouth resuscitation? Check this out, Woodrow." My father shambled over to see the dead bird on the bottom of the cage. "What," he said. Mama said, "They sure do die funny, like a gunslinger or something." I took one look at poor Samuel. I laughed myself silly. When I saw a slit of shiny black through the membrane of his eye, I cried. Then I pictured him with his skinny legs in cowboy boots pointing skyward. I laughed again.

"Hey, your father was just as asleep as me when he died," Mama says.

"I was remembering Samuel. He died when I was sleeping."

"Well, your father didn't die with his legs up in the air." She turns and walks away. All proud of herself.

I tiptoe into the bedroom. Maybe I expect him to be there. Alive, having tricked me. Though he's not the type. Maybe I expect to find some clue. A message from him. Except for the bed, the room's just the way it was in April. The bed is unmade on Pop's side. Mama's side is pulled tight. She hasn't slept there in months. I lie down on his side of the bed. It smells of him. It still seems warm. I curl up, close my eyes. I hear nothing, see nothing. I smell the must of him and I start to cry. Quietly. Mama walks in, sees me, backs out. "All right," she says.

I make myself as miserable as I can. Remembering my father. Pop sitting in front of the TV watching old cowboy movies. Nobody watches cowboy movies anymore. But you couldn't tell him that. It all made him happy. The sound of horses' hooves, dozens of horses times four. A cavalry kicking up dust. It did for him what the theme music on *Jeopardy* does for me. I can hear that tocking tune and pretend I'm home from school. Sick and full of hot soup. Pop probably spent his Saturdays in dark, cool picture shows. Eating Milk Duds. Forgetting that outside was the choking wet New Orleans heat. And a family that wasn't sure why he was born. I picture him in detail, right down to his brown fake-leather house slippers. I keep on crying. Pop sending a birthday cake from Gambino's to me at school when I was sixteen. Lemon *doberge* with white icing and pink roses. A big sacrifice for a man who brought a mayonnaise jar filled with pennies to the bank every six months. "Your dad, Zib? Are you hard up or what?" Angela said when she saw the cake. Of course Pop didn't know about that. I see him walking in the front door after work. "Any surprises today?" he is saying. I cry harder. A crude wooden tow truck. With towline made from baling string. Hand-cut paper letters, *CB,* glued on the door. I give my nephew credit. He played with it for hours. Even tangled the cord so badly Pop had to make a new one. In my picture, Connor is standing patiently by Pop's TV chair. He's waiting for a commercial. Fiddling with the string until it's a hopeless mess. Pop looks around proudly; Mama's told Connor to watch out for splinters. I'm the only one there who sees him. He doesn't know I'm there. I sob loudly.

I don't care what Wilson says. Pop hasn't bailed me out since my troubles began costing more than five dollars. Wilson likes to take a chunk of the past and save it in Lucite. Pretending that it holds forever. Pop paid my library fines. As long as the book wasn't overdue more than a week. He gave me money for school pictures. As long as I didn't expect the eight-by-ten with twenty-four wallet-sized. Pop never paid a speeding ticket. Or cosigned a loan. But that's not part of what Wilson remembers.

Wilson slips into the room. He closes the door quickly be-hind himself. But he lets in the smell of Mama's cigarettes. Like someone coming in from outdoors might let in a gust of hot air on a summer day. I say, "Hey."

"Hello," he says. He sits down on the edge of the bed. Folds his hands politely in his lap. He's not the kind who'd pat me on the rump. This is his best, kindest offer. "You ought to go back, you know. If you are smart, you will drink a cup of coffee and go back."

"I ought to do something here." I prop myself up in the bed a little. I look around the room for clues. Really, the house is all Mama's. Pop's just been someone who hung his clothes here and controlled several major appliances. "Though I'll be damned if I know what."

"He is not here. You came to see that for yourself; now you should go home. Mother is looking for somebody to kick around, and I am already here. It is not exactly a circumstance in which a major estate has to be divided up." I ask him if we won't inherit a piece of something. Mama's been crowing about Louisiana law for so long that I figure I know a lot about it. Even if everything I know may be wrong. I'm not expecting a big life change. I'm just curious.

"Well, technically, I think we each own about an eighth of this house, but that is the square root of nothing." I picture the house sliced into eight pieces. Like a one-layer cake in a shal-low pan. I want to own my old room. Which Mama turned into a sewing room the day I left home. I have a sense of power over her. The crazed power only Louisiana laws can give. "Okay," I say, giving him a sad smile.

Angela's boy is on her front porch. Cross-legged and blinking like he's never seen the sun. Around him on the buckling, half-painted boards are what look like a hundred dollars' worth of old Jurassic Park figures. Foot-high dinosaurs, each with a chunk of meat cut out of its flank. Muscular little men in khaki with nets and guns. He's playing with them like a four-year-old girl in a doll corner. High, shrieky voices for the men, growls for the dinosaurs. He's using the accessories the way they're probably shown on the box. "Hey," I say. He looks up, squints in the late sun. "Your father died," he says. I haven't seen this kid since he was a baby. Dustin. Angela decided to name her first baby Dustin in 1979. She sat through *Kramer vs. Kramer* twenty-eight times in the theater. Dustin. Boy *or* girl.

I nod my head. "I'm Zib."

"I know," he says. "Mr. Bailey made me a fire truck once. But don't tell Mrs. Bailey. Okay?"

"She can't exactly holler at him now," I say. I may cry. My eyes haven't recovered from my jag an hour ago. It'd be easy to start up again.

Dustin smiles at me. "Probably she *could* holler at him."

"Where'd Angela get you?" I say. The tears are flowing, but I'm smiling.

He shrugs. Aims a velociraptor at the flesh door on the tyrannosaurus's rib cage. Makes a spit-sloshing, gnashing sound. Shrugs again.

I'm back at my apartment by nightfall. I stay in for four days. Not eating, remembering my dreams. On the fourth day, I get a priority-mail package. Three unused bottles of Vaseline Intensive Care lotion. There's a note. "So you don't dry up. Love, Mama." Pop was hoping to live a lot longer, itching and screaming. I open a bottle. Take in the cream scent. Feel all right for some reason. A clipping has wrapped itself around one of the bottles. It's the shortest obituary I've ever seen.

BAILEY, WOODROW WILSON, SR. On Monday, June 12, at his home.

Beloved husband of Jerusha Ferguson Bailey. Father of Woodrow Wilson Bailey, Jr., and Elizabeth Bailey. Also survived by a brother, George Bailey.

Funeral arrangement incomplete.

I make a photocopy, take it in to Mr. Scamardo. "When was the funeral?" he says. Not unkindly. He flips the paper over like there's something on the back. "Hard to say," I tell him.

4

Jerusha

THEY BOTH BLAME ME FOR KILLING WOODROW. I TELL THAT
to Gloretta, and she says, "Well, Ru, they say when you get a
divorce, the one the kids're still living with, that's the one
they're meanest to." Gloretta watches too much television, and
I tell her that all the time. You can't phone her before eleven or
between three and five, no matter what. Woodrow was pro-
nounced dead during *Live with Regis,* and I didn't dare let her
know until after *Rosie O'Donnell.* By which time Woodrow
was long on his way to the funeral home. That might not mean
much, but it was the last chance anyone had to see him.
Woodrow wanted to be cremated, not for any good reason except he was so cheap he thought he was getting away with
something.

"Chrissakes," I say, "first of all, I didn't divorce him, I killed
him. I mean, they say I killed him. You are getting me totally
mixed up here. And second, it's not exactly like they're living
in this house, eating my food or anything. They're both forty-
some years old. And far as I can tell, they both got the hell out
as soon as they'd figured they'd drained every penny out of
their daddy and me, no looking back."

"Well, they're mad at you," Gloretta says.

"Shit, they're always mad at me. You can't leave your mama unless you're particularly mad at her." Wilson lives in Chicago, well, outside Chicago, in Evanston, where everyone from there that I meet at his house is a professor and knows everything and looks at me like I have three heads. Zib has been in Florida so long I'm surprised she has any skin left. "Well, if how far they go is any indication, your two are *furious*," says Gloretta. What Gloretta neglects to tell you is that her two girls live in walking distance of her house, of course on the good side of St. Charles Avenue, and that practically the only time she ever sees one is if she accidentally bumps into one in KB's. Which has become less and less likely these days, since KB's, which sold out to a chain but nobody cares, had the great idea of being at every major corner on St. Charles, which means the only people who shop there anymore are the ones getting off at the streetcar stops. Colored kids going to Wright Junior High and colored maids going to work on Soniat Street, mostly; just about the only white people that go in there these days are the ones on fixed incomes like Gloretta and the tourists who don't know any better or they'd be in Disney World. The parking lots are empty; if you've got a car, you drive someplace cleaner and cheaper, for Lord's sake.

"I don't think those two of yours are exactly brimming over with love and devotion," I say.

"Nobody asked you, Ru."

When Gloretta gets like that, I generally find some reason to get off the phone, though she knows too much about everything I do for that to be easy. I can't tell her the doorbell's ringing because she knows mine's been broken since 1983, and she also knows my phone's in the back of the house where I can't hear anybody knocking. Not that I'd answer, anyway, especially not that I'd get off the phone to do it. All that's been to my door in quite a while is Jehovah's Witnesses, and never white ones, either. I usually know when they're in the neighborhood, because it's not Sunday and they're walking up and down the street with one or two starched-up little colored kids, looking so important. So I don't move around in the front of the house until I figure they're off the block. Anyway, one time I tried to tell Gloretta that I didn't feel like talking to her right then, and she hung up on me and didn't talk to me for seven months, I counted. So I say, "I got to go to the john, Gloretta; you want me to bring the phone in the john?" and she knows I've got a long enough cord and little enough shame to do it, and she says, "Go, go, I need to get off anyway," a little huffy, but people don't hurt my feelings like that, and I hang up the phone, and I look at it like Gloretta is sitting right inside it, and I say, "You're too sensitive, you old fool," and I feel pretty terrific.

Lest anyone gets the wrong idea, Wilson and Zib are not accusing me of murder. They're not even coming right out and saying I killed Woodrow. They're not like that: that much they have in common. Neither one has said anything direct since I knocked all the disrespect out of them before they were five, and they get disrespect and straight talk completely mixed up. It gets on my nerves. What they both did—and I fully believe each one did it without talking to the other because they generally can't stand each other—they both sent me an article from the *Wall Street Journal*. Well, Wilson sent me the front page of the *Wall Street Journal* with the article circled in black marker so I'd see the banner up top and know how educated he is, and Zib just sent me a raggedy clipping of the same article, with part of one sentence set off in yellow, just in case I didn't get the point. SECONDHAND SMOKE LINKED TO DISEASE. They believe everything they see in print, no matter how stupid it is. First of all, I don't see how I can go through two packs, filter tips but two packs, every day since I was eleven, and never have a sick day in my life, and then Woodrow is supposed to die from a couple of wisps of smoke that already have been through my lungs, thank you very much. And he doesn't even die of lung cancer; he dies of this giant grapefruit in his brain. Woodrow was a man who breathed through his mouth day and night with those big funny bucky teeth that never had a cavity even though they were out in the air all the time. Anything he took in went straight down his windpipe; it didn't go anywhere near his brain. The way I see it, there are too many colleges with too many science majors, and these colleges are sending out all these picky people who have to think about something brand new or they won't have jobs, and they have to forget about common sense very fast. If you believe everything they say, you might as well lie down and die. I pitched both copies in the trash.

Woodrow died June 12, and it's almost October and he's still sitting in a box in the bottom drawer of my dresser. The house is directly across from the Valence Street Cemetery, and I've lived in it since a year after we got married, and I've always said it'd be very nice if whoever went first was buried there so the other one could get over and visit all the time. For about the past twenty years, there's been this fat colored man and what I guess is his wife tending the graves and walkways and little patches of grass. In summer they get a bunch of lazy boys from the archdiocese who pick up grass clippings and pine needles, but otherwise the two of them take care of the whole place by themselves, and sometimes it's not a pretty sight. There've been two floods in recent memory, and both times bones have floated up. I used to walk the dog over there, but after a while I got too nervous about what I was going to see, and I walk him down toward St. Charles Avenue now. He's only a chihuahua, dropping wet rabbit pellets, but it gives me a bit of satisfaction for him to go on those fancy lawns. Anyway, *I* wouldn't have minded being buried in the Valence Street Cemetery, because Woodrow could have gone over there every day or so and raked the gravel on my grave, but he had better plans for himself. Woodrow had to have himself cremated so he can be put in Arlington. The man got about as far as Subic Bay and crab lice during the Korean War, but he's had this idea of having a flag draped over a coffin and a twenty-one-gun salute ever since he watched the Kennedy funeral on TV. I don't know how they're going to work this, since the cardboard box he's in you could cover with a handkerchief, but I don't mess with the dead, and I'm going to take the dog over to Gloretta's, water the yard, get myself a plane ticket if I can find all our money, and take Woodrow up to Arlington. I just need to get both of his children to decide when they are not too busy to give their father a funeral. There's something about seeing him wheeled out of the house and then getting this box back a week later that isn't exactly right. I haven't been inside a church *except* for funerals since Wilson got married the first time. But now I can almost see why people go to church, just so they'll have someplace to go and look at that casket when the time comes and know for sure that somebody in particular has died. For all I know, Woodrow rolled out of here and sent me the box UPS. I certainly haven't looked inside. As tight as Woodrow was, he probably didn't pay to have himself reduced to pure ash. I read in *The Star* about a cut-rate crematorium in California that crammed fifteen bodies in one oven, smashed up the bones with a shot put, then shoveled ashes out of big oil drums with coffee cans: three pounds for a woman, five pounds for a man. There're probably more surprises in that box than you'd find in the Valence Street Cemetery after a hurricane.

I wait until nine o'clock to call Wilson. You'd think that after teaching the same classes for ten years, he'd know his lines by heart, put in his fifteen hours a week lecturing from memory, then go home and relax. Especially when he teaches things like Organic Evolution. I don't know the first thing about Organic Evolution, but I can tell from the name of it that it has nothing to do with fast-breaking news. There are bound to be subjects where finally everything there is to know has been figured out, and Wilson probably teaches half of them. But I can call him up when I assume the rates go down at five, and that girl he's married to now will answer all out of breath and act like I'm crazy to think anyone would be off work at five; she's only home herself because she has this little business set up in the basement of their house so she can ignore her children and pretend she's better than me. I've said in front of her, "There may be some people worse than me, but nobody's better than me," and I think she gets the idea of where I stand, but she still looks awfully satisfied all the time.

"He's not in yet, Jerusha, but he ought to be," she says. That's another thing about her that drives me crazy. Wilson's first wife never called me anything, just waited until I was looking straight at her. She'd call me Gammy to her kids, "Give Gammy a kiss," Jesus! But she couldn't settle on what to call me herself until after the divorce, when she took back her maiden name and started calling me Mrs. Bailey, very polite. So when Wilson up and got married again while he was still asking Woodrow for help with his child support, I said to the girl, "Okay, right off, figure what you're going to call me, and then get used to it." She laughed, not at all nervous I thought, and she said, "So, what are my options?" and I felt like saying, "Well, how about Mrs. Bailey or Mrs. Bailey?" But instead I said, "Well, the first one calls me Mrs. Bailey, and Zib calls me

Mama, and Wilson calls me Mother, and my friends call me Ru." "I don't know my category yet, do I?" she said, as flip as hell I thought, and then she asked me what Ru was for, though lots of people do, thinking about that little Roo in the cartoons or that actress Rue McClanahan on TV. I always say, "R–U, like in Je*ru*sha," and then I sit back and wait for them to say, "That's a beautiful name. Is it Russian?" Even a couple of ministers never heard of it; I'd get a kick out of trying it out on a Jehovah's Witness one day when I have absolutely nothing else to do. The truth is, I was born two weeks late, and finally my mother said to God, "You get this damn baby out of here, I swear I'll give it a religious name," and then I came out about eight hours later. My mother said, "Well, no sense pulling a fast one on God," so she got my father to bring her a Bible, which was no small feat considering they didn't have one, and she closed her eyes, still half asleep from the gas, and she let the Bible fall open. Lucky for her, it fell open to the Old Testament, because there are a lot more women in the Old Testament, the New Testament being the story of a bunch of men who generally didn't fool around. Right in the middle of Second Kings, there was exactly one female, somebody's mother, though that somebody was a king, and that's how I got my name. My father wanted to name me Mildred, so I'm just as happy that's the way things turned out. I am strictly not a Millie type. I am also not a Jerusha type, but Wilson's wife jumped on it as though she'd picked it out herself. "From the Bible, right? I remember: the missionary's wife in *Hawaii*—you ever read *Hawaii*? Her name was Jerusha, I've always loved that name, we'll probably name one of our daughters after you, oh, this is terrific." So far they've got one girl and one boy, and they're named Morgan and Connor. No one ever knows which is which, but I guess she's sobered up considerably since she got married. Her name is Barbara, but I don't call her anything. It's sort of a private joke with myself. "So," I say.

"So, you want him to call you when he comes in?"

"So, how are things?" I don't feel like letting her off so easily.

"Good, good." I can picture her, looking around that big old farmy kitchen, hoping something will make a huge noise so she'll have to excuse herself. I've been there twice, and the best way to describe that kitchen is that everything teeters. She has sweet-potato vines covering practically half the room from a single jar, pots of thyme and basil that she plucks from, an overhead rack of unscoured pots that bump and rattle and look like they're all going to come crashing down any minute, and wooden toys all over the floor; give one of those kids a plastic toy, and it'll have disappeared the next day. The house has three stories plus a basement, with about three times as many rooms as my house, and everyone sits in that kitchen and waits for huge, disastrous noises, I swear. Nothing happens, and I sit and wait, smiling. "Connor is going to start reading any day now," she says finally.

"It's about time," I say. Connor is five and has been in kindergarten two months now. "Wilson picked up the newspaper and started to read 'Dondi' when he wasn't quite three," I say.

"I know." The woman is proud of her husband except when he's my son. "Regression toward the mean," she says after a while.

"Whatever."

She doesn't say anything, and even though I'm paying for the call, I don't mind waiting. "How've you been?" she says finally, and I think she is stifling a yawn.

"Pretty good," I say, and the suggestion of a yawn makes me launch into a full-sized one. It's so big it's trembly.

"You know, it's only been, what, four months? It's all right to feel bad." I count back, just to be sure she's talking about Woodrow and remembering correctly while she's at it.

"Three and a half months," I say.

"If anything happened to Wilson, I don't think I'd ever get over it," she says.

"Wait till you've been married another forty years."

"I imagine it's worse."

"Not really." I'm not in the mood for sympathy, to tell the truth. But I'm not going to tell her that. This is the first she's said about Woodrow since he died. Her parents look like they're both in their fifties and have skinny legs and a tan even in winter; they play golf like it matters, and they live in a Chicago suburb so fancy that the household help is all Polish. The girl isn't going to know a whole lot about death for a long time; I'll cut her slack on that.

"Maybe you're still kind of numb," she says, her voice very soft. "I mean, it was so sudden."

"Are you crazy? You call a man lying around screaming in pain for three months sudden? You want time to stretch out forever, you sit in a house and listen to somebody holler for help, like you can do a thing about it, every day, all day, for *three* months. I almost lost my mind. No, honey, I'm not numb."

"Okay, okay."

"Look," I say after a while, "I just called up to tell Wilson one thing, just tell him one thing. Tell him I am getting to be a nervous wreck with that box sitting in my bottom drawer. Tell him to call up that sister of his, pick a date, let me know, and I'll fly Woodrow up there. Okay?"

"Sure," she says, "I understand." And she actually sounds like she does.

I let the dog out onto the front lawn after I hang up. The street is completely quiet.

Usually this time of night, bands of grinning colored boys come walking by, hammering on each other with drumsticks and talking to each other in loud, happy, challenging voices. I think it's quite fine when there is a lot of noise in the street, because it means no one is trying to sneak and hide and hurt somebody. I don't see anyone for three blocks in either direction, and I wish the grass weren't so wet, and the dog weren't taking such a long time sniffing and wiggling his little butt and making false starts and then sniffing again. "Get a move on, Mealworm," I say, loud enough to surprise him and scare myself a little. All that's out here to hear me are the dead people across the street. He drops a few sweet, tiny turds on the grass, and I pick them up with a Kleenex and carry them back inside and flush them down the toilet.

The house is as quiet as the street, and I hear every small sound: the tic-tac of the dog's nails on the wood floor; water dripping from a clogged gutter at the back, even though it hasn't rained since late morning; the refrigerator kicking on so it can cool a half a jar of mayonnaise, two sticks of margarine, and two jars of blackberry jam that Woodrow didn't live long enough to eat. It takes me a hell of a long time to go to sleep, to tell the truth.

5

Wilson

YESTERDAY I PUT UP THE SHADOW BOXES IN MY OFFICE, AND THIS morning one of the secretaries in the department came in and said, "I wouldn't expect that of *you*." I am sitting here considering whether to take them down. I have just two, but they are large and costly for a small office. The first holds his medals: the Korean campaign, the rifle and pistol marksmanship, the good conduct, the last of which fills me with regret when I look at it. Mother says that all it took was the avoidance of venereal disease, and so it is possible that my father never had sexual relations in his life with anyone but my mother. In the second box are his other souvenirs: the clothing stamp with his name on it, the K-bar combat knife, five brass buttons, his corporal's shoulder patch, and the Tokarev pistol that Mother says he bought in San Diego from someone who made it all the way to Korea and saw death, unlike my father. The woman in the frame shop gave me a look of mild disgust, and that should have been a warning, but I see these as all my father's treasures, not as symbols of anything, except perhaps the wish I once had that I would be the son of a man of ferocity, not in his muscles and blood, but in his eyes. These two boxes are his record, as inaccurate as a biography written by a lover. Men who come in will understand, because even small boys and gay men know one war from another, and so can see this collection as history. It is the women who concern me, coming in and guessing that I myself fought some campaign, breathed in teratogenic chemicals, absorbed the impact of metal, came back proud of myself. Barbara told me to get that crap out of the house, she was not going to let Connor ever see a gun if she could help it. Connor, who stood in the middle of the bathroom when he was three and peed in a circle while making the sound of a semiautomatic.

Fifty percent of all Americans claim to have had a communication from the dead, and I believe those statistics; believe, too, that most of those claims are real, that a barrier has been crossed. These messages are no more the product of wishful thinking than near-death experiences are. But they come to people who seem to have no expectations at the time, and I wonder if I am trying too hard. I am sitting here late at night in a building that is empty even of janitorial staff. I have no window, no lake view; I am difficult for a spirit to reach, if I can judge by the stories of others' encounters—on country roads, in bedrooms with open curtains. I think my father would visit here, where I have his rewards on display, before he would go to my mother, even though she has his remains in a box. I listen, imagining that he will come as a voice, and the phone rings.

"You're there?" Barbara says.

"More or less." My voice shakes, and I realize that the sound of the phone has scared me more than I know.

She asks me whether I know what time it is. She is peckish and tired, but I do not know what time it is, and I am surprised to learn it is 9:30. I have not eaten since eleven, when I had processed turkey on white bread, no mayonnaise, shredded lettuce with a few brown strands, coffee to force it down. My bowels turned to concrete, leaving me nauseated, making me forget food. Without hunger these days, I do not track time well. I tell her I am sorry. "*She* called," Barbara says. "Mother?" I say, knowing that Barbara reserves that tone of voice for only one person. "Mmm-hmm." "Sorry not to have been there to protect you," I say.

"Drop dead, Wilson," she says, and I think she is being good-natured, but I have not been certain for a while now. "*You* have to pick a time for the funeral. I've never heard such bullshit. Usually you kind of work around the dead person's schedule, you know?"

"My mother cannot win for losing," I say. "If she called up here and said, *Wilson, be in Virginia on the twenty-first,* you would be annoyed about *that.*"

Barbara lays New Orleans port vowels on her Chicago ones, creating what is not my mother's accent but nevertheless the world's worst possible delivery of the English language. "'Give me a day's notice and I'll fly him up,' she says. "Like she's got a private plane. That's even *worse.*"

My mother never has flown, as far as I know. My father would have said, "No, Ru," and she would not have flown because, I sense, she would not have known how to book a flight or enrage my father. "Mother does not fly," I say.

"Now she does," Barbara says, and in this split second I have the sickening realization that this is the first time I know absolutely that my mother does not know what she is doing. "We are *not* going to help her," Barbara says, reading my mind. Before I can think of what to say next, she apologizes, and I start to laugh. She asks me what is so funny, and there is petulance in her voice. She was rarely querulous before we married, and back then any time I would sense over the phone that her arms were crossed over her chest I would be afraid that that was going to be our last conversation. She has grown more comfortable being a scold from time to time, and in so doing has lost power over me. "The best defense is a good offense," I say. "That is the *male* credo; I would expect more from you." I think she will be disarmed; Barbara enjoys being married to a man who knows clinically that all women are better than he is. Every spring she comes to my lecture on how the prophets were so spiritually evolved that society had to destroy them. I say that women, being more spiritually keen than men, tend to draw a similar fate, and afterward she always says that she is crushingly in love with me.

"You know, I'm not in the mood for being co-opted right now," she says. "I'm in this house all day, I get these children out, I pick them up, I feed them, I wash them, and I swear you wouldn't know how to find the baby shampoo if someone *paid* you, and then finally it gets quiet, and I'm almost capable of sitting still and maybe falling asleep before one o'clock in the morning, and she calls up and puts a stick in the shit and stirs it up. The least you could do would be to be where I can't find you so I can figure you're having an affair and I can be furious."

"I am sitting here thinking maybe I will hear from my father." I speak softly, for maximum impact.

"When are you going to get over this dead father shit?" she says, and bursts out laughing. I begin to laugh, too, repeat what she said, laugh until I get a catch in my side. "I'm not joking," she says, then laughs again.

I know what she wants to hear; she wants me to be more self-flagellating than any man has a right to be, to say something like, "Oh, Barbara, I have to be honest with you, I have enjoyed walking around looking sensitive and having a reason for everyone to give me attention, and it is hard to give it up." And I am trained to say that when it is the truth.

"You will not believe me, but I hate like hell feeling this way," I say.

"You're milking it, Wilson."

"I am sure that is the way you see it, but. . . "

She begins to scream, a piercing, breath-sucking scream that will waken the children and frighten the neighbors so badly that they will call the police rather than come over to check. She continues for a good half minute, and I am holding the phone away from my ear and struggling for breath for her, and then she inhales, ready to scream again, and I manage to cry, "Stop!" before she lets out one more ear-splitter. "Where are you?" I say.

"Relax. I'm in my darkroom." It is her normal voice, without even a scratch in it. The darkroom is in the basement, a contained space in the middle of the unfinished area under the living room. The previous owners rented to graduate students in the seventies, and the darkroom was then a primal-therapy room. Barbara left the padding on the walls because it blocked out light, even if it also blocked out heat in winter. The real-estate agent said to us, confidentially, "The landlord came over one day to pick up the rent, and he thought a cat was being killed in the basement. Turns out some kid was in there thinking he was going through his mother's birth canal. Sheesh! What'll they think of next?" "Oh," Barbara said, looking overhead at the exposed pipes, "it'd take nothing at all to convert this into a darkroom." "But I have never seen you take a photograph," I said. "You can't buy a house with a space that has no light and *waste* it," she said. "Barbara is Jewish," I said to the agent. Over time I have learned from Barbara's parents that being Jewish means picking one's rules, eating a ham-and-cheese sandwich on Passover one year, then sitting in synagogue with an empty stomach on Yom Kippur the next. It depends on how much they think God and Fate and Mr. Goodman up the block are watching. The real-estate agent did not laugh. Even though her name was Friedlander.

I ask Barbara if she is all right, now that I know I do not have to come running home one step ahead of the EMTs. It is remarkable how quickly I can map out my moves for running out of a room. "No, I'm not all right," she says.

"Look, you are *tired*."

"Don't tell me what I am, Wilson."

I tell her that I am on my way home right now; having planned to leave quickly, I feel a need to do the motions, to stack the papers on my desk, two seconds, to slip into my coat, leave my scarf, it slides to the floor, I pick it up, put it on the coat tree, five seconds, pack my apple back into my briefcase, close it, five seconds, no, wait, the zipper jams, forget it, leave it, adjust the lower left corner of the shadow box over my desk, one second, order, good, my abdominal muscles loosen at the thought, I am ready to turn off the light, the phone rings again. "Give me an hour," Barbara says, "okay?" Her voice is soft, tremulous, almost seductive, but I do not feel even the smallest flicker of sexual interest.

I settle back at my desk, put my feet up, stare at the fluorescent light on the ceiling until it starts sending little translucent worms across my retina. I consider phoning Zib, but this is the time of night when she usually cannot be bothered. She says she has not had a man in a long time, but she must be out looking for one most nights, because she does not pick up her phone, and whoever answers at the Winn-Dixie tells me most times that she has punched out. I never have been to that part of Florida, and I cannot imagine what her life is there. I think the palm trees are as stunted as the ones in New Orleans, and I gather that most of the chain stores are familiar to me, so Zib may have found a place that offers nothing new to her. I will go down there one day, take Connor and Morgan to the beach in the winter, try to do so when I also have Eric and Jessica. I want to find out what kind of furniture my sister buys, having lived in my mother's house with its orange-and-yellow upholstery; I wonder what she sits on these days while she is watching Bergman movies and British comedies. I do not picture Zib embracing discomfort or discomfiture; she happily would use air-conditioning to re-create the bone-chilling temperatures of her film fantasy places, though she might avoid color. Mother claims Zib likes the kind of luxury she can throw away. She is the only person I know with disposable contact lenses, having passed up photorefractive keratotomy because she likes flicking that perfect little piece of plastic into the toilet each evening. I check my watch; only ten minutes since Barbara's call. I am too tired to put my feet down on the floor for anything. I reach for the telephone, but it is past arm's length. I think I will call Zib in the morning. Eight o'clock is fair. I can be up. I fall into a doze, in the light, and I do not waken until morning.

6

Zib

I ANSWER MY PHONE ONLY IN DAYLIGHT NOW. NOT BECAUSE Mama called me right at dawn to say Pop was dead. I'm not the type to get all bent out of shape over a bad experience. I think I'm sending a message. What I do in the dark is *personal.* I don't want intrusions. The only person this message is aimed at is Mr. Scamardo. If it were somebody else, I'd say *Leave me the hell alone.* But Mr. Scamardo's hit some snag in his middle years. If I tried I could probably pinpoint the day. The day his hormones went to his unprotected head. And bubbled around until he quit making sense.

It was mid-August. That's the time of year when no right-thinking person would set foot where I live. Right northwest of the fat squash-shaped part of Florida. Afternoon rains give relief. But up here the sun has no mercy. The spaces are wide and uncovered. And it's too far from the Gulf for the air to move. I can't arrive at work without being soaked with sweat. Even with an air-conditioned car. The top of my head gets so hot in the time it takes to walk from the employees' lot that I think the blood under my scalp will congeal into pudding. Mr.

Scamardo has no hair on the top of his head. I think the heat was too much for him that day.

It was the middle of the morning. He paged me into the bakery. Behind the deli. Nobody else was in there. But then that was a lull time of day. Hot baked goods were already cool on the shelves, ready to be bought in the afternoon rush. I avoid the bakery. The smell forces me to eat. I can go in there right after a huge supper, and the scent of melted shortening will make me grab six glazed doughnuts and pack them down my throat. *Before* I realize I'm not hungry. In fact I'm so sick I want to throw up. I walked in and breathed in deeply. Warm bread, fried pies, a touch of chocolate. Mr. Scamardo looked at me in my moment of weakness, pulled a cannoli off a baking sheet. Offered it to me in the palm of his hand, like I'd never stolen a sweet before. I put it away in three bites.

"You never gain weight, huh?" he said. He patted his flat chest. Reminding me of mine. I patted his belly. "But you do," I said. He laughed like he'd get something for it.

"I've come to a conclusion." He said it in a way that made me nervous. The chocolate end of the cannoli rose back up my throat. I hiccuped. He didn't notice. He took a deep breath. I hiccuped again. He ran for a paper cup of water from the sink. I told him to calm down. Though I didn't want him to. The jumpier a man acts, the cooler I get.

"I'm tired of bimbos," he said in a rush. Like he'd re-hearsed a line for a school play. All he wanted right then was to have delivered his part so he could step to the back of the stage. I was expecting something a little less personal. I said nothing, held my breath. But he was waiting for applause. Or something else. After a while I said, "Okay." His eyes got wide. He gave one nod of his head. Here was a guy who thought nothing of standing at the end of the flour and sugar aisle and bellowing threats. At a seventy-year-old snowbird, no less. Who was cleaning up spilled safflower oil with a new string mop. Now Mr. Scamardo couldn't bleat out more than four words. "So why're you telling me this?" I said.

"You're not a bimbo."

He was looking at my chest. I tried to think of something else. The way men who come too fast scan scoreboards in their minds. Wilson. When I was in school I'd say Wilson's name to myself to empty my head out. Wilson. He was down the hall somewhere, a head taller. Wilson. Wilson can measure almost anything that has to do with the human body. And mind. And probably spirit. Bra size less than a D cup? No bimbo here. But what about a wish for a D cup? What about a D cup stuffed with polystyrene? Wilson could pull a doctoral dissertation out of bimbohood. But Wilson is too serious. Wilson first saw breasts in *National Geographic* like the rest of them. The difference with Wilson is that he goes to Third World countries looking for the real thing. The saggy, brown, honest breasts. All the rest, including Mr. Scamardo, keep looking for something more like what they glimpsed in their mothers' bedrooms when they were small boys. I shrugged.

"Look, Zib, don't make this difficult for me. I want a woman who's my equal." He cocked his head. Not a cute move for a man who's only halfway to bald.

I could stifle a laugh easily. Because I was so quavery inside. "You have no equals at Winn-Dixie," I said. Meaning Winn-Dixie had no women managers. As far as I knew. Assistant managers, yes. An occasional tigress from corporate headquarters, yes. Either type was too disgusted with her place in the organization to want anything from Mr. Scamardo. Except maybe a chance to pummel him.

He smiled shyly. He turned pink all the way to the shiny peak of his head. "I mean, if you're looking for a woman on a *par* with you, you're not going to find her at the Winn–Dixie." His grin got more idiotic. "I'm not complimenting you." I said it as nicely as I could.

"That's what I like about you."

"Hey, I can't win here." I gave him a playful little punch in the belly. It was surprisingly hard. Like the cheapest pillow at-Wal-Mart. Full of fat that had been there so long it had decided to harden and protect him.

"Come on, Zib," he said. His voice was husky. I guess he thought that passed for emotion. He took my wrist. He tried to get me to look him in the eye by following my face with his. Finally he was ready to give up. So I looked him straight in the eye. "You're married," I said. "And I've been faithful, too," he said. I laughed. "No, that ought to be worth something to you." "Like what?" "Like I'm not the type to mess around. A clean bill of health, you know what I mean?" I nodded, tired. "And it means I take you seriously as a person. I'm *discriminating*."

That's not what I'd heard. Cashiers were nothing more to him than a kind of produce. Worth something as long as they were shiny and ripe. Then put out in the Dumpster when they got spotty and misshapen. To him patting a butt was like plucking a grape. A privilege. Something he could do while walking at a good clip through the store. Not breaking stride. He didn't try to diddle more than one woman on a shift. So the cashiers couldn't complain among themselves. Instead they were silent. They took it good-naturedly when they had children to support. They quit if they weren't strugglers. Once in a while they came to me. "Go over his head or file suit," was all I could tell them. Until they quit they looked at me differently. Not with disgust or pity, but with disinterest, I thought. After a few years I could sense which ones he'd want. They had a quality about them. It wasn't in their coloring. Though of course he left the black women alone. And it wasn't in the shapes of their bodies. If anything, it was something in their eyes, close-set and narrow. A dumbness, maybe, a dullness that they may have been born with. Or that they may have gotten through too many nights of crying their eyes out over things that didn't matter. A measure for Wilson, distance between the inside corners of the eyes. I have wide-spaced eyes.

When I was a child people said I looked like a young Jackie Kennedy. I thought Jackie Kennedy was walleyed. Fish-like. I took it as an insult. I can look back and wonder how I came to that conclusion. Little girls are so taken with anything pink. And of course Jackie Kennedy was in all the magazines in that suit when I was four. But Mama didn't have a good word to say about her. Mama fussed that she was a spendthrift. Jackie Kennedy cared far too much about having every hair in place, Mama said.

"Don't you think I know you pretty well?" I said to Mr. Scamardo.

"Not really," he said. He sounded like a man who thinks he's kept all his secrets.

He moved closer. I could smell yesterday's salami on his breath. I could see little gray hairs growing out his nose. I noticed for the first time that his upper lateral incisor was the size of a baby tooth. It was white. All the rest of his teeth were almost the color of sweet potatoes. I don't dismiss options lightly. I gave myself about half a second to think about whether I could sleep with Mr. Scamardo. And make my life easy. So far no one I knew had taken him up on his offers. He'd picked at them, sometimes for months. Until either they quit or someone who looked more like Karen Black came in for an interview. The smell of him made me cough. I breathed through my mouth until I could shift my weight. Move away. I wouldn't be able to do it. Not even with a fifth of bourbon to freshen the air. And dull my senses.

"I've never said these things to a woman before." His voice was low. Trying to sound like Elvis.

I smiled. "That's true," I said. Usually he talked with his hands. He smiled back. With those teeth I'd never smile back. Smiling is for winning something. "I don't fuck where I work," I said.

He threw back his head and laughed. Now I could see that his molars were full of silver. Somebody'd spent a lot of money on his teeth. I was sad for him. "God, I like your style," he said.

"There're millions like me who *don't* work for Winn-Dixie. I could probably introduce you to a dozen." I didn't know anybody outside of work here. I didn't even know anybody *at* work too well. Angelas are hard to find. And Angela herself doesn't leave New Orleans. I was sure in an emergency I could hang out in the laundry room of my apartment complex. The right woman would come along. For all I knew, the right *man* had come along. I'd just been too busy dumping other people's clothes on the floor from the dryer, loading mine in, scurrying out.

A deli worker came through the bakery to get potato salad from the fridge. "I can do a lot for you," Mr. Scamardo whispered in my ear. He was close enough to leave breath steam on my cheek. I waited until he turned. Then I wiped that side of my face with the heel of my hand. Hard. After that day, he kept phoning me at home. Never for a work reason, always to invite himself over. I did it backward. I started out telling him the truth, that I didn't want to start anything. Then I worked back to lying. I said I had a headache or a date. I didn't discourage him either way. For two months now, I've quit answering between dusk and dawn. I've thought about getting caller ID. But knowing where a call comes from seems too much like knowing what happens after death. On a lower level, of course. Some things are best left wished about. Wilson would disagree. But I notice he doesn't have it on his phone, either.

I'm in the bathroom. My mouth is full of toothpaste. The phone rings. I spit, run for the phone. Say *hello, please hold*. Spit twice without covering the phone. In case it's Mr. Scamardo.

"Hey." It's a man's voice. Whispering. I don't recognize it. So I don't say anything. "You there, Zib?" It's Wilson. I'm so relieved I giggle.

"What's the matter with you?" I say. He sounds more beaten down than usual. I look at my watch. Ten after eight. I think long-distance rates go up at eight. A shock of alarm goes through me. I'm the only one in the family who believes a phone call should be made when the mood is right. Never mind the cost. I ask him if Mama is all right. I know the answer. Mama is always all right. Mama will never have a traffic accident or a heart attack. Mama won't even find out she's dying slowly. Mama will bury Wilson and me. And probably all of Wilson's children. Mama has brine in her veins. "Oh, I am bone weary," he says. From what? Wilson lives like a wealthy man who hates golf. Wilson hires somebody to put up his storm windows. He pays somebody to weed his flower bed. His heart rate probably's never gone over seventy-two. "I always am annoying someone these days."

"So you called to make it unanimous?"

"Forget it."

I apologize.

"Look, Barbara thinks I am going insane, for which she thinks I should be punished, never mind all the horseshit she can spout about trauma and self-esteem and whatever else is a teaser on the cover of the *Ladies' Home Journal* when it comes to *her* family."

"What'd you do?" This is bound to be ridiculous. Which is good.

"I fell asleep in my office."

"I don't blame you." I congratulate myself with a little chuckle. Which is met by silence.

"I am not in the mood for this," Wilson says.

"*Now* you're acting like a man." I sent him a card one time. This fat lady is on the front. She's saying, "Stand up and face your problems like a man!" Then you open the card. And it says, "Blame someone else." I wrote *Happy Birthday* on it. He never thanked me.

He gets out a *goddammit*. Then my other line beeps. I'm not the type to have call waiting. I don't talk to one person on the phone in any given week. Let alone two. But I have a limit on how many mysteries I want in my life. I don't want to worry in the middle of a conversation about whether I'm missing out. "Hold," I say, before Wilson can tell me anything.

It's Mr. Scamardo. "What, what?" I say. Wilson's put me in an excellent frame of mind. He asks me if I know who this is. "I'm on the other line, Mr. Scamardo." "Al," he says. "I'll hold," he says. "It's long distance." "I'll hold."

I switch back over to Wilson. To tell him it's my boss. "I'll hold," he says. He's still angry. I tell him I'll call him back. Which is generous of me. Considering I know he's ready to holler at me. And he still will be ten minutes from now. I don't like to pay to be fussed at.

"You do not have to," he says. He sounds awfully tired. "I only called to tell you one thing. Mother is getting positively neurotic over that box in the drawer. She says we should pick a date, and she will meet us in Arlington. When can you get out of there for three days? I can do a weekend, almost any weekend. I have no Friday classes, no Monday classes, just office hours, and many times no one comes, anyway."

"People buy groceries on weekends, Wilson."

"With you or without you."

"People figure out Organic Evolution. With you or without you, too," I say. I dread a click on the line. That would mean Mr. Scamardo's hung up, pissed. And I've gone to so much trouble not to piss him off.

"Thursday, Friday, back Saturday night?" Wilson offers.

"You can't get a cheap ticket if you don't stay over Saturday night," I say. Such things matter to Wilson.

"Another concession on my part," he says.

I tell him to hold. I click over. I ask Mr. Scamardo if he can hold one more minute. "Not really," he says. "Half a minute," I say. "You're the boss," he says. I switch back to Wilson without giving Mr. Scamardo the laugh he wants.

I tell Wilson that I have to go. It's my goddamn boss on the other line. "Tell him you are making arrangements to attend your father's funeral," Wilson says.

"He'll ask me if Pop didn't die one time before."

"What in the name of God are you doing down there?"

"I don't know," I say softly. When I'm feeble enough, Wilson backs off. At which time I feel rotten. Mama always said I was going to make him into a homosexual if I didn't quit hurting him and tricking him. He's been married twice. And he's fertilized four eggs, like somebody's prize rooster. I know that doesn't mean anything about a lot of men. I'm sure I haven't made Wilson gay. But he's gentle enough to hate football. And he finds conversation with other men difficult. Most of the time I realize that's ruinous enough.

"Look, you book any reservations you want, and I will take off," Wilson says. "Your father can die as often as you want up here."

Tears start. "I love you, Wilson," I say. Then I click over to the other line. Before he can recover enough to say anything.

"So," I say. I hear silence. I'm on hold. I wish I knew how long I've been on hold. I could hang up all righteously. I watch the second hand on my watch. It moves only twenty seconds before Mr. Scamardo comes back. "Mr. Scamardo," I say. "Al," he says. "Okay," I say.

"You want company?"

"It's eight o'clock in the morning."

"You've brushed your teeth, haven't you?"

"But you haven't," I say. I drop the receiver into the cradle. From a height of about six inches. A perfect landing.

7

Jerusha

IT'S A WONDER ANYONE EVER GOES ON AN AIRPLANE. YOU ASK
for a reservation and they want a credit card. You say I don't
have a credit card; my husband didn't believe in credit. So they
say, Oh, come into our office, which is in a part of Metairie
that was a swamp last time I was out that far, and by the way,
that'll be $835. I have about two hundred dollars in cash, and
I've misplaced Woodrow's checkbook, and a plane crashed
somewhere with no white people on board, probably, which
means something's wrong with equipment and a plane in
America will be next, and I'm not ready for my time to be up.

So Wilson and Zib are flying up to meet me, and Woodrow
is in a mahogany box on the front seat. I couldn't stand the idea
of walking into Arlington Cemetery with a cardboard carton,
so I took him over to the funeral home last week and had him
transferred. They were discreet, taking him into the back where
I didn't have to see, like he was in his underwear in a dressing
room in a department store; if I wanted to watch, I only had to
ask. I'm curious about most things, but I could live forever
without seeing Woodrow looking like something at the bottom
of a barbecue pit. Arlington is overcrowded; they won't let you
in unless you're cremated or famous. Woodrow's not getting a
horse with backward stirrups or anything, but they told me

they'd get three guys out there to shoot off seven rounds. Or seven guys to shoot off three. I didn't write it down.

I stay in the Bull Dog Inn just past Atlanta. Everything flushes, flows, and blows when it's supposed to, and I don't see any reason to look for anything fancier. I'm somewhere in between Woodrow and Zib when it comes to motels. Woodrow figured you could reach any point in the continental United States with only one motel stop: drive twenty-four hours, stop twenty-two hours, check-in to check-out, get your money's worth, drive twenty-four more, get to Maine or Washington State for forty dollars plus food and gas. Zib wants to stop in city hotels, tour and swim and spend. Zib will not go more than two hundred miles by car; then she has to take a plane. "Suit yourself, but I am not going to act like a poor person," she says. This from someone who lives like a nun, one room, no furniture to speak of. She never goes to the doctor. Zib puts all her money in clothes and throwaways. She's like these colored people in my neighborhood. They live in about six hundred square feet, roof leaking, no air-conditioning, but they drive up and down in top-of-the-line Buicks.

I don't understand a thing about Wilson. Wilson goes wherever and however anybody tells him to: he gets a wife who wants to stay in the Plaza in New York, so he stays in the Plaza in New York; he gets a grant that puts him in a lean-to in darkest Africa, so he sits for three months in a lean-to in darkest Africa. When he teaches Organic Evolution, he says we're all going to be like Buddha one day. I don't know why I surround myself with people who are so *extreme*.

The last time Woodrow and I drove this route, it was two-lane undivided highways, and I had two children who pounded each other senseless in the back seat. We took both cars because Woodrow said we couldn't agree on what we were supposed to be doing on vacation. I wanted to go see my great aunt in Richmond, Virginia, since there was a good chance she might leave me something one day, but Woodrow thought that a vacation meant going to a battlefield and standing by a termite-infested cannon and pretending you could see men blowing holes in each other across what was now nicely mown grass. I think Woodrow didn't want to fight over the cigarette smoke. I took Wilson and Zib in the car with me because Woodrow wouldn't know what to do with them, and I made it as far as Atlanta before I told him to pick one, either one, or I'd kill both of them. Naturally he picked Zib, which made me happy because, even though she was the girl, she was the heller of the two, and you could count on Wilson to sit in the front seat with a Big Chief tablet and write down all the states he saw license plates from. Trouble was, halfway across South Carolina, I got a flat tire. I was following Woodrow because, all else aside, Woodrow could read a map, and I'd rather not. I slowed up, started to pull over to the shoulder, realized he was no more paying attention to me than he ever had; he was going to get all the way into North Carolina before he noticed I wasn't behind him. So I went tearing behind him, blasting the horn, riding on the rim, sixty miles an hour, and Wilson was screaming, "Mother, no, Mother, no," and I leaned on the horn, but Woodrow never looked in the rearview mirror. I couldn't see Zib, who'd flapped around in the motel pool the night before until she was so crazy about herself that she couldn't sleep. I pushed the accelerator to seventy, and the car was rocketing along like it was going to explode, and right after we came out of a curve I pulled into the other lane until I was riding next to him, and I stayed there until he looked over to see who the fool was, playing chicken on a two-lane undivided highway. We had to get a tow truck, the wheel was so messed up. Turned out he was listening to a boxing match on the radio.

While the car was in the shop, we checked into a motel court, expecting to stay two nights, and Woodrow was beside himself over the unplanned expense. "We're halfway north, what're these people doing with air-conditioning?" he said, like it was costing us extra. Woodrow worked security at the Whitney Bank vault in New Orleans, so all he heard all day were the sounds of downtown air-conditioning and boxes full of valuables, and he came home nights beat and fussy and turned off our only unit. He paid off the mortgage in ten years with what he saved on electricity bills, never mind that Wilson kept saying that with a mortgage he could get himself another tax form and have enough left over every year that I could have bought my underwear someplace besides Krauss's.

"We take one car up to Virginia, we come back for yours on the way home," he said. "Save on the gas, too." I told him I'd consider his plan, though I didn't intend to go all the way across North Carolina and most of Virginia without a cigarette. We'd be in his car, his rules, and he didn't like the smell of smoke, even though he didn't mind the smell of mildew from the time Zib left the windows open in a rainstorm. I figured something would come up. All that ever got me my way with Woodrow was dumb luck.

That night Zib woke up moaning that she was going to throw up. All of us in that one room, Woodrow snoring like a fool, Wilson with his arms crossed over his face like he was going to block out something, naturally I was the only one going to hear Zib. "Serves you right," I said, not opening my eyes, trying to stay asleep. She had put away five burgers from White Castle. Five minutes later, she was over the toilet, three feet from my bed, barfing her guts up. "Serves *you* right," she said when I jumped out of bed. Zib had said she wanted to eat in a restaurant where they starched the napkins, said to Woodrow, "You all act like we're poor. This is too embarrassing for words." I pulled her outside the cabin, and her big yellow Jackie Kennedy walleyes got wide. At home I smacked her for sass; in the yard I chased her with the garden hose, nozzle loose, even though it wasn't any of the neighbors' business. "Calm down, I just don't want you waking your brother with all that racket," I whispered.

Some valve in her must have shut to spite me, because the color came back into her face. I waited with my arms folded across my chest. The air filled with mosquitos, and I slapped at them with no patience. "I can't just throw up because you want me to," Zib said.

"Get some air," I told her, and we stood out there staring at the highway. We had a sliver moon and clouds; I could see nothing beyond what light we were giving off ourselves. No cars were passing, only one other cabin was occupied, and I found myself wishing for a little traffic. The owner was an old talker, and I figured he needed to average four customers a night or he would have to die long before he looked like he was going to. I thought about going in and getting a cigarette. I was straining for the sound of cars on the road, and Zib was rocking side to side like she was trying to put herself to sleep standing up. She let out a yelp, like a puppy dog when you step on its tail. I clapped my hand over her mouth, and her lips were still wet with bile and thick spit. She tried to talk, and I pulled my hand away, sticky. "Don't move," a man's voice said from behind me.

Naturally I turned around. No man is going to talk to me like that. Especially in the middle of nowhere. I saw the gun before I saw his face. Woodrow. His service revolver pointed right at me. I broke up laughing. I'd always figured that if I needed an operation or something, the first thing I'd do was rob the Whitney Bank vault. Woodrow and that rusty old Tinkertoy couldn't scare anybody. His hand was shaking. I could see it in the dark.

"It is illegal to have that, Father," Wilson said, coming up from behind him.

"It's illegal to steal pens from the Whitney Bank, too, but your father has reasons," I said, working hard not to laugh.

"Shut up, Jerusha," Woodrow said, all insulted. "You wouldn't think it was so funny, some nigger out here in the bushes trying to rob us." He put his arm around Wilson's shoulder, led him back into the cabin. "I got a marksmanship medal in Korea," I heard him telling the child. And Wilson shook his head up and down like it mattered to him. Wilson was an odd boy from the start. "Sorry," I hollered behind Woodrow. I don't know if he heard me.

As it turned out, my car was ready the next afternoon, and we pulled off while there was still five hours of daylight. When I got home I told the whole story to Gloretta, and it got sad instead of funny. "That man's proud of himself," Gloretta said.

Right now it would be nice to see that old blue Ford station wagon bucking down the interstate ahead of me, all the windows closed and everything. I'd still think Woodrow was foolish, but it'd be nice.

When you live in a city like New Orleans your entire life, and then you get out on the road, I guess it's natural to get careless. Or to dare fate. I don't feel like being a prisoner all the time, locking this and locking that, and when I go down the highway a few miles and find a McDonald's, I leave the car windows open so I won't burn my backside when I come back. Here it is, late October, and a heat wave over the entire southern United States is moving east like it's chasing me. Woodrow picked out this car, and we didn't figure out why we got such a bargain until the first time we tried to sit on black vinyl seats. The dealer must've gotten one car with black interior in the bunch and couldn't unload it on anybody else. Woodrow always told me to stop complaining, but then he never wore skirts.

Everything is in the trunk, except a road map, a brown paper bag with four apples left in it, and a yellow throw pillow from my living room sofa that I sometimes tuck behind me when I'm driving. And Woodrow. I put Woodrow and the apples down on the floor to get them out of the sun. I swear I've only been in McDonald's for ten minutes; how long can it take to put away a cold sweet roll and coffee that tastes like unpurified Mississippi River water. When I come out, the apples are still there, but Woodrow is gone.

I run back into McDonald's, and I guess I look like a crazy woman, but I don't care. There are only about a dozen people in the whole place, and I stand where you line up to put in your order, and I scream. "My husband's gone. I left him on the floor of the car, and somebody took him." The girl who sold me my breakfast backs away from her register with the kind of look on her face she'd have if I was swinging an AK-47 rifle around the place and asking for nothing except revenge. I always thought I liked going in for fast food in the boonies, because they hire these Amy Carter–looking girls who twang and smile, but I guess in an emergency it's better to get one of those moody colored women you find in New Orleans. At least in the city nothing surprises anybody. "Look, you fool, I don't mean my real husband," I say to the girl. "I mean my husband's ashes. He's in a box, and the box is gone." She has a smile on the bottom half of her face. I'm crying now, and I don't like to cry even in private. I tell her to get me the manager, and she scoots off, relieved like I've told her she can have the week off with pay.

Even the managers in these places are white and about nineteen years old. "Oh, Jesus," I say when I see him. "What good are you going to be?"

"Ma'am?" he says, and I have to start all over.

"My husband died. I had him cremated. I'm taking him up to Arlington. National Cemetery. Outside Washington. In a box. Okay?"

He nods, and I can tell he wishes he'd gone into watch repair or something else instead.

"So I come in here to eat. I eat. I go back to the car. *And the box isn't there!*"

"Oh, God," he says. Probably he's never known a dead person before. And McDonald's is not where you expect to find dead people. They go off somewhere else to die, like mice who eat rat poison. "Call 911," he says to my cashier, who is standing behind the display case that is full of salads at 8:30 in the morning.

I'm tempted to tell him, "No, don't do that." For all I know, transporting Woodrow across state lines is a federal offense. Though how else I'm supposed to get him up there is beyond me. I can see telling my grandchildren, *Oh, Grandpa Woodrow got lost in the mail.* Wilson isn't the sort to raise children with any sense of humor. Though the idea of saying, *Oh, Grandpa Woodrow got stolen in a parking lot of the McDonald's someplace outside East Jesus, Georgia,* is not a lot better. Not to mention how Woodrow himself is feeling about this now. I've known ever since I married him that Woodrow was going to come back and haunt me if he died first. Even if he died in his sleep. From what I see on *Unsolved Mysteries,* the only people who come back as ghosts are the ones who were murdered or killed themselves. I figure that has to do with having unfinished business, and all his life Woodrow had unfinished business. Really, he had *unstarted* business. Woodrow needs to be in Arlington Cemetery.

The manager has given me a cup of coffee, and I sit in a booth for a few minutes trying to decide if I'm going to drink it to be polite. I'm thinking in my head, in case Woodrow can hear me, "Look, Woodrow, I am terribly sorry. I could've brought you inside, but I didn't want people sitting in here to see me hugging this box, acting like I'm some nutcase or like I've got a million dollars in unmarked bills inside."

Not that Woodrow would say anything. He was the kind who stewed. Very quietly, and it sometimes took a year to figure out that I'd done something that got on his nerves. And then only if I did it again. "Remember last July when you let the brake tag expire? Once is stupid, Jerusha, twice is *damn* stupid. What you pay in penalty'd buy a bag of groceries." A bag of groceries to Woodrow was the international standard of currency, though I don't know how, since he had the idea that nothing had changed since 1939, which is about when he bought his last bag of groceries. Anyway, I don't know how spirits let you know they're stewing, but I imagine they have their ways, and I don't want to spend the next year being jumpy about going into rooms by myself.

It takes the police over an hour to come. It's breaking into my driving time, but I can't leave and cut my losses since the whole point of going up there is to have Woodrow with me. The manager brings me another cup of coffee, and I line it up next to the first one, which is still full. I don't think he realizes that I'm on my way somewhere, and the last thing I need is to be so full of coffee that I shake and pee all the way down the road. I light up a cigarette, dare anyone to say anything. For all I know, Wilson and Zib are not the only people born in the South who read the *Wall Street Journal*.

Two officers walk in, and they both order a sausage biscuit and a Coke before they come sit down at the table with me. "How much you pay for the box?" one asks me when I've told him the whole story. "See, I'm not sure what kind of crime this is exactly."

"The *box* cost me $79.95 plus tax, but the stuff inside the box cost me nearly fifty years of pure aggravation," I say. They both look at me like I'm using big words. "That's my husband in that box. *Human* remains. Grave robbing. Whatever you want to call it, it's not stealing a $79.95–plus-tax box."

They tell me to stay there. It's getting to the fringes of the lunch hour, and I can tell the manager is unnerved that I am still going to be sitting here when all his happy, hungry customers come in. He's at an interstate exit, for Chrissakes, you'd think he'd be used to everybody coming in on some level of adventure, then going away without remembering they've been here, but I can tell he wants me out of here before I scare people off, sending a message up and down the highway that crazy old women are sitting in his restaurant telling stories about grave robbers.

This is the first time in my life that I see myself as an old lady. Generally I figure I'm still a kid. After all, I can ride a bicycle and rollerskate.

The policemen come back in in a few minutes. They look full of self-importance, and they beckon me out of the restaurant. I pick up my purse, and the manager smiles and waves good-bye. "I might be back," I say. "Fine, fine," he says, with that mushmouth accent of his. *Fahn, fahn.*

This little strip of feeder highway may look like it's nothing but one franchise after another, but there's a lot of pieces of red raw land lying around the parking lots, full of bulldozer and truck tracks. The policemen take me out into the McDonald's parking lot, and one says, "You think you could identify the remains?" I tell him no, that I made a point of not seeing what Woodrow looked like burned to a crisp. "Just ashes, maybe five pounds of ashes," I say, remembering that article in *The Star* about that cut-rate crematorium in California. They walk me past the usual parking-lot droppings, a disposable diaper that is coming unwrapped and stinking in the sun, the dumpings from a car ashtray. I look at the ashtray mess—Doublemint gum wrapper, a couple of butts, some ashes that haven't blown away—and I hope that this is not what the funeral home was sending up to Arlington. "That's not him," I say to the officer. "Didn't think so," he says seriously.

They walk me over to a construction area next to McDonald's, and I see what looks to me like a stomped ant pile in the middle of the red Georgia clay. It takes me a second to realize that ants use what's available, that ant piles take on the color of the land, that the little mound of gray is probably Woodrow. "Aw, shit," I say, not daring to get closer.

"Think that's it?" the other officer says, and I nod my head. They walk over to the Woodrow pile, and I stay where I am. They are used to dead people, but they move quietly, like they're going to disturb somebody who's sleeping with a gun tucked under him. "Yeh, fresh footprints," I hear one say. Men get such a charge out of that detective game. They come back to me, tell me there's nothing more they can do. "What'm *I* supposed to do?" I say. The idea of scooping up Woodrow my-self makes me crazy. After all, every handful was at one time some part of him that was full of nerves. "Mother, you realize that if I were doing this while the chicken was alive it would be screaming with pain?" Wilson said once at the dinner table when he was no more than ten. "You realize if someone took a bite this big out of you that they would go rush you into sur-gery and try to connect everything back again?" I told him to get away from the table and not to come back until he could stop the disgusting talk. Wilson said, "Well, now I am not par-ticularly hungry, anyway," and he refused to eat meat for about six months after that. I can see myself scooping up every part of Woodrow except a hand or a liver, only to get to Judgment Day and find him standing there without all his parts and refusing to talk to me. "I'll *pay* you," I call to the officers. "Ma'am?" one says. I could grow to hate that form of respect. "I said I'll pay you to help me get him back in my car." They look at each other, like boys shooting dares, and one says, "Aw, ma'am, no need to pay."

Half an hour later I am back on the road. Woodrow, along with a few little bits of Georgia clay, is lying inside a brown pa-per sack from McDonald's. I figure I'll get to the motel before the kids, mold the bag around until you can't see the red clumps anymore, and run out and buy a new wooden box. I can't leave Woodrow in a McDonald's bag. McDonald's is all into saving the earth, so the bag is not made to last an eternity. Besides, I wouldn't want to hear what Zib'd say.

8

Zib

MAMA DOESN'T LET ON, BUT SHE'S IMPRESSED. A HALF DOZEN strangers go running around Arlington Cemetery just to give my father a funeral. I think it's pitiful. When I die, I give everybody two choices. I want a string of a hundred late-model cars with their headlights on tying up traffic for miles. Or I'll donate my body to science. A bunch of guys hanging around on the government payroll so men like my father can feel heroic after they're dead and can't feel anything? That's about as bad as an Italian funeral. All these women come in and cry and scream. Like it's their job.

A couple of times when I was a kid, Angela and I went to those all-night funerals. They have them down at Lamana-Panno-Fallo. Angela had Puglia uncles dropping like flies for a few years. We'd sit in a corner with lapful after lapful of garlicky food. We'd eat and belch quietly. And get punchy from no sleep. At first Mama didn't believe I was staying out all night at a funeral. But after about the third one, she quit asking Angela's mother Miss Hazel if I was lying. So I managed to spend a few nights out in high school in places I wasn't supposed to. By telling my parents that another one of Angela's uncles had died. By then, of course, Angela had run out of uncles. There are limits even in Catholic families. But Mama never knew. Instead, Mama would marvel for a few minutes about how many children Catholics could have. At least three times I heard her say to my father, "Remember that dog I had when you met me, Woodrow? Little puggy thing we called Peggy? She runs off, gets knocked up by what must be a giant German shepherd or something, comes home, eight weeks later looks like a balloon on legs, starts moaning like she's going to die; finally we take her to the vet, out pops one lousy pup. Beau, we called him Beau. The terror of the neighborhood." Pop nodded. He was tired of the story. Even though she only trotted it out every few years. So she turned to me. "We got Peggy's box cut out right after that; no sense taking that sort of risk again. I figure Angela's like Beau. Hazel quit while she was behind. Only reason I can think why she didn't have six more." As big as he was, Beau lived to be sixteen. Mama figured the world would probably get just as much mileage out of Angela.

We get back to the motel after Pop's funeral. I'm wishing I could crawl off into a dark corner. I'd curl up and rock back and forth until it's time to go to the airport. But Mama made all the arrangements. Two cheap rooms with a connecting door. Her and me in one room together. Wilson by himself in the other. That's the way our family's traveled since I was about three. Wilson sleeping with Pop, me with Mama. Even if we had only one room. They'd get the bed; we'd get the cots.

When I was about fifteen, it occurred to me that we'd had that setup far longer than necessary. "You could've put me and

Wilson in a room together when we were little," I told her one night. We were in a motel room somewhere in eastern Colorado. I'd been lying there. Dreading a night full of her phlegmy noises. "Wait till you have a husband," she said. "You'll look for every out you can get." When I went to sleep that night, I pushed away dreams of faceless boys. Those dreams made me slip my fingers under my nightgown until I was making wet little noises under the sheets. Noises that I was sure filled a room.

Mama lies down on one of the beds in our motel room. We're just outside Arlington. She's asleep faster than a kid who falls in his tracks after a crying fit. For a while I sit and look at her. I try to imagine what it's like. To have been full of disgust all her life. And then to have to come to this. She's driven halfway across the country with her sad, cheap husband in a paper bag. She slapped my face when I got hysterical at the sight of it. She can tell anybody she wants that she did it for my own good. But I know better.

When we were children, Mama hit only in anger. Never for teaching. Never even for getting silence or cooperation or whatever she wanted at the time. She beat us only to feel better. By wiping the smiles off our faces.

She's on her back. She starts to cough in her sleep. So hard that her feet, shoes and all, fly up a few inches off the bed. I rap quietly on Wilson's door. Open it. Beckon him to come in and take a look. "Watch," I say. In a minute she coughs again. Stick-straight legs come up off the bed. I look to Wilson to see if he'll laugh with me. "Disgusting," he says. And he goes back into his room.

She mumbles threats in her sleep when I turn on the television. I look around for something to read. I consider trying

Wilson again. Then I see her car keys. If I don't get out of here soon, I'm going to start to scream. And I may never stop. If I do that while she's sound asleep, it'll be the chance she's been waiting for my whole life. To go so far out of control that she'll beat my head against a wall. Then strangle me to death. I take the keys.

I live in Florida. A good part of the year most of the people driving around have no idea where anything is. That almost makes it possible for me to stay sane in Washington traffic. I don't have anywhere I want to go. Just away from the motel. I'm not concerned that I'm going to get lost. I'm just driving along, trying to find a radio station, *trying* to get as lost as possible. I can't play that game I used to play with Angela. Toss a penny at the corner, heads go left, tails go right, reach another corner, toss the penny again. Eventually we were so turned around that we had to call her mother and ask for directions home. I have no Angela. Besides, there are no corners on the Beltway.

I'll find a car that appeals to me and follow it. Not that I believe in fate. I'm as scientific and godless as Wilson. I just don't see any reason to make a living out of it. I'm not going to follow a 1974 pickup truck with a bed full of black men. Even if it's worth riling Mama. I'm scientific and godless. I don't take crazy chances. I'm also not going to follow an Infiniti that's so new it still has cardboard temporary tags in the back window. That would rile Mama, too. She hates people who look down on her. Almost as much as she hates people she looks down on. The reason I liked Fellini's *Orchestra Rehearsal* was that they set the metronome and followed it instead of the conductor. I decide to look for license plates. Maybe from Louisiana. Or Florida. Kindred lost spirits. Kindred adventurers. If you're not trying to get anywhere in a hurry, all you have to do is maintain the speed of the car in front of yours. A red Saab from the eighties passes. Its bumper sticker says TOO SMART TO BE RICH. It has New York plates. It's weaving confidently. I fall in line behind it. I don't need to know the driver.

He loses me in Old Town Alexandria. That's good enough. It's not like I expect to follow him to the end of the earth, corner him, marry him.

I'm never going to get married. The only reason to get married is to have children. I'm not the type to have children. I don't hate them. I buy presents for all of Wilson's kids. I'll read them stories if they don't interrupt. Children these days are selfish. I don't have the patience for that.

I've learned in twenty years of meeting men that I'm attractive as hell to them. It's not my looks. Which I can take or leave. The only interesting thing about me is that my eyes are so green they're yellow. Same as my father's. What draws men is that they know I want absolutely nothing. They may tell me I'm the most beautiful woman they've ever seen. But I know what they see long before they do. I find that secret knowledge a lot of fun. Most of the time.

I find a parking meter. That's something I couldn't do in the French Quarter. I go over to Union Street. I want a view of the river. I figure I'll get oriented to the geography of the place. People raised in New Orleans tell direction by the river. I suppose Wilson'd argue that in five thousand years their descendants'll lose all sense of east and west. I walk into the pub. Late afternoon and the place is nearly empty. It's one of those places that attracts people who don't think it's chic to eat dinner before eight o'clock. Even if they're starving. Brick and glass and dim lighting. A magnet for the self-important. Like Washington itself.

I take a seat at the bar. I'm going to get stinking drunk. Not quickly. But thoroughly drunk. I ask for chablis cassis. Sip slowly but without stopping. I begin to blur around my own edges. Order another. I'm staring at the image of the top half of my head in the bar mirror. I'm trying to stare down my own yellow fish-eyes. A man sits next to me. I pay no attention. My wine comes. "You're the white Chevy wagon," he says to me. He orders a draft beer. "It's my mother's," I say. I'm still staring at the top of my own reflection. I'm curious now as to how I look when I talk to other people. It's possible to stand in front of the bathroom mirror and mouth the words you might say to somebody else. But it's quite another thing to see yourself in action. I don't look like I give a damn. I check him out in the mirror. Shifting my eyes, not turning my head. As far as he knows I haven't paid attention to him. The silhouette of his hair is the same as the Saab man's.

"You were following me," he says. "You took two exits. And three turns. Then I lost you."

"That should tell you something," I say. I'm looking myself straight in the eye in the mirror. I have a wonderfully sad smile on my face. From what I can see of me.

"Well, either this is deliberate, or it's a coincidence. I'll take it either way."

"Good for you."

His beer arrives. He takes a sip of it. Like he's only got three dollars in his pocket. And he's going to stretch it out over an hour.

"You're from Louisiana," he says.

Maybe he can pick up something in my accent. But people in north Louisiana sound like Texans or Mississippians.

And people in New Orleans sound like lower-class New Yorkers. I spent half my teens and most of my twenties ridding myself of any accent whatsoever. I watched national news reporters the way Mama said Mrs. Khrushchev read the Sears catalogue.

Then I remember the car. "My mother's from Louisiana," I say.

"Then you are, too."

"I'm around forty," I say. Daring him. He has a thick head of hair. I know only two people of indeterminate age with that much hair. Ronald Reagan and Ronald McDonald. This guy has a long wait for forty.

"I bet when you go to Louisiana you say 'I'm going *home.*' I bet when people ask you where you're from, you say Louisiana. I'll tell you right off I'm from New York, and I haven't lived there in five years."

"I don't want to know about you." I say it pleasantly. I'm not lying. I want this day to pass like a dream. No sharp edges. No definitions. No clues. The funeral had such a grim cast of look-alike men with razor-cut hair. Nameless cyborgs. Like in a bad techno-thriller. I'm sure I'm going to have nightmares years from now. Military trucks will roll in. Filled with square-jawed boys who come to bury the dead. I'll waken with a jolt when they get to be too much to handle. Then I'll drift off again into a sweeter sleep. I'll find myself in a bar with more anonymous men. Men whose hair hasn't been touched by a razor since their mamas took them to the barbershop.

"A zipless fuck," he says, equally pleasant.

I turn, don't look him in the eye. I slap his face hard. Startled, he slaps me back. Nowhere near as hard. But still enough to make a great smack. It feels right. I want him to do it again. I'm not a person who enjoys pain. But today I can appreciate sensation. As long as it's over in a fraction of a second. It's like having an orgasm when I'm too drunk to move.

"I don't read," I say. I turn away again. I've read that book. And probably a thousand others. I like to make people think I have a certain brilliance that doesn't come from books. My mother reads only historical romances. My father read only cheap westerns. And my brother reads only clinical texts and primary source materials. Each has been convinced that any sort of books other than his own is foolish. So I've had a life-long habit of reading only in library stacks or under bedcovers. Never letting on. I can send my mother a clipping from the *Wall Street Journal* and leave her wondering where I got it.

I'm on my third glass of fast wine. The man runs his hand slowly across my thigh and down between my legs. I feel nothing on my skin. Only in my cunt. I order more chablis. With extra cassis. Makes it go down faster. Like sweet, thick water. I don't like the taste of alcohol. I like the senselessness it leaves behind. "Okay," I whisper. Tears stream down my face for no reason. I turn to look at his face. Only for a second. It's a quite terrific face to be seen through a haze. Dark thick brows, sharp black eyes, a sheepish lap-toothed grin. I look away. If he tries to murder me, I'll remember nothing for a police artist. If I get pregnant and bear his child, I'll remember everything. "My father had a funeral this morning," I say. I'm explaining. I think.

"His own?" he says. I begin to laugh hysterically.

We fuck in the back of my mother's station wagon. At an expired meter under a street lamp. For all I know, people are walking past. They're putting their fingers to their lips. Beckoning their friends to come over and watch. There's no shame in anonymity. I find the idea of an audience inspiring. I let myself be especially naked and lithe. The man seems to have no such thought. He's concentrating on my pleasure, oddly enough. "Are you Jewish?" I say when it's over. Not because he's generous and circumcised. But because the secret of having fucked in the back of my mother's car with a Jewish man is extra splendid. Jewish people all have more money than my mother. When I was small, they owned every department store on Canal Street. She made sure everyone knew it. The notion of mixing with Jews makes her crazier than the notion of mixing with blacks. "At least you know a colored person when you see one," she'll say. "Except in the Seventh Ward."

He asks if he'll see me again. He's slipping back into his clothes. My arms are folded across my face so I won't see anything. "Of course not," I say. "But you'll remember me."

He laughs. Sits up. I suppose he's dressed. I can feel the jerky movements of someone tying tennis shoes. "You can go," I whisper.

"You look like a dead body."

"Don't worry, they'll never convict you," I say. After a while he clambers over the seat. Lets himself out the door. I feel no cold. I fall into a deep sleep of release. I don't waken until my blood lets go of enough alcohol for me to shiver.

It's 11:40 on the car clock. That's one thing about American-made cars. You can drive down the street for fifteen years in one. You can let chunks break and drop off. But the clock will never stop working. One day you'll find yourself standing there with a steering wheel and a clock.

Mama and Wilson are waiting up. All the lights are on in the motel room. "Another minute or so, and we would have called the highway patrol," Wilson says. "Are you all right?"

Mama takes one look at me. I haven't bothered to check myself in the rearview mirror. Usually running my fingers through my hair does enough to put me as right as I ever am. "See her face? She's gotten herself laid," Mama says. My hand goes up to my cheek involuntarily.

It's been twenty years since I've had to sneak in with whisker burns on my face. As a matter of fact, it's been about ten years since I wondered what I looked like after sex. As another matter of fact, I haven't had sex in over a year. People say having sex is like riding a bicycle. You never forget how. But covering up the traces afterward is something else.

I glare at my mother. "I don't care what you do," she says. "I don't care if you go lie down in the middle of Interstate 95 buck naked. Just don't use my car to get there."

"You were sleeping," I say.

"But how's this for laughs? I *woke up*. Ever hear of that happening when somebody falls asleep before bedtime? And guess what else normal people do before bedtime. They *eat*. Ever think of that?"

The motel is next to a huge outdoor shopping mall. It's even named after the shopping mall. I can see at least three national food franchises right out the motel window. "There's enough food over there to feed half of Africa," I say. I point in the direction of the mall.

"People in Africa don't care what they eat," Mama says. She looks sideways at Wilson.

Wilson rolls his eyes so both of us see him. "You ate very well, Mother," he says. He turns to me. "Are you okay?"

"No," I say.

"Well, I'm not, either," Mama says.

9

Wilson

THE TRIP IN FROM O'HARE IS FAST AND MINDLESS THIS TIME of afternoon. With no traffic, I let peristalsis work along, so that I will be ready to move my bowels when I saunter into the house and into the bathroom. I have not gone in three days, traveling and sharing connecting rooms with my mother and sister. I grew up in a house with only one bathroom, a centrally located one at that, and we might as well have had no door for all the privacy a boy could have. A bout of flatulence, a good stink, and my mother would stand outside the door and say, "Been eating old socks again, Wilson?" I never masturbated in a bathroom until I was a grown man and out of her house. I even could not linger on the toilet for too long, or my mother would cry out, "I know what you're doing in there, Wilson. Get out and let somebody else have some fun." I do not need a psychiatrist to tell me that the chronic knots in my gastrointestinal tract were tied by my mother with the skill of a boatswain's mate.

I pull into the alley behind the house, and I am trying to decide whether to phone my mother to be certain she has made it to New Orleans safely, so I can forget about her for a while, when I see that Barbara's minivan is not there. I suppose that somewhere in the back of my mind is the idea that I will have time to go to the bathroom, phone my mother, listen to her complain about something she has found wrong upon her return to New Orleans, and still be able to tug Barbara into the bedroom for a quiet half hour before she has to go pick up Connor at school. Morgan stays at nursery until five on Mondays, Wednesdays, and Fridays for reasons that Barbara thinks are valid enough.

I find the note on the kitchen table. "Morgan still at nursery. Connor out at 3:00. They'll eat anything from Brown's. Don't know when I'll be back." No signature, cursive handwriting, skewed this way and that; Barbara normally prints like a schoolteacher, the bar of her lowercase *e*'s parallel to the blue lines. Barbara has not done this before, not in all the years we have been married, even when she has had a client push her on an impossible deadline. This can have to do only with David. Her brother is my closest friend, acquired in college here because, unlike Zib, I did not have an arbitrary lifelong friend provided by the next-door neighbor. David has been so despondent for the past three years that I expected his death would precede my father's. If it has to come now, at least I am numb; that may be why bad events come in threes. That is the human limit before the pain becomes unbearable.

I dial her parents' house. I have not spoken to her father since early September, when he insulted me so surprisingly that I stumbled off into silence. I was excited, and I still am, about biotechnology, about genetic alterations. Not so much for practical reasons, because a strawberry that has been crossed with an Arctic flounder is going to taste the same as a garden strawberry by the time it is piled atop my shortcake. I was thinking about the arguments, the position papers, the classrooms full of indignation. We were at the Greenes' house for Friday night dinner, and I looked over at Connor, who still does not know how to blow his nose, preferring to suck it back until his ears explode. He was snorting away like Felix Unger, and I said, "Oh, Connor, someone must have slipped some pig DNA in your test tube." Connor giggled and sniffed the next dribble back with more decorum, but Barbara's father Bernie must have decided right then that he had had enough of something. "Can't you just teach the kid to blow his nose, for God's sake?" He looked at Barbara, but he was talking to me. "That's the trouble with all you overeducated idiots. You can't do anything direct. If it takes one week, you take five, if it takes one syllable, you take a dozen. If I'd known that the more years you spend in school the stupider you'd get, I'd've jerked you and your brother out in fifth grade."

I did not leave the table; I had seconds on the beef brisket. But I kept my mouth shut for the rest of the evening, deciding each time I had a thought worth throwing into a lull that I was inviting trouble. I sat back and watched Morgan become the only one with anything to say by the end of the evening. Since that night, I have managed to stay away from Bernie, and the one time he phoned, he said, "Hey, Wilson," as if nothing were wrong, and I said, "Hold on a second, I will get her," and that was that.

I get a busy signal at the Greenes' house. I dial my mother, get a busy signal, too, dial the Greenes' again. The busy signal at their number seems less distant, less insistent. Suddenly I rush to the bathroom, the pain in my belly so severe that I think I am going to vomit.

The children in Connor's kindergarten class are going, table by table, to get their sweaters, and when I open the door the teacher is saying, "Well, you can go outside and play until three o'clock, or you can sit in here for thirty minutes and think about what it means to be quiet." The din falls to secure whispers, and I step inside, tell the teacher that I have to take Connor; it is an emergency. "Have you cleared it with the office?" she says, looking at me as if I am a psychopath who has to be handled carefully. I shake my head, which I suppose is an admission of guilt to a kindergarten teacher. "Christ, this is an emergency," I say. Connor is looking at me blankly, and it is possible that he will be too embarrassed to admit he ever has seen me before in his life.

"What sort of emergency?"

"Look, I just drove in from the airport, and there is a note that says, 'Get Connor, get his sister, too,' and my wife has a thing about being the one to pick them both up, she never has asked me to do this, she never has asked *anyone* to do this, *ever*, so I do not *know* what kind of emergency, but I assume someone is dead."

The room is silent, filled only with the straining of little suburban ears that are used to eavesdropping in case this is the time mommy is going to ask daddy for a divorce. I catch a glimpse of Connor. He has heard the word *dead,* which means sure drama to a child his age. "Daddy!" he says, as if a stranger has walked into the room and announced that one Connor Bailey has been given a million dollars, all twenties.

"Go, go," the teacher says, and I make a mental note to consider the ease with which my son can be kidnapped.

With Connor in tow, it is easy to take Morgan from her school. I head for Brown's, put in my order, dial the Greenes' again from the phone behind the counter, get a busy signal, change my plan, throw a ten-dollar bill at the clerk without getting my chicken, head toward Highland Park. "That was stupid, Daddy," Connor keeps saying; Morgan hears no protest from me, echoes him, "That was stupid, Daddy." I press the accelerator hard, take the curves in the road as poorly as I might in an ice storm, fail to stay within the lines.

Perhaps when I was taking off from Washington, David was blowing his brains out. Every time I get on a plane, I busy myself, thinking or reading or working, but at the precise second when we become airborne, I catch myself at whatever I am doing and check my watch.

I want to know the date and time I die, even if only for a second, and I figure that my chances of that happening on an airplane are as good as any. So at 10:37 A.M. Eastern Daylight Time, as I was sitting in my seat thinking about the distinct possibility that I was not going to see my mother again before she died, I imagine David Greene was sitting in his office just outside Skokie with a .38 special jammed up against his soft palate, getting ready to pull the trigger and splatter 160 points' worth of IQ all over the plate-glass window behind his desk. I picture the curtains open, the bullet going through his head and through the glass and then following a fine bloody arc out into the street, falling in slow motion, as if pleased with its own thoroughness. I take a curve on two wheels. "Somebody's dead," Connor says to his sister. "Okay," she says.

It is not until I am halfway up Green Bay Road that it occurs to me that maybe David is not the emergency; maybe someone is lying gruesomely dead in Barbara's parents' house on Oakland Avenue. Bernie and Marge Greene are both too sickeningly healthy to have died suddenly and neatly. Their house, a rambling white colonial, always has struck me as one a movie company would rent to do a film in which a couple of suburban swells are murdered during a robbery. They will be lying in pools of blood in the foyer; Bernie will have opened the front door without asking who is there. He will have tried to tell the robbers that he is living on a fixed income and has nothing; never mind that it is possible to see a thirty-five-inch television in the solarium from there, and then Marge will have come up to see what all the commotion is, and they will have been shot, one after the other, Marge first if the robbers have any decency. Yellow tape will mark the yard; Barbara will be standing out on the Goodmans' lawn next door, dry-eyed and stunned. The image makes enough sense to me for it to emerge full-blown, and I tell Morgan and Connor when we pull into Oakland Avenue to stay in the car, but I make the turn, see no police cars, no crowds on the Greenes' property, and now I figure Bernie and Marge, clean and bloodless, are going to come to the door and tell me something about David.

I ring the bell, and no one answers, so I go back to expecting to find Marge and Bernie dead; then I realize that in such a case Barbara would not know. I try to rearrange a few facts, and Bernie opens the door. The image of what his murderer saw was so vivid in my mind a few minutes ago that I find myself looking beyond him, to confirm that the TV set is visible from the doorway. I see it; I see Marge come padding up, curious, and now I know something is wrong with David, and I am again filled with horror. I do not hate the Greenes, certainly do not want them murdered, but it goes with the business of marrying that one begins to wait for one's wife's parents to die almost as soon as the wedding reception is over. Not to be rid of them exactly, though that is part of the anticipation, but more to become the oldest members of the family, to have all the riddles solved, to know what every succeeding generation is going to look like, to know how far one's generation is going to get in one's lifetime. "What happened to David?" I say. I am out of breath, and the sprint across their lawn is no more than thirty yards.

I feel nothing, absolutely nothing. I am standing on the step, and the grass and leaves still hold the perfect yellow-green of late summer, and I see nothing else, a funny world of the palest green. The sounds of cars on Sheridan Road, half a block away, stop, as if a traffic light has trapped them, and Morgan, who has been shrilling inside my car, muffled by airtight doors, falls quiet. Some small part of me has been expecting David to threaten to kill himself for the past ten years. To threaten and give me a chance to save him; that has been a bad enough possibility. Not that David ever has said he is sad; on the contrary, he always is brimming with the goofiest jokes, the kind that make prepubescent children roll their eyes with embarrassment for him. I have been waiting for the anger to go to exactly the wrong place. But I have imagined that he only would come out and say that he wished to die, maybe even take some pills that made him slip in and out of a coma for a week, anything so that he would be around to see how surprised everyone was by his terrible sadness. I begin to sob.

"Nothing's wrong with David," Marge says.

"I think there is," I say, still crying.

"He was on the phone when you rang the bell," she says. "He didn't *act* like anything was wrong." She puts her hand on my arm, signals Bernie to get the children out of the car, pulls me into the house. "What in God's name is wrong with you?" she whispers. I do not want to go into the house. Finding Bernie and Marge dead on the floor is a less frightening prospect than having to walk in and look foolish in front of them. The Greenes are Jewish, and they are hypersensitive. I am not stereotyping them because, being Jerusha Bailey's son, I eschew ethnic slurs.

When I wrote to my mother and told her I was marrying a friend's sister named Barbara Greene, she wrote back full of anger and said, "You didn't tell me a thing about her, if she's a

Jew or a Negro or what." I phoned her and asked her what on earth her problem was, and all she said was, "Don't you know anything, with all your Ph.D.s? You got a person with a color name, you got a person with color. You ever know a white person named White? Or Green? Colored people have no god-damn imagination, they only got last names about a hundred years ago, and they took color names or presidents' names. You ever see a white person named Washington? And the Jews. They got something to hide, they come over here and get to the Statue of Liberty and all of a sudden they're Mr. Gold or Mrs. Rose. Am I right?" I told her I knew a lot of people, of every race and creed, named Brown. "But mostly Jews and col-oreds, right?" she said. "Barbara's Jewish, all right, are you satis-fied?" I said. To give her credit, she has not had to bring out the Jewish issue more than once or twice since I got married, having made her point. The Greenes are different. They never have come out and said a word about my being Presbyterian by birth, if they even know the exact denomination, but they are always looking for slights, for bad manners that they take as insults, for flaws.

Marge sits me down on the sofa, puts her arm around me. That sort of closeness makes me uncomfortable. The last time I touched my own mother, I was probably about three years old and throwing my arms around her thick, jelly-filled thigh. "Barbara has had some kind of emergency," I say. She asks me how I know, and I tell her about the note and follow what she must be thinking; I see that I have not been clearheaded.

She removes her arm from around my shoulder, folds her arms, recoils. "You've scared these children to death," she says. I look up and see that Bernie has ushered Morgan and Connor in. Their expressions change from bored to accusatory. "See?" she says.

I like Marge; I remember that she is not the same person as her husband. Barbara looks like her mother, only Marge works like the devil to keep herself looking as if she eternally will stay in that vague age range between thirty-seven and fifty-seven, while Barbara happily is pressing for middle age, pushing every springy silver hair into view, wearing less makeup than a sneaky schoolgirl, never exercising on purpose. Sometimes I look at Marge, thick-skinned from the sun, except around the perimeters of her face, where a surgeon has excised a fistful of flesh so that her features all pull away from center, skewing every expression, and I know I have no clues about what Barbara is going to look like. "Don't worry," Barbara used to say. "My parents will both die and leave us rich, and then I'll be magically transformed, and I'll sit by the pool all day and go off to the spa and get my face lifted every six months until I can see people coming behind me." "Do not expect me to touch you," I would say. "Expect you to touch me? I'll forbid you to touch me," she would say back, laughing so hard that she would make lines in her face that I hoped were permanent.

Bernie signals Marge with one motion of his head, and she takes Morgan and Connor into the kitchen. I am the oldest child, the only one left in the room, ready to hear bad news.

"What in God's name is wrong with you?" he says.

He does not frighten me. Most men do not. I can be called down by a woman—a dean, a clerk, a salad-bar waitress—and I will look at the floor, struggle for words, put back whatever I took. But a man can bluster at me for hours, and I will see him as nothing more than a large boy, playing a game. "Nothing is wrong with me, Bernie," I say. "I am the most rational person you ever will meet, and you know it."

"If that's what you really think, you need help. You're being a jackass, or is that not a technical enough word for you? Matter of fact, you've been a jackass for a while now." He smiles at me. "See, I'm not saying you've been one *forever*."

"If you are referring to today, tell me what anyone else would have done. Barbara is so fucking predictable that she is boring—she breaks pattern, and I am not supposed to be alarmed?"

"Don't call Barbara boring or I'll throw you out of here."

I laugh. I expected him to take the opportunity to berate me for using a four-letter word when I have a doctoral degree. He asks me what is so funny, and I say, "Your priorities."

"You've been drinking."

I had a Scotch-and-water after the plane took off this morning, but alcohol leaches out into the pressurized air, leaving me no more stunned than if I were flying without it. I do not consider drinking on planes to be true drinking, any more than eating a dessert soaked in whiskey and then set afire.

"I have been traveling, Bernie."

We sit in the living room in silence for a long time, and Bernie says, "So, how was your father's funeral?" Now I laugh and cannot stop. "Marge!" he bellows, and Marge scurries in. The children do not follow, but I am not surprised. Nothing Marge does interests them. I am still laughing. Bernie points at me. "I asked him how his father's funeral was."

"But you should have heard his delivery," I say, my voice high-pitched. Connor shambles into the room, carrying by the leg the naked Barbie doll his sister keeps here, as if it were a weapon. "Bang," he says, shooting me as if the bullet were coming straight out of the top of Barbie's balding head. He falls back in peals of laughter, and now I am laughing so hard my diaphragm hurts.

"Christ, get the hell out of here," Bernie hollers at me.

"Why?" I say, suddenly feeling sorry.

"Because you're being an irresponsible son of a bitch."

"Sorry," I say.

"He's exhausted," Marge says. "Punchy. Right, Wilson?"

I nod vigorously. I am crying again, but I am crying with relief.

The children leave with me. I know they have fried chicken on their minds. The clerk at Brown's remembers me. He looks at his watch, then hands me a sack of chicken. "I'm getting off in twenty minutes," he says. "Twenty minutes, and this chicken would've been in the garbage."

Morgan wants her chicken heated in the microwave, and Connor prefers his cold. I wrap a drumstick in a paper towel, set the microwave for ten minutes, hear popping sounds after three. The microwave oven has bits of chicken skin on its walls, and Morgan peers in. "You sploded it," she wails. Connor tells me to get out, lays another leg on a paper plate, sets the oven for one minute, hands the chicken to his sister. I eat nothing.

Barbara slips into bed at two in the morning. I am in a thin doze, waiting, and I do not stir. She has come straight up the stairs, removed her dress; I can smell her. She smells of Safeguard soap. I try to find what to say, but she is snoring when I am still considering, and I think I lie awake the rest of the night.

10

Jerusha

LUCKY I PUT MEALWORM IN THE VET, SINCE GLORETTA IS IN the hospital. I dialed her house for three days after I got back from Virginia, and no one answered. For one whole day I let it ring nonstop, and I carted that phone around as far as the cord would reach, waiting to hear her squealy old voice come on in place of the ringing sound. I got the creeps thinking about going over there to check on her, because if anything she'd be dead, long and smelly dead, so finally I called her older one. Cheryl. Gloretta had a stroke, she told me like Gloretta had a varicose vein or something. I learned with Woodrow that a stroke is no big deal compared to *some* things, but Cheryl has no experience with strokes, so she shouldn't be so casual about it. "Just the left side," she said. Fifty percent of her mama was out of commission, and she had to get off the phone to get her nails done. All twenty of them, with all the nerves firing around them the way they were supposed to.

I figure I'll go over to the hospital eventually to see Gloretta, but I'm too sorry for myself to walk into some hospital room and find Gloretta drooling and complaining. With Cheryl in charge of her recovery, it's guaranteed she'll be there for a while; Cheryl's not driving anybody home who can't be dropped at the curb. I'll get myself under control in a couple of days. For today, I sit on the front porch and wait for somebody to pass by. In this neighborhood, if a person dies in the house, the word will have traveled in every direction for four blocks before the body temperature drops below 98.6. White and colored, everybody knows who everybody else is, and it's only a matter of time before someone walks past and tells me, "I'm sorry about poor old Mr. Bailey; how you doing?" If it's a white person, I'll say, "Come sit a while." If it's one of the coloreds, I'll come down the steps and talk on the sidewalk for as long as both of us can stand the sun. I like the way their hair gets all shiny when it heats up.

Of all people, Angela comes out her front door. I forgot about Angela after I hosed her down and closed all the windows for the summer. I am not going to look at her. The way that girl lives is a shame. Right before Hazel died, which is ten years ago, Angela got knocked up by one of the four men Hazel said she was sleeping with; Hazel told it like her daughter just won a popularity contest. They gave Angela a blood transfusion at Charity Hospital, and she got something called Hepatitis C. She found out she had it after Hazel died, when that poor baby of hers was a few months old. The only change that made in Angela's life, far as I could tell, was that she switched from AFDC to SSI. Her checks still came on the first and fifteenth of the month, only she said the SSI was bigger than the welfare so she could buy Benson & Hedges instead of generic cigarettes. As gray-yellow as she is, Angela still has sex with men worse looking than that desert nigger I hosed down with her. No one can blame me for calling him that; that was Woodrow's expression. To Angela's credit, the kid has a Sony PlayStation and a shar-pei puppy. Hazel left her the house and as much freedom as she ever had, and for a long time I made sure she wasn't outside when I used my front door. The boy was three before I found out his name was Dustin and he had yellow-colored hair. It's not that I think Angela's a piece of trash, though of course that's what she is. It's that she sits in that house doing jackshit nothing all day except sleeping, and if she catches you looking like you have nothing better to do, she talks your ear off. Today, though, I might be happy to sit here and listen to Angela until she says something disgusting, which shouldn't take long, and then I could holler at her.

I don't turn my head in her direction, and I sit here on the porch watching the caretakers raking pine needles over at the cemetery. That place could be one giant mulch pile inside a month if people let it go. I saw a lady with a good haircut and a linen dress stop by the fence one day, scoop up a couple garbage bags full of pine needles, keeping her back straight the whole time, I swear. She was picky, like she was getting snap beans at the grocery, throwing backs stems like she was paying by the pound. Didn't even rip her panty hose. I saw some nice azalea beds in the 1600 block a week later, all full of pine needles.

I hear the door open at Angela's house, I hear her go back in, and then out of the corner of my eye I can see her bounding out with her dog on a new purple leash. The dog hasn't had any more schooling than Angela has, and it jerks her along down the steps so fast I think she's going to fall. Angela likes everyone to think she and her liver are too delicate to move, but Angela is one nimble girl. She gets down those steps with two skips and a bounce, same as she did when she was no bigger than a peanut and running out like crazy to brag to Zib about something that wasn't true. She had my Zib believing anything. Hazel had a 1958 Chevrolet station wagon painted Windex blue, and Angela had Zib convinced that car was custom ordered from London. Which Angela probably thought was somewhere in Mississippi.

"Hey," I say, daring her to ignore me.

"Hey," she says, and she jerks the dog in my direction. It's like she's hoping the dog will pull her the other way, and she'll be able to shrug and keep moving. But the dog is happy to see a real human, and he comes flapping toward me. The one thing I like about that dog is the way his jowls make this funny clapping sound whenever he moves. Shar-pei dogs are fun to look at, but a person on food stamps shouldn't be able to have one. "Sorry about Mr. Bailey," Angela says. Never mind that the man's been dead over four months. *Usually,* Angela is queen of the door-poppers. The dog lifts his leg on my camellia bush for a long time, then sits down in front of me. "Might as well sit," I say to Angela.

"So how's my running buddy?" she says after a while. Angela might be almost middle-aged, but I bet she figures all those fools who used to get in trouble with her are just ready and waiting for her next cockamamie plan. Including Zib. Angela ran away from home more often than she was there when she was supposedly in high school, and any girl who was willing to go with her as far as boarding a public-service bus was considered her running buddy. She got Zib to cut out of class at McMain High School one day and go running around the Wildlife and Fisheries Museum looking at the great frigate bird and making dumb jokes, so Zib ranks right up there with the girl who went all the way to San Diego with her.

Ordinarily I would snap at Angela, tell her that she better not put Zib in her class, that Zib was a normal girl. But I'm wishing I'd never laid eyes on Zib. "Your running buddy's as big a pain in the ass as ever," I say.

"Yeah?" Angela always wanted to beat out Zib at anything. She's probably thinking, *Well, I can make Zib's mama like me better than her.* Like I haven't known this girl her whole life.

"I just went up to bury Mr. Bailey week before last."

"Oh." Her eyes glaze over. That fast. Usually people have some interest in knowing what I did with him in the four months in between.

"Zib flew up."

"Oh!"

"She stole my car."

"Whoa!"

"You speak English?" I say.

"Sorry," she says. "I haven't talked to nobody over the age of about ten in a week. I thought Mr. Bailey died last summer. Yeh, last summer. I remember, Dustin already'd been out of school about a *day*, I swear, and the kid is driving me crazy, and I tell him, 'Go outside and play, for God's sake, before I have to strangle you,' and he comes running in, and he's hollering that they're taking a dead body out your house. I figured somebody was dying in there anyway, you know how you can always tell, like if nobody ever comes out, and these sort of nurses come by. That was definitely June, maybe even end of May. No, wait, his school don't let out until after Memorial Day. Except sometimes they push Memorial Day back, you know?"

"For Chrissakes, he died June 12."

"You sure? Right before that you come at me with the hose, remember?" She giggles. "It was *cold.*"

"Jesus," I say.

"So how come you're burying him in October?" Now that she's thought about it, she's mildly curious. Angela has lived directly across the street from the Valence Street Cemetery since the day her mama brought her home from the hospital. That's almost as good as living over a funeral home, if you're interested in death.

"We had a military funeral at Arlington National Cemetery outside Washington, D.C."

"I saw that about Kennedy. Remember? They showed the whole show on TV when I was in high school. You *still* didn't have a color set. Must have been the ten-year anniversary or something. I watched at your house, remember? Mr. Bailey thought it was important as hell. I mean, the guy had been dead ten years, probably even the *horse* was dead by then."

I liked it better when she was saying *Oh?* "So we all went up to Arlington Cemetery," I say. I'm thinking about telling her about McDonald's, see how it plays. It didn't take Wilson and Zib long to find out what had happened, since they were both at the motel when I got there, and they insisted on unloading the car for me. Wilson went into this long lecture about how fitting it was that a man from the end of the twentieth century would wind up in a McDonald's bag, and he told me not to change it, to take Woodrow to Arlington like that, give the archaeologists or anthropologists or whatever you call them something to think about. I didn't go into how McDonald's is putting its food in paper instead of Styrofoam now because paper is natural and rots. I just told him, 'We'll put it *inside* the box, good enough?' Zib, on the other hand, took one look at her father's remains in that bag and started to laugh so hard I thought she'd never stop. She kept it up, getting red in the face and coughing and losing her breath, and finally I slapped her face to bring her around.

"They have a twenty-one-gun salute? And, you know, the parade with the Marines and the horse and all?" Angela says.

"Mr. Bailey was not exactly a fallen leader," I say, more for my benefit than for hers. "But we did have a twenty-one-gun salute."

"They brought twenty-one guys out there with guns for Mr. Bailey?"

"No, seven. Each one got off three rounds." I thought seven was impressive. Not to mention the man from the administration building, the chaplain, and six pallbearers. Luckily, pallbearers don't *have* to carry a casket.

"They do that across the street, every nigger in town'd be diving under their house," Angela says, and I try not to laugh. "My daddy's over there." She points toward the back of the cemetery, where the weeds sometimes get three feet high in summer. "One time, I come right up on this rat, ain't been back since. Daddy can watch me from where I'm at. Though Mama said he had his eye someplace else when he lived with us, no point thinking he got his eye on us now." She falls quiet, and the dog squirms. "She stole your car?" she says, and the dog lies back down, jowls flapping while he gets himself comfortable. I like that. This is one resigned dog. It must lie around praying for Angela to go to sleep. Which, luckily for the dog, I'm sure Angela does as much as possible.

"Well, good as. I mean, I guess you can't steal a car from your own mother, at least not if you bring it back."

"You mean she borrowed your car."

"Yeah, she borrowed my car like you used to borrow lipstick from Woolworth's on Canal Street."

"I never brought no lipstick back." She sounds proud of herself. Not for stealing, but for having a quick legal mind.

"Well, by the time she brought that car back, it had about as much appeal to me as a mashed-down lipstick."

Angela looks toward my car, which is sitting in my driveway. "I don't see nothing wrong with it."

I tell her never mind. I don't say anything else, and I hope she'll go away. It takes her a while to get the hint. It even takes the dog a while to get the hint.

It's past two o'clock in the morning when Angela comes pounding on the back wall of my house. To be sound asleep one second and then to have that kind of noise ten inches from my ear is enough to give me a stroke. "What? What?" I holler through the wall. I can't make out what she's saying, but I know that it's somebody female who's not trying to sneak up on me.

"I remember where all the rooms are at in your house. You still got your bed up against the back wall, right?" she says when I come to the front door to see what she wants. "You still got no doorbell, huh?"

"This better be good, Angela." I'm clutching the front of my housecoat like I'm having a heart attack.

"I got to borrow your car." She grins at me, like she's young enough to be cute again. Not that she ever was to begin with. "See, I don't steal cars like Zib."

"Zib didn't steal my car. She borrowed my car." For six hours. To go sit in some barroom where nobody knew where she was. But there's no need to tell that to Angela. Angela's going to make me forgive Zib if she's not careful.

"It's an emergency." Angela doesn't act like somebody who's having an emergency. And she doesn't look like it, either. She's got on makeup.

"What, you ran out of beer?"

She's grinning again. If she were my daughter, I'd smack her. "I got to take somebody to the hospital. It'll just take a minute. I just got to drop him off."

I watch enough television to know that Angela is the kind of girl who'll find a dead married man in her bed one day and drop him off on the ramp at the emergency room at Charity Hospital and gun the motor so fast out of there that no one will see the license plate. Unless it's *my* license plate. "Somebody die in your house?" I ask her. Straight out, nothing personal. Not that Angela'd be offended. She's probably flattered I think she's so cool-headed.

"No, but just about now he wishes he did."

I tell her to come into the living room. I flip the light on, and I can tell Angela's wearing an extra-large 1984 World's Fair T-shirt and nothing else. Not even shoes. "Okay, what," I say.

"The guy tries to give me fifty bucks."

I shrug.

"I mean, buy me dinner, buy my kid a present or something, bring me a bottle of champagne that'll wreck my liver because you don't know no better, but don't go offering me no money. That's an insult."

I fold my arms across my chest, and I nod at her. At two o'clock in the morning, you can have any set of rules you want.

"So he goes to sleep. And I am sitting there in the bed, getting madder and madder every minute. I mean, on top of everything else, I can't even sleep, I am so pissed off. But this bastard is laying there, buck naked, laying on his back like I don't got a kid that's going to walk in any minute, and then he starts to snore. Well, that's the limit."

I think about guns and hatchets, but I don't see any blood on Angela. I read enough about murders to know there are blood-spatter experts who can tell you how a murder was committed by the stains on the suspect's clothes. You may be able to see Angela's privates through her shirt, but you can't see any blood on her. I won't have to have any blood all over my car. Blood can give you AIDS, and I'm sure everybody who visits Angela already has a terminal disease. Or at least a death wish.

"I superglued his cock to his belly," she says, matter-of-fact.

"Oh, shit," I say, and I sit down. I don't want to hear about men's things. Woodrow was always trying to keep his happy, even when it didn't work anymore and he went out and spent more money than he'd ever paid for any appliance, including a refrigerator, and the doctor put in a bulb that pumped up his thing when he was in the mood. I was happy when he decided to give that little chicken neck a permanent rest, and I never had to look at it or think about it again until it was just something to wash every few days, like an ear or a toe.

"He is fucking furious. He can't pee. It'll go straight in his eye." Angela is acting all thrilled, but she's got that look I've seen on her most of her life. That look that says she went too far, and while it feels like fun she knows some part of her body's about to get a good stinging soon.

She sees my car keys lying in a bowl on top of my rolltop desk. She picks them up. "You still don't put them on the ring with the house key, huh." Woodrow told me to keep keys separate, so if somebody stole my car he couldn't race me back to the house and break in and take everything. I said to him, "You steal a car, you head for some border, Woodrow," but he kept after me about it, and it was one of those things I gave in on. I pluck the keys out of Angela's hand, drop them back into the bowl.

"Heloise says use polish remover," I tell her.

"Heloise? Like used to be in the paper? The one you couldn't tell how old she was but you figured it didn't matter?"

"Yeh, that one," I say.

"You telling me Heloise got a man in her laboratory she done this to? You seen that picture of Heloise. If that woman ever saw dick, I'd be surprised."

"You can get superglue on other parts of your body, you know."

"Yeah," she says, like I'm a genius. She looks at her fingernails, which are yellow and ripped down to the quick, splays her hand out in front of me like she's a hand model. "I don't buy polish remover," she says. This from a girl who never wore the same shade of polish two days in a row, and who never paid Woolworth's a cent, either.

I have a big bottle of it in my bathroom. I bought it two years ago when Woodrow was on this tear with his woodcrafting. He liked the way superglue held two pieces of wood together, instead of having hammer dents around the nails. I told him he was going to get it all over his hands, but he never did, to spite me. I bring out the bottle, and Angela goes for it, and I say, "Hold your horses." She looks at my nails, which I cut short with scissors once a week to get even with the woman at the beauty parlor at the corner who gets my catalogs by accident and keeps them. I walk around this neighborhood with stubbly fingernails, and people will drive up and think I'm her customer and wonder how she's staying in business, doing lousy looking nails. "What use you got for polish remover?" Angela says.

"You're bad as Zib," I say. When Zib was a child, she'd look in my pocketbook, see I had a five-dollar bill, come ask me for ice cream. I'd say, I can't afford to buy you ice cream, and she'd say, "You got a five-dollar bill, Mama."

I get one of Woodrow's empty pill bottles, fill it up; Angela takes it, holds it up like she's pretending it's a crystal vase, says, "Sure you got no use for this?" and runs out the front door like I'm going to swat her. She looks back, runs in and gives me a hug. I think I'll get a blood test tomorrow.

I almost don't have time to get off all the lights before she's back, banging on the front door. "I got to have more," she says. She edges her way into my living room. "That's not the way you ask a person," I say. I don't know why I've never given up on Angela's upbringing. Maybe because I owe it to Hazel. I know I gave up on Wilson and Zib because I *didn't* owe it to Woodrow.

She's waltzing and fidgeting all over the room, and then she tells me never mind, scurries out the door. I go in the bedroom, where I've left the bottle, and I throw it in the metal trash can next to the bed. I dare her to come ask again in the middle of the night. I'll show her the bathroom cabinet, defy her to find polish remover anywhere in there.

I need a new muffler soon, so it's easy for me to hear my car starting up in the driveway. By the time I get to the front door, all I can see are my taillights going up Valence Street. I wonder how she had time to walk that poor man to the car, roust her boy out of bed, push him out because he's too big to carry, figure out my sticky ignition, and pull off. I dial her phone, and this time it's back in order, ringing and ringing. At least she didn't leave the boy. She probably had them both sitting up in that car before she came to my door. I have to remember to lock my car next time. This must be the only neighborhood in New Orleans where colored boys walk past all hours of the night and leave a raggedy car alone, and then a white woman comes and takes it. She'd write to Zib and brag about this tomorrow, if she could write.

I settle down on my bed, figure I'll wait until I hear her coming back. Angela can kill herself, and I won't shed a tear, since she looks like she's dying anyway, but my car is something else. Angela is the type to total a car, and the blue-book value on mine is probably less than the deductible, knowing Woodrow's money sense. She better not harm that Dustin. She better not even bleed on the boy. Her blood is poison. I've got the latest issue of *Family Circle,* which ought to keep me entertained long enough for someone to drive down to Charity, let a man out of the car, and drive back. I start looking at the recipes. It used to be that they'd tell you how many calories are in everything. Then how much fiber. Then how much fat. This time it's how many minutes it takes. I don't need recipes for six that take twenty minutes. I take out a cigarette. My lighter's out of fluid.

The decorating ideas are too frilly. Who needs to decorate when you're nearly seventy and haven't had company in thirty years? I have a pack of matches from the old KB's in the drawer next to the bed. Thought they'd be worth something, now that KB's is closed. Well, at least they're worth more than an empty lighter. I light up, pitch the match in the metal trash basket.

The next thing I know, I'm on the sidewalk in front of Angela's house. It's wetter out than right before a rainstorm, the air is full of a radio squawking and flashes of red and white light from a fire engine, and I am lying on a stretcher, breathing through a plastic mask.

11

Wilson

WHEN I WAS A CHILD IN NEW ORLEANS, AUTUMN WAS ONE of those foreign phenomena—Dutch windmills, Egyptian pyramids, and such—that decorated school bulletin boards. It was supposed to be familiar: like the families in the Scott-Foresman readers, red maple leaves were something I thought should be in my world, but they never were, except as line-drawn dittos on construction stock. When Connor brings home school papers that make sense to him, stories in which the brown-skinned people are middle class, coloring sheets with apple trees, I am honored to know him, this normal child, who is one of those who were in the Midwest when I was growing up and puzzling about deciduous trees and mothers who shrilled in the kitchen.

He is sitting at the kitchen table, ignoring a bowl of oatmeal and honey and soy milk, gluing leaves, elm and oak, yellow and orange, on a sheaf of blue construction paper and looking at me. "You should press them first," I say. "Otherwise they will turn brown and crumple." "It's supposed to be for today," he says with annoyance. "Remember?" I shake my head no. I think I would remember such a thing. Barbara walks into the room and I catch her eye, wishing she would tell me where she was Monday night. We have not been in the same room alone and awake for days now. "I heard him tell you two weeks ago," she says and moves on. "It would've taken you ten minutes."

"He scared us half to death the other day," Connor announces.

"Kick me while I am down, Connor," I say.

"I already know," Barbara says wearily. "And don't call your father 'he.'" She fixes Morgan's hair while Morgan is drawing slow circles in her oatmeal. Morgan's hair is fine and long, pale and straight as Zib's once was. It is the kind of hair that I can find in my food and not throw out the entire plate, and Barbara is pulling the brush through it in her open palm, her motions gentle, as if Morgan were going to lose her hair and grow no more. "You're not supposed to brush your hair at the table," Connor says. "She's brushing away from the table," Morgan says and leans back into Barbara, thinking she is being helpful. "Don't call her 'she,'" Connor says. Barbara pushes Morgan's head away with the heel of the hand that is holding the brush, and the bristles press into Morgan's scalp. She lets out a yelp of pain, and Barbara drops the hairbrush on the floor. The handle is wood, and it splits down the handle shaft; I recall she paid thirty dollars for it and complained about the price until she convinced herself that it would last a lifetime. "In the car," she says, and the children stare at her and do not move. "In the car!" "I haven't done my teeth," Connor says patiently. He screws the cap back onto the glue, aligns his leaf papers neatly one on top of the other. "I am giving you ten seconds to get in the car," Barbara says, her voice shaking at the highest register.

"I didn't brush my teeth," Connor says.

"I don't care about your teeth," Barbara says, and Connor begins sobbing. His cries have had a broad range of meaning since he was a newborn; in that respect he was simple to tend. This is a fearful cry, and I know he is thinking that the threats are going to be realized, that by tonight his teeth will be full of holes that will take a jackhammer and no novocaine to fix, as his mother has promised for years. "Five seconds," Barbara says, and Connor is screaming now. I tell him I will meet him at the car, and I dash for his toothbrush, cover it with some of my tartar-control Crest, reach the car as Barbara is backing out of the driveway. Connor sees me. "I have to have the *sparkle* kind," he shouts through his closed window, but Barbara has not taken her foot off the accelerator, and I have to jump back to avoid being swiped by the car. The daub of toothpaste flies onto my shirt.

I wait for Barbara in the kitchen. I know she will be back. Barbara has not adopted her mother's fancy ways of leaving the house only in full maquillage, but Barbara goes nowhere without showering and brushing her teeth. It is not eight o'clock yet, and I dial my mother's number. No answer. I try again, to be sure I have dialed correctly. I let it go twenty rings. Seven-fifty in the morning; she cannot be out. Mother became a poor sleeper when my father was first diagnosed as truly sick, napping like a watchdog, smoking into the early hours, dozing sometimes until midmorning. She has no one to talk to, any-way, since Gloretta Higgins is her main visiting partner, and Gloretta is on a tight schedule, scurrying through her house in the early mornings so that she can have everything in what she considers the right place in time for the talk shows. Mother re-spects Gloretta's routine or, rather, Mother cannot be bothered with the consequences of interrupting it. I go over my mother's geography, a small scape, a one-block radius. Mother may have been adventuresome as a child, if I can gauge from the kinds of risks she takes when she opens her mouth, but she has come to believe that there is nothing new for her to see, and so she has no reason to stray far from home unless forced. In New Orleans, it is as possible as it is in any small town to find all a person needs in shouting distance: foodstuffs, sundries, ideological battles. I dial Angela's house. No one answers. I cannot remember the name of the beauty parlor on the other side of Mother. It changes every five years, in name, not in ownership, as if an *e* with an *accent aigu* or a sorry pun will bring in more customers. Gloretta Higgins. No one answers. I consider turning on CNN to see whether New Orleans is flooded right up to the phone lines. Except for slow, insidious termites, water is New Orleans's only natural enemy, though when the globe warms another ten degrees in the next fifty years, as I expect it will, New Orleans will have to be placed under a sky-blue mirrored-glass dome or it will turn into a fishy-smelling puddle.

I dial Uncle George. Speaking to Uncle George is high treason in Jerusha Bailey's book of statutes. Mother does not believe in mental retardation: to her, simple-minded behavior is an act of will that can be overcome. When I was working on my bachelor's degree, I sneaked over to see George during my freshman vacations, when I was tingling with knowledge. I did not want to insult him, in case my suspicions were wrong, so I disguised the intelligence puzzles by copying them in pencil. "I can't see nothing without my glasses," he said when he failed to fill in the next number in a two-digit repeating sequence. "You can't draw worth shit," he said when I tested him for congruence of shape. I went home later that day and told Mother that Uncle George probably had the IQ of a trainable mentally retarded person, and she said, "Trainable my eyeball. You've got to *want* to learn something before somebody's going to train you. Your Uncle George learned his mama'd take care of him till he died, and he didn't see reason to learn anything else." My father came in right then and told me to hush, that you get your brains from your mother and father, and if George got stupidity from Grandma and Granddaddy Bailey, then how come he wasn't stupid, too? I tried to explain birth trauma, and Mother said, "Birth trauma? Grandma Bailey took one look at that ugly thing popping out on her quilt and fainted dead away; that's birth trauma."

Uncle George answers the phone, disbelief in his voice. "Hello, Uncle George, this is Wilson." "Yeh." As if we have hung up moments ago. I ask him how he is doing. "Who's this?" he says. I tell him Wilson, Woodrow's boy. "Oh, Wilson." Silence. I ask him how he is doing. "Cat had kittens under the house," he says. "Woke up in the night, hear this hollering, like it's been hit by a car, you know? One big holler, then all this little peeping. I go out on the front porch, I don't see nothing. I got pretty good eyes, you know? Not for reading, no, but I can see fine in the dark. I keep looking for something smashed out on Carondelet Street. You know how them niggers come barrel-assing up Carondelet Street? They won't take St. Charles, no. Just like they won't walk on the sidewalk to save their lives. Got to walk in the middle of the street, dare a car to hit them. What was I telling you about?"

"You were telling me you had kittens under your house." I look at my watch. Barbara will return soon, and I do not want to be on the phone when she walks in. But I don't think George has spoken to a soul in weeks, the way he is going on.

"I crawl under there this morning. All different colors, I pull them out. You know it's a story you can't touch no baby animal or its mama going to kick it out the nest? That mama's in here nurring away. Hope no cars don't hit them. They sad-looking, yeah."

"Have you seen my mother?"

"Who's this?" he says. I tell him, give him as much of my lineage as I think he needs. "She's a good-looking woman, your mama, yeah, I've seen your mama." I tell him she is not answering her phone. "So how come Woodrow's not answering the phone?" he says.

I do not want to do this. Uncle George does not hold threads of information long; maybe I do not have to tell him at all. "He died in June," I say. "No one told you?" George breaks into loud sobs, then takes in a breath. "Oh, I'm scaring that poor mama cat. Shhh, shhh." I am crying now. I tell him I am sorry. "It's okay, shhh, shhh," he says. "When he died?" I tell him June. "She didn't call me, no. It was in the *Picayune*?" I tell him it was. Mother sent me the obituary, the sorriest obituary I ever have read. He might as well have been a dog. "I can't read a thing without my glasses, you know," he says. I nod, though he cannot see me. "My name was in it?" Of course. "Nobody called me. Not the *Picayune*, not your mama, nobody. Woodrow probably told her to call me. Mean as cat shit sometimes, that woman." Mother told me once that George had made a pass at her, and I tried to explain that people with limited mental capabilities have sexual drives, too, but no finesse, and she should not blame him. "He knew what he was doing, Wilson," she said, and I let it go at that.

I hear Barbara pulling into the driveway. "Is everything all right in New Orleans?" I say to George.

"Woodrow died," he says.

"I am so sorry, Uncle George."

"Four kittens, all different colors, too."

"You let them stay with their mother for six weeks, you know that, right?" When I was small a stray had a litter under Angela's house. Hazel took the mother to the SPCA before the babies were ready to be weaned, reasoning that they would scatter, find homes, but within a month we had a half dozen psychotic cats howling and fussing all day and night on the block. They disappeared one day, and Zib asked Mother how that happened. I told her that she did not want to know, and Mother told me to hush, I was too softhearted for my own good, and Zib figured it out and bawled loud enough for Hazel to ring the phone. Zib could not look at a cat for years after that, and then one day she began learning cruelty jokes from Angela, and she has been hard ever since.

"The mama knows better than me," George says.

I tell him that I will come see him soon, and he says my mother will holler at me. His voice has the same timbre as my father's. Tears are streaming down my face when Barbara walks into the kitchen and sees me hang up the phone.

"You're supposed to be gone by now," she says. I tell her she has to talk to me. She walks over to the sink and turns her back to the room. There are no dishes in the sink, and she has not turned on the water. "What's the point?" she says.

"You came home smelling like soap."

"I always smell like soap, Wilson." She picks up the bottle of clear Ivory liquid from the counter and waves it at me.

The image of Uncle George in Grandma Bailey's living room is so clear that I ache. Grandma Bailey left George with her dark Victorian furniture set around a rose-patterned linoleum rug that was chipping away at the corners before she died, revealing unvarnished wood underneath. Last time I visited, George still had not moved anything an inch out of place. I should call him back and tell him he needs a litter box. "What?" I say.

Barbara hefts the bottle of Ivory at me, and the clear soap spews out of the top in an arc that leaves a straight line on the floor. She misses me by far, but throws a dishrag right into my face. "Look," she says, "I am very tired of you. I don't *want* to be tired of you, but I am."

She walks out, and I mean to wipe up the detergent, but I have a nine o'clock class. I call after her, tell her I will clean up when I get home, take it back, say I will come home at ten and do it.

After class I know I need to do something. What I need to do is sleep. But I have an eleven o'clock. What I need to do is get a cup of coffee.

12

Zib

Mr. Scamardo is furious. I haven't been to work since I came back from the funeral. I have two weeks of vacation time coming to me. I've only missed five working days. But when I call up every morning and tell him I'm not going to make it in, he hollers. "You want to go on a Caribbean cruise, you want to fly to Paris, you want to sit in your apartment and get drunk for a week, you tell me in advance, I don't care, I'll get somebody to cover for you. But you are pushing me past my limit with this every-morning stuff." "I swear I'll be in tomorrow," I tell him. He offers to punch me in. If I'll do him a favor. I tell him I'm too repulsive to be seen. He says, "Let me be the judge of that." Maybe I'll let him see me dripping grease from every pore and hair shaft. I'm also sure I have AIDS. A man like him deserves a fatal sexually transmitted disease. But I'd have to have sex with him in order to kill him. "I think I have AIDS," I say. He says nothing for a while. "You can't work around food if you have AIDS," he says hotly. I tell him that's not true. I'm from New Orleans. Half the waiters and busboys, slicing lemons and scooping ice and pouring coffee, are probably HIV-positive. That's half the fun of being in New Orleans. "There're a couple dozen women in the personnel files who'd do anything to have your job," he says. I tell him I appreciate his kindness and interest. If I have AIDS, I'll need my health insurance.

I lie around the apartment and think too much. Five A.M. comes again. I'm sitting straight up in bed unable to do a thing. If I run to the drugstore for a few bags of chips and a six-pack of Coke, I'm exhausted. I can't imagine standing around the Winn-Dixie. Two-hundred-dollar basketfuls of groceries roll past. Minute after minute. Every penny has to be accounted for. Every tomato. Every cashier.

I have no symptoms of AIDS. I can't have incubated since Saturday. Whenever my life is wonderful or horrible, I know I'm about to die. I had a boyfriend who was a medical student about twenty years ago. He left his *Merck Manual* in my apartment. I can take any symptom, a twenty-four-day menstrual period, an ache in the base of my skull, a sour belch, and know I have an obscure and fatal disease. I know the *Merck Manual* is twenty years old. So it's missing both new and treatment-resistant afflictions. As well as now-sure cures. But I can't help myself. I lie in the bed, and I think about a certain and messy death. The tic of a neuron explodes into a tumor as big as my head. The smear of nose-blood in a tissue turns mucus into spinal fluid. A moment of breathlessness means a giant hole in my heart. The man in the red Saab gets more evil every second. All his moves were a bisexual's. All his behaviors were an IV drug user's. I lie here and try to figure out everything about him. Why'd he have nothing better to do than pull off the highway and walk into a pub and fuck the first woman he saw? Why'd he live in Washington instead of New York; because his family scorned him for his nasty ways? Why didn't he get regular haircuts? I'm sure he has AIDS. So I have it, too. It only takes one time. He didn't have condoms. Why protect himself when he's already got the disease? But I was so drunk. It was easy, slow. Nothing tore. Poisons had no way into my bloodstream. But no one's ever said a man has to rip you up for the virus to get in. I've felt my cervix. It has a hole in it for semen to skibble inside and make babies. Right up there in my womb. Which I picture as being a balloon full of blood. Just waiting to spill its contents every twenty-eight days. Or more often if I'm dying of ovarian cancer. Flooding estrogen and tearing closer to a hideous death every twenty-four days. Page 1191 of the *Merck Manual*.

I've had this worry habit for most of my life. I've refined it only by saving up more complicated facts. Usually I can talk to my mother. She'll fix me up with very few words. "You're not going to die. You're too mean to die," she'll say. "Only the good die young," we'll say at the same time. Then I'll list the mean people who've died young. My third grade teacher. Angela's father. Adolf Hitler. Zelda Fitzgerald. A mean person for whatever life stage I've been in at the time. "Well, you're not an alcoholic or a madman who's about to be assassinated, right?" I nod. Even if we're on the phone long distance. "So your cycle's twenty-four days? So you shouldn't stay up so late. You sleep five hours a night, sure your body's going to think twenty-four days is twenty-eight days. Get a calculator." "You got a headache? Quit drinking so much." She's always been right. When it's come to *me*. On the other hand, my father had headaches and stumbled around. She looked for liquor bottles all over the house. Then his brain stem got taken over by all these alien cells that gave him a real death. I have no symptoms now. Except this tiredness that ties me to my bed. While bad ideas dance in front of me. Even when I close my eyes. Even when I sleep. I can't call her to tell her I'm sure I have AIDS. She'd say, *Well, only the good die young,* except *that bad people get AIDS;*

*that's what you get for taking my car and running off; of course you
have AIDS, and it serves you right.*

I don't have many friends here. When I started as a cashier,
I had a million friends. Bag boys who wanted to brush up
against my breasts. Checkout girls who liked to giggle with me
about fucking the boy in the warehouse. The one with no
neck and a cock so big we could see it through his pants.
No matter what mood he was in. Each summer a friend or
two would snare a lonely man coming through her line with
frozen entrées and canned ravioli. She'd marry him and
promptly quit. The girls who took their places were younger
and huffier every year. I've been an assistant manager seven
years now. Everybody's required to hate me. If not at first, then
eventually. It's company policy to make cashiers and bag boys
miserable. I schedule them to close on Saturday nights. Their
boyfriends and girlfriends have to amble around the parking
lot while I have them putting Life Savers in the racks by
checkout. Mr. Scamardo hates anybody who's got a life of
promise. It's *my* responsibility to treat them all badly. I'm driving great numbers of kids into staying in college and getting
jobs in high-rise office buildings in big cities. What Mr. Scamardo *ought* to want me to do is sing a siren's song. Lure them
into a life played out under the fluorescent lights of a supermarket. Have them listening to Barry Manilow music and cash
register beeps. Fill their noses with the smell of produce that'll
rot tomorrow if it's not sold today.

I'm going to phone Ellie. She married a man five years
younger than she was. He came through her line in the summer
of 1994 with nothing but a watermelon and a fifth of vodka.
Took her to the beach the next day. In a soup of alcohol, sweet
red juice, and Gulf water, he decided right then to marry her.
And take her back to Atlanta. Ellie has four well-fed-looking

children. She's gotten wisdom from being forced to be a grown-up in a plastic city where nobody's crazy. Not the wealthy, not even the poor.

Somebody shrills hello into the phone. I say, "Can I talk to your mommy, please?" I say each word clearly, like the child's hard of hearing. I hear silence for a second. I hope I'm not going to be holding long-distance while the receiver hangs loose half an hour at Ellie's house. I hate to talk to kids. If I call a cashier to come in early, I tell her I'll cut her hours if her kid ever leaves me waiting again for more than thirty seconds. She laughs, and then I say I'm serious. The next time I call her, if a kid answers, she'll jerk the phone away and say, "I *told* you I'd get it." The kid will wail, and I'll say, "Well, you don't have to kill him, for Chrissakes."

"Zib?" says the same voice after a moment.

"That you?" I say.

"Where are you?" Ellie is out of breath. Though she answered on the second ring. I tell her I'm home, why. "Because my kitchen is knee-deep in Jell-O, that's why," she says. Like that's an accomplishment. I ask her what she's doing giving Jell-O to four children under the age of six. Ellie'd read the ingredients panels on every prepackaged food at the Winn-Dixie by the time she quit. And she eliminated everything from *her* diet that didn't come straight from the farm.

"Hey, they like it, what can I tell you?" she says. "I don't eat it. I don't eat horses' hooves."

"It doesn't say horses' hooves on the box," I tell her.

I hear a high-treble howl in the background. "Shh, shh. Here," she says.

"Ever consider birth control?" I say.

"Hey, this's what I want." She's more pissed at me than at her kids. She's jealous of me. "Well, you're never bored," I say.

She laughs. Then she asks me if I can hold a second. And I hold two minutes. I'm getting ready to hang up. She comes back. "A psychiatrist'd be cheaper than trying to talk to you long distance," I say.

"Oh, Zib, I got to go," she says. She's not as sorry as she wants me to think she is.

"What if I told you I was dying?" I say.

"You're not dying," she says cheerfully and hangs up.

"Hey, you're one terrific mama," I holler into the dead phone line.

I can't explain why I decide to call Wilson. I came close to liking him in Arlington. There's something about being with your brother and your mother all day. Sharing space, going everywhere together. It drags you back. You're four, and your brother is five, and you're in Woolworth's on Magazine Street. You run off to the toy shelf while he's standing there holding her hand. Staring at nothing while she picks out one spool of blue thread. She comes after you and smacks your butt in front of everybody. And he looks more sorry than pious. By the time we were both in junior high, he'd slipped into constant excellence. It made my mother furious. She had to work so hard at finding reasons to be angry at him. I made that part of her life easy. I was still smaller than she was. And I gave her grounds at least once a week to slap my face. I thought I was required by some code to despise people like Wilson. I spent the better part of five years making fun of him with my girlfriends. So I was convinced that, like my mother, I should work hard at picking at him. We drew an imaginary line through the universe. One side for him, the other for me. He couldn't be mean if I was. Couldn't be lonely if I was. In turn, I couldn't let on that I'd ever read a book that didn't come off the rack at K&B. Couldn't pretend to like children.

I call his office at the university. I've never done it before. But I have his direct-line number. Mama sent it to me once. Along with a list of people she wanted for pallbearers. "Hey, Wilson," I say. He recognizes my voice. He says, "Oh, Christ, please do not tell me that Mother is dead, because frankly I cannot handle it."

"What?"

"Is she dead?" he says. He sounds like he's going to cry.

"Not that I know of," I tell him. "Though she might very well be."

He starts to laugh. I hear that nervous relief that's worth being scared to death for. "You never called me before," he says.

"I never particularly liked you before."

He asks me if I can hold on for a second. I groan. My phone bill is going to be so inflated by dead air. Really, a second, he says. Then he covers the receiver enough for someone to see him doing it. But not enough to keep me from hearing him. "Look, can you wait in the hall? I have not talked to my sister in years." I hear a postpubescent male voice say, "Sure." He's got the tone of somebody who's teetering between a D-plus and a C-minus.

"Hey, you really scare them," I say when he comes back.

"You flatter me, Zib." He laughs a little.

I have him on the phone. A Cerberus is waiting outside his door ready to tell all comers that Dr. Bailey can't be bothered. And I don't know what to say. I'm lying in bed, in an XL T-shirt with the must of three days of fretting on it. I close my eyes, try to get out of my apartment and all its sourness. It's easier to talk like this. "What do you know about AIDS?" I finally say.

"Oh, Christ," Wilson says.

"I'm serious."

"You are not going through that again."

It always surprises me that Wilson doesn't forget my flaws. He's kept a mental file on me. With every embarrassing moment given equal weight. I can joke to a friend that I wet my pants when I was seven, never bother to mention it to another. Then I hear about it from *Wilson*, and I'm seven years old and totally humiliated. "Hey, Pop had a headache, and he fucking *died* from it," I say.

"You do this only when you are miserable, Zib."

"All I asked you was what you know about AIDS. I didn't say, 'Oh, God, Wilson, I need you to fly down here right now, I know I've got AIDS, I'm going to die in three months.' All I said was, 'What do you know about AIDS.' Jesus!"

"I know you can get it from taking your mother's car and driving all over Virginia until you find some guy with a five o'clock shadow who is not very picky."

"You're a riot, Alice." Mama always said that when I was funnier than she wanted to admit. I was grown, watching *Honeymooners* reruns on cable at three in the morning, before I found out where she got the line. I'd never have given her the pleasure of my asking.

"Look, if you are worried, go and get a test."

"You can't get a test for six months."

"If you know so much, why are you calling me?"

I tell him I don't know. Which is true. I don't have a reason. Just a comfortable feeling about talking to him. I've told him once that I like him. I'm not going to give him any more anxiety than that. I didn't hug him good-bye when I left for the plane Monday. Though we'd sat up all night together after Mama left. Eating sandwich cookies, drinking Pepsi, and watching *Shenandoah* on the TV set in his room. "As long as we are regressing, we might as well go all the way," was about all he said to me that night. I laughed and went off to the vending machines whenever supplies ran low. My hand was full of Wilson's money. I was happy enough. He paid the motel bill before I woke up. "May I tell you something?" he says after a while. I nod. My eyes are still closed. I'm in the mood for a lot of sugar and caffeine. "You are spoiled," he says good-naturedly.

"Thanks a lot," I say, equally pleasant.

"No, hey, it is not as if being spoiled is your *fault*; it is a passive way of being, if you think about it; it is something someone else did to you."

I do a quick mental review of my life. When was I lavished with so much attention and material excess that I expect a lot out of life? Mama's flyback paddle and her unfailing ability to say no to me cover all the years I was growing up. I don't recall men who've come into my life and showered me with anything but deceit. "You've got the wrong person, Wilson," I say. I want to say, *How about that woman you're married to? Who had her own car when she was sixteen? And a million stuffed animals on her bed? And a trust fund that gives you more income than I make?* But Barbara is sloppy. She goes out of her way to give the impression that she grew up in a slum. And that she doesn't expect a thing out of life. To me it's show-offy. Though sometimes I have conversations with her that are funny and mean and low-class.

"You owe Father money, right?" Wilson says.

"He's dead, Wilson."

"I am not trying to collect. I am trying to make a point."

"You sure you're not trying to collect?"

"I would be doing it for Mother, and she is not at the top of my list of people whom I am going to call up and offer to help. I have not talked to her since you did. What do you owe him, four, five thousand?"

"Are you insane? He gave me about three *hundred*. All in fives. Over about twenty years. And he didn't say anything about paying him back, either."

He's silent. "Sorry I asked," he says. He owes Mama $1,900. He borrowed it to pay child support after his divorce. He hasn't paid her back. Naturally she told me about it. "I got them both where I want them. Woodrow's got a hole in his bank account that he can't figure out, and I dare Wilson to complain about me." If Wilson thought about it, he'd know Mama hasn't kept his secret.

"I think Barbara is having an affair," he says.

"You jerk," I say. I'd throw up if I didn't have a belly full of sweets. Wilson's been sitting there. Listening to me, thinking about Barbara. Waiting to trump me.

"Is that all you can say?"

"Well, you're making me look like an asshole."

"Jesus, Zib, *res ipsa loquitur*."

"*Res ipsa loquitur* yourself. I happen to know what that means. I say you're making me look like an asshole. Then you go trying to make me look like an asshole. The thing speaks for itself."

Wilson starts to cry. I've never heard a man cry except in the movies. If I have to hear one, I'm glad it's my brother. He wailed if he stubbed a toe when he was small. My discomfort is the same, man and woman, six-year-old boy and five-year-old girl. I want to make it stop. "I'm sorry, I'm sorry," I say.

"You are really spoiled," he says. His voice is all wet. I can tell he's trying to smile.

"I'm sorry about the Barbara news. How'd you know?" His first wife didn't give him another man to blame. She said it had to do with Wilson, period.

"I don't *know*. I *think* she's having an affair."

"You *think* she's having an affair. Jesus, Wilson, what makes you *think* she's having an affair? You have a list of indicators in a book?"

"She smelled like soap," he says. I laugh. "Shut up, Zib. She smelled like Safeguard soap. Barbara will not buy anything from Procter & Gamble. Not because of Satan, but because of red dye number four."

I sigh. "She probably showered at her mother's house." Marge Greene strikes me as the type to overkill. To have Drano under her sink. And malathion in her potting shed. She disdains her son because he went to Valparaiso University instead of the University of Chicago. Because he set up offices in Skokie instead of downtown. Because she wanted him to marry a Jewish girl and have smart, gnomish children. And he married a blond paralegal who was taller than he was. She divorced him when she figured she might have kids that looked like Bernie. Marge prefers toxicity. Marge uses antibacterial soap.

"At two in the morning?" Wilson says.

I have no argument for that. "You tell Mama?" I wonder if he let *her* get on the phone and go on about Gloretta or the coloreds and then gave her his more important news. Though Mama can't be shamed that way. She's capable of saying, "Wilson, you're interrupting me."

"I have not talked to Mother. Her line was busy forever after I returned, and then it rang without an answer, so I figured she was exasperated with us and keeping it off the hook or unplugged except to call out."

"Mama can be a bitch," I say. I feel better for the first time in days.

13

Jerusha

I DON'T KNOW WHY I'M SO ALL-FIRED READY TO GET OUT. These fat nurses talk to me like I'm a child or a lunatic, even the colored ones, and if I see one more social worker I'll scream, but I have no place to go, and nothing to do when I get there. Which is information I keep to myself. Since Woodrow never let me give a dime to the Red Cross or the United Fund, I don't take charity, and I'm going to have to if I don't do something fast: either they are going to pet all over me and let me stay in Baptist for a few more days because even the doctors feel sorry for me, or they are going to put me in a shelter or a housing project or a cheap apartment and give me food stamps and make me no better than sixteen-year-old girls on welfare. Or Angela. I've been able to throw every social worker out of my room as soon as I've read her ID tag, and I've coughed up a lung when the doctor's come in, but I'm running out of time. I have to have somebody come pick me up because the hospital administrators think I'm going to collapse on their sidewalk and sue them. And I can't think of anybody who owes me big enough to call. Gloretta isn't answering her phone, so I guess she's on some other floor of the hospital, staring at the ceiling and dribbling baby food down her chin.

Angela doesn't answer her phone. And I'm not about to call Wilson or Zib, much less tell anybody they exist. Last time I spoke to either one of them, we were in a motel room in Woodbridge, Virginia, and Zib had just come back from being a slut out in the open where her father's ghost could watch her. The woman lives in Florida, and if she's still got urges when she's that close to menopause, she could *wait*. Living across from a cemetery, I believe that spirits hang around where you expect them to, either where they went to a violent death or where they went to a peaceful burial. Woodrow died believing Zib was a virgin; she could've crossed a few state lines away from his grave before she started messing around. *And* she took my car. She went on this tear about how I didn't need the car, how I could've gone tromping over to McDonald's in the mall, like I ever wanted to set foot in McDonald's again. Or in a mall where I had to ask a dozen clerks, "You got a nice box for ashes?" Not to mention that I'm almost seventy years old and had come from burying my husband, or whatever you call shoving him in a drawer. All Zib knew was that her father died, and she had all the rights in the world, and she huffed and sulked, and then her brother, who's read too many books, said, "Listen, we are all upset here. This has been a trying day." So I said, "You two don't have any right to be upset, nothing's changed in your spoiled little lives," and I packed my bag and was off in my car. It was one o'clock in the morning, and neither one tried to stop me. I drove nonstop to New Orleans, because the only satisfaction I had was knowing the two of them were going to have to squabble over paying our motel bill, and I was damned if I was going to run one up on myself somewhere in Georgia. I haven't heard from either one, and my phone is probably giving out one of those I'm-sorry-the-number-you-have-reached-is-not-in-service-at-this-time messages. I dial it for fun, and what I get is a hacking ringing sound. Let them try for a couple of days. Then they'll call the operator, and she'll have it in her computer that my house has burned to the ground, and they'll both look like fools, running around, trying to find out if I'm dead.

I try Angela's number again. I'll let it ring twenty times, in case Angela is home sleeping off her adventure, but someone picks up on the first ring. "Ange*la*," I say, so she'll know she's in a world of trouble. "No, this's Dustin." It's eleven o'clock in the morning. "What's a healthy boy like you doing, sitting home at eleven o'clock in the morning?"

"Who's this?" he says. He sounds like somebody who expects a password or an explanation, not like one of those colored kids who dial your number by accident, then say to you, "Who this?"

I tell him it's Mrs. Bailey, next door.

"I know who you are," he says pleasantly.

"Yeh?"

"You got a dog. One of those little dogs like they had on the commercial. My dog wants to eat your dog."

I forgot all about Mealworm. Mealworm is no Lassie; he didn't bark and tug my sleeve when he saw the explosion. Maybe he's dead. He's got lungs the size of spit bubbles. I ask Dustin where my dog is. "In your yard," he says, all matter-of-fact. I'm relieved. I like that little dog. I can live forever without going in and finding him like a charcoal rat. He'll get out of the yard, I say. "But he goes right back in," Dustin says. "He's smart as a cat." I thank him, feeling pleased. "And he doesn't eat hardly nothing. I mean, he's so little. I give him food."

"Where's your mama?" I say.

"I don't know. You know your house burned down night before last?"

"Yeah, I know my house burned down night before last. Good thing I know; you go off telling people something like that, you could give them a heart attack."

"Sorry."

I ask him again where his mama is. I can tell he's a patient kid when he tells me again that he doesn't know. To be Angela's kid, you've got to be patient. There's no other choice. "She bring my car back?"

"The white one?" I tell him yes. He says he'll go look. I say never mind, it was a stupid question.

"She tells me don't answer the phone," he says.

"So why'd you answer it?" I know he wants me to ask him that, and I feel sorry for him.

"I didn't answer it yesterday." I tell him I know that. "But then I figured today maybe I'm supposed to answer it. I mean, Angela might call." The boy calls his mama by her first name. She deserves it. "Or school might call. I'm absent, you know."

"Look," I tell him, "you call 911. You're not supposed to be there all by yourself."

"They'll put my mother in jail."

"Your mother's probably in jail already."

He gets quiet, and then he's sniffling, and I ought to feel sorry for him, but this is Angela's fault, and she deserves to have her kid hate her. I tell him I'm going to call him tonight, though I don't know how I'm going to do that when I've got so much mess to fool with. It's not that I like the boy; it's that I can't stand Angela. "Don't leave Mealworm there by himself," I say.

"He's okay," Dustin says.

My doctor is younger than both of my children, and he can't play that God stuff with me. "Look," I say, "give me five dollars,

I'll take a taxi out of here." He asks me where I'll go, like he gives a damn. "A hotel," I say. For all he knows, I can check into the Windsor Court.

Everybody's the same when they're over sixty-five and wearing a hospital gown. He fishes in his pocket, gives me a ten, playing God.

I don't make up my mind till I'm sitting in a White Fleet cab in the housecoat I wore when they brought me in. My housecoat is damp, because it smelled like smoke and I washed it out in the sink with one of those little bars of Ivory. It takes anything thicker than a Kleenex a week to dry out in New Orleans, and if you leave folds in it, it'll mildew. I give the cab-driver my address. "You could've walked there," he says.

"You want a twenty-four-dollar fare, you work the air-port, not a damn hospital," I tell him. We pull up in front of my house, and I'm too busy waiting to see if the meter'll go over a dollar, so I don't see my house till I'm out of the cab. It clicks to a dollar, I hand him the ten, tell him give me nine back, and slam the door before he can get even.

I don't know what it is about a fire that would make a person cry, but when I go halfway up the steps and look in where my front door used to be, I bawl like a baby. The living room is full of pictures, and every week I dusted the frames and cleaned the glass with Windex. I'm not like these women who put new pictures on their refrigerators; these are old pic-tures. The glass is brown, and the pictures are in ashes, and there is no color in the room except a patch of my orange and yellow slipcovers. Zib'll be happy. I've had those slipcovers since she was newborn and spitting up on them, and she says that after a nuclear explosion all that'd be left are those slip-covers and Ronald Reagan and a bunch of cockroaches. I step through the doorway, and the floor holds me, and I'd walk in here anyway, even if I had to balance on burnt matchsticks. I don't have a lot to lose. Winding up back in Baptist with both legs in traction sounds good all of a sudden.

All the way to the back, everything is burned. I wish I knew how I got out of here alive, because I should be a Spam mold on top of my mattress. I hear somebody tipping in behind me, and I turn around without being afraid, because nobody with bad intentions can be walking into this house. There's nothing to steal, and who'd want to rape an old lady in a pile of charcoal.

"It stinks in here," Dustin says. "Matter of fact, the whole neighborhood stinks."

"You get out of here; all I need's a lawsuit," I say. Angela's the type who'd be just as happy if her son were a paraplegic, as long as she got a million dollars in the bargain. I probably should have worried about her driving my car. But things didn't feel so shaky two days ago.

"I'm not going to fall. I've been in here three times already," Dustin says, and he edges past me like he's going to show me around.

In the kitchen, some light comes in through the back window, and now I can see how much water is in the house. I wonder if the electricity is on, if one of us is going to step in a wet spot and die. "They said to tell you they cut the power," Dustin says. He's smart for a kid whose mother would have to be watered twice a week if she got any stupider. "Yeah?" I say.

"It could kill you," he says, missing the point.

"Who said?" I don't have patience with kids. Even kids who act like they've never been kids. Dustin probably had to go home from the hospital the day he was born and cook his mama dinner, but he shouldn't be puffed up about it.

"I saved your life, you know."

"Yeah?" I say.

"There wasn't nobody home. Excepting me. If I hadn't've been there, you'd be dead probably. Not probably. Definitely. You'd definitely be dead."

I look at him. He's a chunky little guy, all full of cheap vanilla ice cream that Angela paid for with food stamps. I saw her in our old KB's the first of one month with a basket loaded to the top with Nutty Buddies, Fudgsicles, and store-brand ice cream. She liked the way the clerk was disgusted, I could tell. Angela is the only white woman on earth who gets food stamps. "Well, I know you didn't *carry* me out. I'd remember something like that."

"I called the fire department."

I can't help laughing. "So then you got a stick and roasted marshmallows," I say. No kid in school can get past the first grade these days without having a friendly fireman and a friendly policeman and God-knows-what-else friendly come in his classroom and tell him little sayings about strangers and fires. Channel 26 has stuff like that after disasters.

"Sorry," he says. "I'm not supposed to go outside in the middle of the night. Technically, I'm not supposed to go outside in the daytime." I fold my arms and give him a hard look. He shrugs, like I'm going to understand that it's all right to break his mama's rules when she's broken every child protection rule in the book, but it's not all right to break his mama's rules when an old woman might be burning to death next door.

"You didn't call the police like I told you," I say.

He shakes his head no. "I'd've done it eventually. But I ought to give her one more day. She's never gone more than three days."

"Good." He is standing here in the middle of a house that could have sent licks of fire right onto his roof while he sat inside behaving, and he probably hasn't had a vegetable that wasn't government subsidized in his mouth in a week, and he's one sure kid. I like that: my car will definitely be back in what's left of my driveway by tomorrow. "Look," I say, "I'll stay at your house until your mama comes back with my car." I expect him to say something off-putting that'll leave him free for jumping on the beds and sitting up all night watching wrestling on television. Instead he says, "I feel better with an adult around."

We walk in the front door of Angela's house, and I say, "I felt safer walking on a burned-out floor; at least I could *see* where the holes were." He laughs good-naturedly. The front room is his room, and you can't see the carpet for the clothes, lint, toys, and candy wrappers. "How come you've got a PlayStation?" I say. He also has about three dozen of those game discs that you can buy for about forty dollars a pop. I could go through this room with a box of thirty-gallon trash bags and throw out everything filthy, and I bet I'd still leave behind a thousand dollars' worth of decent crap. Food stamps don't buy anything made in Japan.

"Angela bought it for me. We got pretty much money, you know." I cock my head to the side. "Yeah, I go with her to Wagner's to cash her check. She gets $522. You can get a PlayStation for about $99." I can't forgive Angela for the blown-up tales she told Zib all those years, but her lies are doing all right by her kid.

I trip through to the back of the house to find the phone, and the boy stays in his room, figuring, I suppose, that there is not one thing in the place to steal. I don't know how men can come into a place like this and have sex with Angela, no matter how free she is. Every shirt, every pair of jeans, every bra, every towel she's owned in her whole life is lying on the floor or draped over some piece of furniture, and half-full pizza boxes and open cans of Coke are all over the place. I need a cigarette. "Your mama got any cigarettes?" I holler back to Dustin. "You can look," he hollers back, breathless, and I can hear those little bleeps and explosions that video games make. She keeps cigarettes in the bathroom. I'm not surprised.

I find the phone book easily: Angela's using it in place of a leg on her dresser, and I slide it out, letting the dresser fall partway over. The dresser's probably empty, anyway. The phone's in the kitchen, a new portable one, without ear grime on it yet. I don't know what person I'm supposed to call. Woodrow took care of the mortgage when we had one, and the electricity bill, and the Sewerage and Water Board bill. Now the bill comes in the mail, I write one of Woodrow's checks, and so far nobody's turned anything off. Except when there's been a major fire. But I have no idea what I'm supposed to do to collect on the insurance.

I look for the yellow pages. Angela has the yellow pages on a high shelf in the kitchen, and when I stand on a chair to get them I find they are new, except the top has a quarter inch of greasy dust on it. I wipe it with a pair of her underpants that are hanging on the back doorknob. There are forty-two pages of insurance companies. In one city. That says something about life in this country. Out of curiosity, I flip back to see how many pages of lawyers. Forty-four. I knew it. I go back to Insurance. They can't all sell fire insurance. Only one does, in fact, and it's for apartments. I try house insurance. Homeowners, now I'm getting somewhere. I start counting again. I must be nervous. Twenty-seven listings. I can manage twenty-seven. I start with the *A*s. A girl answers. Sounds like Angela. I've got Angela on the brain. No surprise. I *smell* Angela. I tell her my name is Mrs. Woodrow Bailey, do I have insurance with her company. "What kind?" she says, and I look back at the phone book fast. "Homeowners," I tell her, "you're listed under Homeowners in the phone book." "Yeh, but we're probably listed under ten other things, too. What's your name?" I tell her again, and she tells me to hold, and I say, "So what'd you ask me my name for?" but she's already transferred me.

I go through six companies before somebody has the decency to say to call where I have my mortgage. "I don't have a mortgage; it's paid off," I tell him. "Call where you *had* your mortgage," he says nicely.

If Woodrow weren't already dead, I'd have to kill him. We haven't had insurance in more than twenty years, not since he paid off the mortgage, says the agent I get from the loan company. "Some guys say, 'You mean I don't have to have it anymore?' and we tell them no, but you *ought* to, but you know how some people are."

"Evidently *not*," I say.

"They say, 'It's not required, I don't pay it.'"

"Yeah," I say, "I do know how some people are," and I hang up. I refuse to think about it.

Angela has let this house go so far that it'd be impossible to clean. I don't know how I'm going to sleep in a bed that'll give me a disease if I don't wrap myself from head to foot in boiled sheets before I lie on it.

Angela owes me a place to stay until she comes back with my car. And her kid is better off with somebody who's raised two children herself than he'd be staying by himself or getting dragged downtown to some agency full of nuns. "*Dustin*," I holler. "What?" He's been playing with that PlayStation since I got here, and I've heard him say "shit" about twice, but other than that he hasn't moved, even to pee. "You don't holler 'What' at me, mister," I say, standing over him now. He's sitting cross-legged on the floor in front of a television set, and I'm sure a thousand fleas have hopped all over him without his noticing. He pushes the buttons very fast, the beeps make a disappointed sound, and he says, "Well, I'm dead, okay?"

"Sounds good to me," I say, and he looks at me to see if I'm kidding. I have my arms folded across my chest, and I'm looking straight down at him, but he's not afraid of me one bit. Zib was like that. You could look crossways at Wilson, and he'd do anything you told him to, but Zib would look back at you and dare you to ask again; she could keep on looking you straight in the eye even when you slapped her in the face, over and over.

"You ever hear of taking baths and eating dinner and going to bed?" I say. He shrugs. I tell him to stand up, and he drags himself up slowly, like a tired old man. I tell him to get me some sheets, we're going to the laundromat, and then we're going to send out for pizza, and then we're going to go to bed. In clean beds. "Angela took her purse," Dustin says, and I remember that I have only nine dollars. "Well, damn," I say, "find me sheets, anyway." The sheets are on the beds, he tells me, like I must be from another country. The *other* sheets, I say, and we both start to laugh.

I'm willing to use up a dollar of my money, so we strip the beds and grab a couple of towels to make a full load. I take off my housecoat, put it on top of the pile, find one denim jumper and a shirt in the back of Angela's closet and put them on after I smell them and make sure she's never worn them. I ask Dustin where the detergent is, and he tells me his mama buys those little boxes at the laundromat, and I say, "It figures, why buy a giant box that'll last two months for seven dollars when you can spend three dollars on little boxes every time, just so long as you don't have to carry anything too heavy around the corner." "Yeh," Dustin says, knowing that money is no object to Angela. We cut over to the laundromat on Dryades Street, and I see a colored woman in there who always stops and talks to me, and I ask her if we can borrow a cup of Tide, and she doesn't flinch, just pours it into my machine. I can't believe I'm asking a person poorer than me for laundry detergent, but a dollar for one of those little boxes would leave me seven instead of eight, and I might need that dollar tomorrow.

"Your house burn?" the woman says.

"Yeah," I say, and I give her this grin, like it's no big deal.

"You got nothing left in that house, far as I can tell," she says.

"Good way to redecorate," I say, and she laughs. "That's a good one," she says.

I wait for the load to finish, look busy so the woman can't come over and offer me charity. I'm not going to have anything much to eat for dinner. Dustin is playing with this big mongrel dog that lives in the laundromat, and I remember I have to go find Mealworm. This dog is some kind of retriever, and I don't know who the owner thinks he's fooling, leaving that dog in the place overnight, like anyone is going to be scared of a retriever dog unless he's a dead duck floating on top of a lagoon. All the dog is good for is shedding long red hairs all over the floor so you have to wash your clothes again if they fall out of your hands accidentally. The one time my dryer wasn't working, I hung my clothes to dry in the bathroom rather than go to this laundromat. "What's Angela got in the refrigerator?" I say to Dustin when I see the colored woman has her head deep inside a big dryer, fishing for socks.

"I still got bologna," Dustin says. "Though I'm kind of sick of it."

"Bologna sounds good to me. You got mayonnaise?"

"Yeh, but no bread."

We have about forty minutes before nightfall. I never sent my kids to the store the whole time they were growing up because Woodrow said that was a nigger thing to do, and I

wouldn't send them now if they were still little because somebody might steal them. Dustin's got some kind of charmed life:
if somebody was going to steal him, it'd have happened before
he became a hundred pounds of dead weight. God wants Angela to have responsibility for as long as possible; even if she
doesn't take it seriously, the kid is here, and she knows it.
"Here," I say, giving him two dollar bills. "Go to Wagner's and
get a loaf of Bunny bread. Big long loaf, you know, the square
kind, with skinnier pieces."

"A sandwich loaf," he says.

"I want change," I say.

"Angela gives me the change," he says. "Unless it's a five."

"I want change," I say. "You want something to hide your
bologna in, you go to Wagner's."

"I'm sick of bologna."

"That's too bad," I say, and he shrugs and shuffles out.
"And be back before dark. Or I'm coming after you." He turns
and smiles at me. I like the boy, even as fat as he is.

"You his grandma?" the colored woman says.

"No," I say, insulted, and I pick up a copy of *Good Housekeeping* that's lying on a chair and flip it open fast. The magazine opens to a page with about ten shiny desserts on it, all set
around this giant torte covered with sliced hexagons of kiwi
fruit. I've never picked up a kiwi fruit, let alone tasted one:
they lie there in the produce case all brown and fuzzy, and they
look to me like they're sending some sort of natural message to
leave them the hell alone. This torte looks good, and I study
the picture hard. I read somewhere that they use Elmer's glue
for milk and put shellac on food in those magazine pictures,
and after I've looked at it long enough I'm able to pretend that
this is nothing more tempting than the Christmas ornaments
made out of bread dough on page 224.

Dustin is back in less time than it takes the load of wash to go through the rinse cycle. His face is red, and he's breathing hard. "You're going to be the first ten-year-old boy to have a heart attack," I tell him.

"Running's good for you," he says.

"Not if you're fat."

The colored lady comes over by us, folding a towel in the air while she's walking. "That boy *healthy*," she says.

"And fat," I say. Sweat is rolling down Dustin's face, which is still red, and he looks like he's going to cry. "Okay, okay, you're not fat."

"Thanks," he says.

By the time the wash is out of the dryer and all folded up, even though Dustin says it's stupid to fold it when you're going to use it, we have eaten half a loaf of plain white bread. It's good like that when you're hungry, and it's enriched as hell according to the wrapper, so I'll let Dustin by with it this time, and to-morrow I'll take the streetcar down to the bank and get money and food and put this kid on a diet without telling him. I've got this feeling Angela and my car aren't showing up tomorrow.

I start to cut over on Cadiz Street, and Dustin says, "An-gela don't let me go this way. The guy in that house deals crack." He points to a double shotgun that hasn't been painted in about a hundred years, and he says it like he's telling me there's a hound dog in that yard that barks a lot. "I've been in this neighborhood since Eisenhower was president, and I don't know anything like that. How come Angela knows that?"

"Angela knows pretty much everything," he says, and I walk us right past that house. "Nothing happened, see?" I say.

Angela is standing on our corner as we come around, and she sees us coming out of Cadiz Street. She puts her hands on her hips, and I walk faster toward her, daring her, though I'm happy out of my mind to see her, because I am going to get in my car and go wherever six dollars will take me. Eight if she'll pay me back, but I'm not counting on that.

"He knows not to take Cadiz," she says as soon as she thinks I can hear her.

"So he told me," I say. "At least nobody's going to call the authorities on *him*."

"You trespassed in my house," she says.

By this time I'm almost in her face, with her sheets and towels under my arm, and they're folded and clean except for a few yellow stains on the sheets that wouldn't come out. My sheets never looked like that even when I was first married. "Like Santa Claus trespasses in your house."

"I don't care if you're John Beresford Tipton; you got no business invading my privacy like that." Hazel always talked about John Beresford Tipton. Angela's taking sidelong glances at her sheets, hoping, I guess, that I didn't notice anything. Like I could have missed.

We're standing on the sidewalk just short of where I can see the front of her house. "You brought my car back?" I say.

"No, I *didn't* bring your car back. Your car got stolen."

"My car got stolen by *you*." I'm shouting, which is all right with me. It's after dark, and I'd be happy for witnesses to come spilling out their doors, waiting for a fight. Anybody could look at an old lady with a pile of clean sheets and a tramp who hasn't combed her hair in three days and pick a side fast. Even a crack dealer.

"Hey, it's not my fucking fault. I leave the car out there on Perdido Street, and they pick me up, and I say, 'Whoa, what about the car,' and they say, 'It ain't got legs, it ain't going nowhere,' and I get out this afternoon, and they give me your keys back, and I run on over to Perdido Street. And believe me,

I didn't want to, because for all I know I'm going to bump into that bastard, who's probably still peeing in his own eye, and the car is fucking gone. I go to the auto pound, I mean *on foot*, and there's no white station wagon there at all."

I don't follow one word she's saying, but I can tell she left my car somewhere that it was guaranteed to be in a chop shop or on its way to Mexico before the motor cooled off. I drop her sheets on the sidewalk. "Look, stupid, what do you mean, they picked you up?"

"Jesus," she says. She doesn't even notice the sheets. "I'll know better next time. *Apparently*, half the murders in town, they drop them off at Emergency at Charity. So they have all these cops standing around like cabdrivers, when they could be out looking for criminals, and they grab you if you have the goddamn decency to realize you made a mistake and bring the guy in. The bastards *laughed* at me. I could *hear* them, 'Hey, get a load of this one.' I swear they almost let me off, they were so goddamn impressed. It been in the paper or anything?"

"You *happen* to notice that the house next door to you, where I happen to have lived for over forty years, where you happen to have walked past to get here, where I used to have the *Times-Picayune* delivered, is now a pile of burned rubble?"

"No," she says, and I believe her.

She takes a few steps back, cranes her neck. "Holy shit," she says. She's fighting the kind of mean grin I'd have smacked off Zib's face; probably her mother smacked enough of them off her face so she learned something. "Hey, it's your fault. That polish remover sits in my bathroom two years, nothing happens, you come pounding on my wall, the next thing my house blows up."

"You should've given me the whole bottle. That's what you get for being so mean-spirited. You're crazy, Mrs. Bailey."

"She's not crazy," Dustin says. He's been fishing in an ant pile with a crumbly old stick from a pecan tree, and I could swear he hasn't been paying attention.

"Get back in the house," Angela says. Dustin shakes his head no, and she shrugs. Wilson told me no once, and after I sent him flying he never did it again. Zib told me no every time she felt like it, and I did a lot of things, but I never stood there and shrugged my shoulders and kept right on talking.

Angela is not going to let me stay in her house now, especially if I ask her. But I have her towels and cigarettes, and that's enough. "I'm not going to stand here in the dark until somebody hits me in the head," I say.

"A man tried to rape Angela, and she got down on her hands and knees and barked like a dog, and he ran off," Dustin says.

"Hush," Angela says, but I can tell she's proud like he's telling me she just won an Academy Award.

I walk toward my house, and Dustin lumps behind me. "Where're you going to sleep?" he says as he pulls up alongside me like an eighteen-wheeler in the passing lane.

"Not in my house," Angela says.

"Goddamn right," I say.

"But you were going to," Dustin says.

"Before your fleabag of a mama came home. You don't need me to babysit you, now you're in *safe* hands."

"I didn't need you to babysit *before*."

"Go on," I tell him, waving him back toward Angela. I can't stand sentimental children. For a while there in the late eighties, I had to turn off half the shows and 99 percent of the commercials on television, it was so full of kids that they hired because they looked like trolls, with shiny little crossed eyes and hair flopping all over. I expected Zib and Wilson to act like adults as soon as they could walk, none of this lap-sitting and snuffling business, particularly for a boy. Wilson came close to being a pansy. Dustin is all right. Even if he knows it. He can take care of himself. But I don't want to be standing there with my arms out in case he decides he wants to act like the kids he sees on television. Aside from Gary Coleman, the kid I hate the most is that set of twins that used to be on *Full House.* Wilson had this theory that kids appeal to adults because they're cartoons of us. That twin kid is a cartoon of a circus monkey, and I don't like looking at circus monkeys even at the circus.

"That wasn't very nice," I hear Dustin saying. I keep walking toward my house, knowing they're right behind me, each one letting me hear what I'm supposed to hear.

"It's not very nice, her coming into my house, smelling my sheets like some pervert, taking my clothes, poking in my business."

"It's not very nice, losing my car," I say, talking straight ahead of myself.

"Well, you didn't know that when you went snooping around my house."

Before I go up my walkway I turn around and look at Angela. "Nobody in her right mind would go snooping around your house. That's like poking a rake handle in the mulch pile, no telling what's going to slither out and bite you." I make a sharp right turn and head for my steps. "Aw, fuck off," Angela says.

I lay the towels down to cover my sofa and lie down on them. A lot of times I slept on this sofa when Woodrow was screaming in the night, and I know all the lumps. Even half burned, the same places mash into my soft parts. I fish out a cigarette, figure there's no harm in lighting up. I don't have a match. That is funny. I don't have a goddamn match.

14

Wilson

THE GIRL SITTING IN MY OFFICE IS NOT YET EIGHTEEN; SHE MAY not be the prodigy that people have told her she is, but she has been talking over her own head for so long that she believes in herself. She has thick, wavy dark hair that shines and looks the same whether she combs it or not, and her eyes are the black of Jews who only have migrated away from the equator in the past half a millennium. Her breasts are too large to be contained by her clothes. I was close to twenty-five when she was born, walking around scared to death of getting a girl pregnant when this girl was a bald, androgynous, free-minded infant. She shifts around on the armless wood chair I chose so that no one would stay in my office too long, and a few tendrils of her hair fall gently over her shoulder and down into the primal well between her breasts, beckoning me to follow, and I force myself to listen to what she is saying, certain that I will be repelled by her ingenuousness and will be able to go on from there. "You know why cats hate men?" she says. "They have a collective memory. Of being hunted by men. And they hate dogs, too, because dogs were the hunting companions. Cats come to women because cats were the familiars of the priest goddesses." She is not fatuous. "You should read that book," she says. She cocks her head to the side, and I sense what she wants from me. I think she would prefer a fantasy, day and night dreams that fill her with tempered hope and make her read dozens of books looking for some new fragment of thought that she can carry into my office, offer up to me, the temple god, then go off to a girlfriend and recite every word I have said in response, compounding her hope, driving her to more obscure corners of the library stacks. "Will you bring me a copy?" I say, and she nods casually, having won something, not needing to be eager.

When she is gone I phone Barbara, wanting to behave because Barbara does not. Unlike my wife, I have learned that it is best to stick with the old choices. At the university I can go from office to classroom and back again and find myself surrounded by young minds that are full of abstractions and thus far spared from solid disappointments. About eight years ago when my first marriage was breaking up, I did the predictable thing: I ached with a desire to be eighteen, and I told anyone who would listen that maybe others would have to go ahead and be bored and empty for the rest of their lives, but I was a man who could not stop thinking, and so it was possible for me, unlike almost anyone else, to spend the rest of my life looking for the secrets hidden under stones, refusing to do anything more except, from time to time, go into a fugue state so that I could deal with health insurance and income tax and child support. After a while, the subtleties came back to me, the need for a woman, the importance of having enough drawers and closets, even pride of ownership. Only then had I begun to convince myself, with echoes of my mother's diatribes resounding, that students were children, wanting to take everything and give nothing; they were people I had to get into and out of my sight fast before they began to sap me of my egocentricity and make me furious.

"Your sister called about half an hour ago," Barbara says as soon as she hears my voice. She has not been referring to Zib by name since my father died, though they used to get along reasonably well. "It's like she thinks she can't interrupt you at your office, but she figures it's perfectly all right to bother me at mine."

"Zib does not think a person is working unless she has had to get dressed and leave the house."

"You, too, probably," Barbara says.

"Hey, I have terrific respect for what you are doing. I could not do anything like that myself; you have to be creative, a true self-starter, you cannot be a drone who hides behind the rules of academia. . . "

"Forget it," she says.

Every muscle in my abdomen tightens, locking up my viscera so they will shoot me full of pain in an hour or so. I do not mind being the object of a woman's rage if I have earned it, but all I have done wrong to Barbara is lose a parent before she did. I beat her to a milestone, where I can take care of everyone. She is punishing me, having an affair or a one-night fling, I do not know which, and finding fault, remaking the bed after me, countermanding what I say to Connor and Morgan. I thought I was safe marrying her because she was tentative when she talked. Now a floodgate has opened and let out what she was fighting. She discovered years ago that she is hollow and sad on the inside, so she goes around acting as if she is the bravest woman ever born. I do not have to see the rancid caramel inside of her, because she covers it, even in her sleep, when she balls up her fists and curls up in a knot so tight that if I touch her in sleep I feel muscles as taut as an athlete's in the thick of competition.

I ask her what Zib wanted. She tells me my sister wants to know if we have heard from my mother. "I told her no; I presume your mother doesn't call you at work, either," she says.

"She called in the middle of the day for that?" I never told Barbara that last week Zib called in the middle of the day because she decided she had AIDS. There is sometimes a grain of truth in Zib's worries. I do not remember much about basic psychology, but I do know that when a girl's mother smacks her for anything she feels like smacking her for, she does not grow up to be a silly fretter.

"Says she keeps getting no answer."

"*I* got no answer. The woman is being passive-aggressive."

"She must want to hear from someone besides the two of you," Barbara says.

"Not really." My mother has not had contact with almost anyone other than Gloretta in about twenty years. Until my father died, she dedicated her time to ragging him; when he retired she could do it full-time, and before that she spent her days cleaning the corners of the house so that she could be in a rage by the time he came home, all innocent, and asked for his supper. My mother prefers strangers, who will stop on the sidewalk in front of her house and talk for a minute or half an hour, leaving her to pass a judgment that she can put in her stockpile, either to tell me and Zib about later or to add to her collection of stereotypes. Lately the edges of her neighborhood have pulled in an Iranian, a few African blacks, and a family of Russian Jews, and Mother has had a field day expanding her horizons. She says all foreigners are selfish, that with a single exception they do not make one effort to speak English correctly, that they expect pity because they were engineers in their countries, where all one needed to get an engineering degree was a shovel and a strong back according to my mother; now the best they can do is pack sausages for $5.15 an hour. Mother calls the Africans black, and she is proud that she is the first person to discover that these people are highly intelligent, talking as if they were from Oxford. "Goes to show you," she says, "that when they went there to get slaves, only the stupid ones let themselves get caught."

"Mother might very well unplug her phone except when she calls out," I say.

"Your sister's called *twice*," Barbara says, and I tell her I will phone Zib.

Zib does not answer her phone, and I decide to try her at the Winn-Dixie. They tell me she is not in the office; they will page her. I tell them I am calling long-distance, and a minute later I hear Zib come puffing up to the phone. "Oh, I know my mother's dead," she is saying to whoever will listen.

"Your mother is not dead," I say into the phone as soon as I hear her breathing into the receiver.

"Jesus, Wilson you scared the holy fuck out of me." I can imagine her standing in an office that smells of wilted lettuce, being watched by a cracker clerk in a red smock who does not respect her, who cannot wait to run into the ladies' room and tell everyone what a mouth Miss Elizabeth has got on her. She waits a second. "How do you know she's not dead? I have this feeling she's dead."

"Because she is not answering her phone? Brilliant deductive reasoning, Zib. Living people ignore their phones much more frequently than dead people do; I am sure I can find statistics. . . "

"You call me off the checkout line to tell me that? You know, you are *never* funny."

I ask her what she is doing working checkout. I have been under the impression that managers, assistant managers, even, do nothing but stand around and infuriate the minimum-wagers. That is how Zib put it when she first worked there. Zib wished a painful death on a long series of managers before she became one of them. "I have to cover when people aren't responsible," she says. "Fuck you, Wilson, you thought I got demoted."

"Call me on your own nickel," I say.

She cries out for me to wait; she has had no answer or a peevish answer for every call she has made today. "Sor-ry," she sings, the way she used to sound when she broke something that I kept on a high shelf.

"'Bad grass don't die,' Zib, remember?"

"You tell your Organic Evolution class that?" she says, and I laugh.

She covers the receiver, but I can hear her barking orders, and an old corner of my mind, where I once stuffed the resignation over her bossiness, fills up at the sound, muffled as it is. "Jesus, are these people immature," she says. "They tell me they have cramps like I never wanted to go home and get laid and used *that* excuse before."

"You want me to call Mother?" I say.

"Trust me, no one is answering. I called a zillion other numbers before I came in, and her phone's not answering."

"Whom did you call?"

"Well, you for starts."

"No one in New Orleans?"

"I just meant there's nothing wrong with my phone."

I tell her to call Gloretta. She acts insulted again, says she even has gone so far as to track down Gloretta's daughter Cheryl; Gloretta is in the hospital. I ask whether she inquired about our mother. "Cheryl barely gives a shit where her own mother is," Zib says. I try to imagine who would know where

Mother is, and I realize her world is full of strangers who know her as that mean old woman across from the cemetery. I could go knocking on half a dozen of the doors in that row of un-painted shotgun houses across from Green School and say *Do you know anything about that mean old woman who lives up in the twenty-hundred block?* and they would know if she left in a stretch limo, an ambulance, or a body bag. But I do not want to go down to New Orleans.

"You could call Angela," Zib says suddenly, though I know she has been thinking of this for hours, perhaps days.

"Angela? Angela-never-knows-what-day-it-is-and-could-not-care-less? That Angela?"

"If anything bad's going on, trust me, Angela's out there watching it," Zib says.

I tell her that she should call Angela. She reminds me that one of the reasons she does not live in New Orleans anymore is that Angela is like an addiction: one gram of Angela and she is drawn in, prepared to tell tremendous lies and take advantage of weak people so she can spend all her time making her body shimmer with pleasure. "She never affected me that way," I say.

"Not for lack of trying," Zib says, and I laugh. She gives me the number, the same one that has been in that house since we were in the TWinbrook exchange, and I ask Zib if they still have a rotary phone. Angela threw it at me once when I was sent over to get my sister home for dinner, and I still have a thick white scar, which is creeping out of hiding as my hairline recedes. My mother did not believe in stitches for boys unless a bone was peeping through the skin. "She probably had it up until the day her mother died," Zib says.

Angela picks up on the first ring. I say, "This is Wilson," and her tone fills with disappointment that borders on disgust. "Yeah?"

"Well," I say, "you are truly happy to hear from me."

"Look, I had to drop call waiting; I'm expecting somebody important, make it quick, okay?" I ask her where my mother is; I am content to keep this call under a minute. "How the hell should I know?" she says, and I remind her that my mother lives next door to her, that my mother drives an old white station wagon, that she can see my mother's car from where she is standing, if her phone is where it used to be. She tells me she has a portable, she is in her bedroom, she is lying down, she does not feel good, and besides, my mother's car was stolen last week. I start to laugh powerfully enough to ward off logical thought. "You in town?" Angela says softly, almost seductively, and I want to say, "If I were in town, why would I be calling you?" but I do not. I tell her no. "Listen, Wilson, I'm going to tell you something. Your mama has gone fucking nuts, I mean we're talking Third Floor psycho ward." "Oh?" I say; Angela is hardly famous for her grasp of the truth.

"She blew up her house. She broke into my house and stole a shitpile of stuff. She was trying to mess with my kid, but I caught her. You want me to go on? That's just the high points."

I am not frazzled in the least. I immediately translate that to mean, *Your mother had a grease fire in her kitchen, your mother borrowed the broom from my porch, your mother told my kid that I am an idiot.* "Right, Angela," I say.

"You don't believe me?"

"I saw my mother only a couple of weeks ago. Aside from the fact that she was cranky, she looked normal to me. The onset of psychosis is not *that* sudden." Right away I lose all conviction. I was in middle school when that quiet man went on top of the Howard Johnson's on Loyola Avenue and started shooting at firemen. I was at an impressionable age when I first heard people say, "I had no *idea!*"

"She blew up the house?" I say.

"It burned to the ground," Angela says, and I am sick with the grief that comes with a sudden death. I ask her if my mother is all right. "Hey, she's the woman always said, 'Bad grass don't die,'" Angela says, as pleased with herself as if she has quoted Herodotus.

"That is what Zib says," I say, but I am not laughing. I am thinking about the house that was supposed to stand forever, with the scent of Camay soap in the bathroom and the crater in the plaster in my old bedroom where, according to my mother, I once slammed my head into the wall in my only display of temper. The crater is about four feet off the ground, and though I do not recall the incident, I imagine I was at an age when hormones had nothing to do with my fury. Great-uncle Randolph's painting, Mother's scrambled-egg-colored kitchen table: the house was full of many things I fought against, and I have taken a secret comfort in going back, checking whether I am right about the kinds of things I like to look at. I make sure we have herbal soap in our bathrooms in Evanston. I have nothing against the smell of Camay, but I can walk into a bathroom and smell it and expect that, even if I close the door, I will be able to see the flood of disappointment that filled my childhood house come seeping under the door, catching me in some state of nakedness.

Angela wants to hear me cry. My mother probably was looking forward to my sadness when she destroyed her house. I fool them both: people on a telephone and people who are not yet in the world of spirits cannot see me, and I let the tears come, quietly, not choking me. "So where is she staying?" I say in a clear, dry voice.

"Somehow I thought you'd be upset."

"Angie, Pangie, puddin' and pie, kissed the boys and made them cry." Zib chanted this more than once when she was young and proud of Angela.

"Yeh," she says, pleased. I tell her that Zib needs to get in touch with our mother. "Well," she says, now warming to the discussion, "tell her to get over here and start looking in the bushes." I tell her to get serious. "Listen, 'heart, I *am* serious. Your mama's probably walking the streets, peeing in the gutters, talking to that stupid little pocket-dog. I told you, the woman's a couple sandwiches short of a picnic." She pauses for effect. "Always was, too, to tell you the truth."

15

Zib

I REMEMBER MEETING A WOMAN WILSON WAS DATING. ONCE. It was in that flash when he was between wives. Living alone in two rooms full of books. He was waiting for a practical woman to come along. She'd take him in under the mistaken idea that he was taking care of her. We were in a restaurant. Wilson had gone to the men's room. He was nursing his spastic colon in private. And eating gut-popping amounts in public. The woman thought she had him. She whispered to me, "Your brother is the most sensitive man in the world." I wanted to say, "Oh, he picks up on everything. And he knows what to do. But try asking him to *feel* something." Instead I said, "Oh, but doesn't he hide it well?" He was sick of her admiration in a few weeks.

Anybody looking at what he did yesterday would say he was protecting me. I know better. It looked like he was waiting until I was home from work. Because he was thinking about my feelings. Not wanting me to go berserk in the middle of Customer Service. But that wasn't it. Wilson wanted me to get home at 1:00 A.M., tired to tears. I'd get the news when I was all by myself in my apartment. The walls in this complex are thin as onionskin. And my next-door neighbor is a man my age with no job and a low fringe of hair. Which from above makes the dome of his bald head look like a gigantic promising egg. In a small yellow nest. He knocks on my door if I fool around with myself and whimper a little. Wilson said Mama burned down the house. I wanted to scream. To be sad about Pop. But I could imagine The Egg throwing back his covers, naked legs flailing, running for my door. So I hissed "Goddamn you, Wilson" into the phone. "*I* did not burn down the house," Wilson said calmly. He was used to the idea. "You could've called me at work when I had people around," I said.

"It is not like someone died, for God's sake."

"As far as you know."

He said he wasn't going to New Orleans. He had two exams to write. "You think your job matters more than mine," I said.

"Well, I am not going to New Orleans. Period."

"Assertiveness training went out in the seventies, Wilson."

"Well, I am not going to New Orleans. Period."

I said, "Well, I'm not going, either." And he said, "Suit yourself." If he thinks I'm calling him when I get there, he's out of his mind.

I come out of the Mobile tunnel. I start to tremble. Like I'm a finalist in an important contest. Waiting for the announcement of the honorable mentions. Knowing I'll hear my name before I want to. I can make it home in just over three hours. Doing eighty so I notice only the obstacles right in my path. But the Mobile tunnel is a transition point. One side and I'm in Florida. In the tunnel and I'm caught up in thoughts of great engineering and boats skimming over my head. Out the other side of the tunnel, and I'm as good as in New Orleans. Braced for insults.

Before I do anything else, I check into the Windsor Court. It's my way of pretending that New Orleans could be any major city. As long as I look out no windows. Take in no river views. No French Quarter roofscapes. All the reminders that this is a port full of cheap accents and hucksters. There are Cokes and Snickers bars in the refrigerator in my room. I'll go out into the streets that are full of chicken bones and skinny stray dogs. I'll look for my mother. And I'll hold my breath while I'm doing it. Knowing I can come back to this room. Turn on the air conditioner though it's in the sixties today. Order a ten-dollar hamburger from room service. Watch television and pretend I'm nowhere in particular.

I drive up Magazine Street. I've noticed over the years of coming back here that I can never get lost. Even when two-way streets become one-way. Even when new bridges and highways rise over old neighborhoods. Their shadows turn pretty little gingerbread houses into paintless shacks. Like they fade from a lack of sun. Street patterns are probably the last thing to go. They're like floor plans of the places I've lived in. If I lost my sight, I could still navigate through any house, any apartment, any school building I've known more than a week. People who shop at Winn-Dixie marvel when I can tell them squirt cheese is on aisle nine.

I pull up in front of my mother's house. And I laugh so hard I can't stop. The house is in its right place. Between Angela's and the hairdresser's. But it's the worst pile of rubble I've seen since the Oklahoma bombing on TV. Mama never wanted a drop of sticky fruit juice on her linoleum. Or a handprint on a doorjamb. Or a scribble on a steamy bathroom mirror. Wilson and I learned to pick up single cookie crumbs from the rug with our fingernails and stuff them into our pockets. We learned how to flip a sofa cushion if we made a tiny pencil mark on it. Wilson kept the neatness inside himself. But for me disorder was a source of comfort. I punish my mother with randomness of thought. She would like to get inside of me. To tack shelves up along the walls of my skull. To set her ideas in neat rows where I can pull them out whenever I want to. I picture her. Standing on the sidewalk across the street. By the cemetery. Watching her house burn down. Trying to decide if this is a clean way to do things.

Angela comes shuffle-kicking down her front steps. While I'm standing in front of Mama's house laughing. "Leave it to you." She says it with what sounds like admiration.

"You got to admit," I say.

"Yeah," she says.

I run up to hug her. I don't ever kiss Angela. We're too close for that. Which is a funny thing to say. Because we've intensely disliked each other for a long time.

Angela doesn't look overweight. But from what I can feel she is all skin and fat. No muscle. No organs. No bones. "Well," I say. I take her by the shoulders and step back like they do in British dramas. "Taking good care of yourself, I see."

"I got about 30 percent liver function."

"And I'm sure you keep that 30 percent damn busy," I say. She laughs. Angela used to say her liver was a toxic waste dump.

"I was expecting Wilson," she says.

"Wilson's too important. To come down looking for his own mother. In the middle of the semester."

"Hell, middle of the semester's the best time for taking off."

I laugh. Even though I planned to come over here and show Angela nothing but disgust.

She doesn't invite me in. I feel a funny relief. Like she's going to lure me into her bedroom closet with promises of Madame Alexander dolls. Only to turn out all the lights and lock me inside without her. We stand on the grass of my mother's lawn. We look at the fragile black frame of the house. Angela says, "The lady went nuts, I'm telling you, totally nuts."

"How?" I say. I'm shaking with fascination.

"Well, I wasn't there when she actually burned down the house, but I was there right beforehand." She pauses. Angela screams if you're not paying attention. "So all I know is, she was becoming this pervert or something, I mean sneaking into my house when my kid is here, a ten-year-old kid. You read about what people do to kids these days, right?"

"My mother was *not* molesting a child. If that's what you're getting at." Angela gives me this look of pity over my ignorance of the ways of the world. I'd recognize that look from a city block away. "Think," I say. "The woman's been dried up since she gave birth to *me*. She doesn't exactly get her jollies off of physical contact." I hear myself saying these things. Even though I've driven from Florida. Even though I've infuriated Mr. Scamardo. Even though I've run my MasterCard up to the limit at the Windsor Court. All because I'm imagining my mother lying near death somewhere. In a hospital, in a Dumpster. With nobody to go looking for her but me. Angela always could turn me around so I believed untruths. And thought I discovered them myself.

"I know what I saw," she says. "She's been hanging around a crack house. And night before last I caught her talking to a dog and shitting out in public."

"Where in public?" I'm horrified. Until she says in my mother's backyard. "Where's she supposed to go to the bathroom?"

"A gas station."

"In the middle of the night?"

"She could've held it."

"That what you tell your kid? Hold it?"

"Damn straight."

"Jesus, Angela."

"I don't see you running around raising no kid. You think it's no big deal, you just put it on your credit card and it takes care of itself."

"I knew something about birth control," I say.

"I knew something about birth control, too. I just got *bored*, that's all. Least when I die I'll leave something behind. What're you going to leave behind, satisfied grocery customers?"

I'm not eight years old. I'm not standing in front of a burned-up house. With no recourse except to stay here. And go down deeper into Angela's hatred of the world. But I start laughing again, punchy from nerves. I imagine myself in a bier at the express checkout of the Winn-Dixie. With thousands of shoppers solemnly walking past. Like I'm in a bin of chicken fryers reduced to forty-nine cents a pound. "You are so mean," I say to Angela.

"That's why I'm your best friend."

We don't go inside her house. Though a front of storm clouds is moving in fast from the direction of the lake. "I can't invite you in; the place is a shitpile," she says.

"Like it never was before," I say. But she doesn't make a move. Except to sit down on her steps.

"If I don't get a transplant, I'm going to die," she says.

"Right."

"I'm fucking serious. I'm filling up with this poison so fast my skin's practically on fire. I mean, I get Dustin to scratch the parts I can't reach, but you can't make a kid sit still and rip at your skin for hour after hour. Doctor gives me Atarax, which, by the way, is as good as some shit you get on the street, if you feel like passing out. But I got a life to live, know what I mean?"

"Sure, Angela." I look at her. She's a dreadful shade of orange. But Angela's always been funny-colored. She gave my mother room for speculating about people from the south of Italy. How easy it might have been for their Negro forebears to fashion rafts from the jungle and paddle across the Mediterranean. After a while, Wilson quit telling her that all of northern Africa is desert. I think it was because he liked the idea of Mama saying bad things about Angela. Though he'd never have admitted it.

She shrugs. That's one thing I liked about Angela. She never cared whether she got sloppy attention. She wanted *undivided* attention when she was showing off. But sympathy or fondness makes Angela nervous.

The longer we sit in silence, the shakier I get. For all I know Angela has bad information about my mother that she can hold on to or let loose. It makes no difference to her. But this is going to scare me out of my wits. It's possible to hate your parents. To say mean things to them as naturally as breathing. But then you see them lying helpless somewhere, and you're three years old again. Clear about your world. Knowing that if one of them leaves the room you'll sink into blackness and never have another sensation. "Where's my mother?" I say.

"You want to know the truth?" I nod slowly. "When I threw her out, I think she went and slept in her house."

I stand up. I'm poised right over Angela. "What do you mean, you threw her out?"

"Hey, hey," she says. She holds one palm up at me. Angela looks like a troll. "You'd've done the same thing. Jesus, it's one thing to be nice to an old lady, it's another thing to have her rummaging through all your shit, stealing clothes and cigarettes and saying God-knows-what to your kid. Look, I didn't call the police or nothing, and I'd've had every right to, her coming into my house when I'm not even there and all."

I fold my arms across my chest. I wait. Angela looks up at me. I notice her eyes are yellow. She looks dirty rather than pitiful.

"She tells my kid I ought to be in jail, that I'm a lousy mother. Great shit to tell a kid."

"Where's he now?" I say. It's after three o'clock.

"Damned if I know. On his way, I guess."

I look around. I try to remember what schools are in the neighborhood. The only school in viewing distance is Green. But it's a middle school. Besides, it's 100 percent black. We all went to Allen. We were at the edge of the district. My mother drove Wilson, me, and Angela every morning. And picked us up every afternoon. Our Lady of Lourdes isn't far. But it costs. I ask her where he goes to school. "Crocker," she says. "Crocker's black," I say.

"Ninety-nine point three percent," she says and smirks. I ask her how she can do that to her kid. "You sound like your mama," she says.

"You know fucking well what I mean."

"Yeah, you're just like your mama. He's in Resource for the Gifted, for your information."

I start to laugh. Angela can't possibly have a child with an IQ over 100. Even if she mated with Vaclav Havel. Evidently her kid took in fewer street drugs during his gestation than most of the other children at Crocker. Angela scowls at me. She tells me to drop dead. "You're not being very nice about my mother. I don't see any reason to be nice about your kid," I say. I forget how much I enjoyed being a child. Everything is out where everybody else can see it. Angela stands up. But she's shorter than I am now. She can't look me in the eye and act like she's going to slug me. "So where is she now?" I say.

"Nowhere I know of."

"Thanks a fucking lot."

"Hey, when my mama dropped dead, I quit having to take care of anybody old and ugly."

I tell her I didn't ask her to take care of my mother. I just thought she'd watch where she went. "If you saw somebody's dog run off, you'd know what direction it ran in."

"She's got her dog," Angela says.

"Jesus God, you don't have a brain cell left," I say. She smiles at the idea. Like she's run out from *using* them.

Mr. Scamardo expects me back at work day after tomorrow. Or else he's going to put me on part-time. He knows that'll force me to quit. It's the threat I make whenever I've decided a cashier is getting too smug. I told him I was sure it wouldn't take that long. My mother's lived in the same house more than forty years. Finding her in her neighborhood is going to be as easy as finding somebody in one of those pig-path towns that are all over Louisiana. "Frankly, I don't believe your mother's missing," Mr. Scamardo said. Then he walked off from me.

I have two hours of daylight. And even less of open bureaucratic offices. So I leave Angela sitting on her steps. I say "got to go" like I see her every day. Angela's going nowhere. She's not even going to have the good luck to die. She's bad grass. And she knows it. Though she's said nothing, I'm sure she figures she's going to be itching and squirming for another forty-two years. As long as she stays away from alcohol. Which is easy when she has so many finer escapes. "Where're you staying?" she hollers after me as I get into my car. "Why?" "In case." I tell her the Windsor Court. At worst she'll phone. And knowing it's Angela, I won't pick up.

16

Jerusha

MONDAY NIGHT I STOOD IN MY BACKYARD FOR SOME AIR, and Mealworm came over to the fence and whimpered at me from Angela's yard. I was nervous about him, thought I'd have to give him away, because Angela is the type to get drunk and throw him down and break all four of his legs and let him drag around on his little splintered bones. I considered finding Gloretta and giving him to her for a companion. I've read about how prisoners and retards and people in retirement homes get talkative or kind or whatever they need to be if they have pets. It's too bad I can't offer myself up to Gloretta instead of the dog. Gloretta doesn't have the world's best house—a half a camelback double that has everything in it Gloretta has owned since she got married, including copies of *Good Housekeeping* from 1958. Gloretta does not believe in yard sales, except as a customer. "You put in a hundred hours, sticking little price tags on stuff that people don't pay no attention to anyway, and maybe you get a hundred dollars out of it, and nobody outside of Mexico makes a dollar an hour anymore," she'd say. "The point of a yard sale is to get rid of stuff," I'd say back. The idea of living in Gloretta's house is sickening. I'd probably spend all my time sneaking around putting price tags on everything, then wait until one day she was out and open the doors and let all those people in low-rider cars come in with their wallets full of dollar bills and clean her out. It doesn't matter. Gloretta is in the hospital, and her daughters will probably keep her there until she's as fit and sharp as a twenty-year-old so Medicare will pay for nurses and the spoiled bitches won't have any tending to do, and when she gets out she won't need me hanging around. We get on each other's nerves.

Tuesday I woke up smelling of wet ashes. The only smell worse than fresh cat shit is wet ashes. All day people looked at me funny, and it took a while to figure out why, having spent all night in the stink of the house. It's like peeing in the bed or living in New Jersey: after time passes you get used to anything. I was standing in line at the Whitney Bank, waiting to talk to one of those vice presidents whose only job is to initial stuff. Only two kinds of people get in that line: colored men with checks that make the teller suspicious and rich white ladies who can't balance their checkbooks and, even though they keep a minimum of five thousand dollars, they have to come into the bank so they can giggle about how elegant the Spring Fiesta was. I was behind one of those women, and she fanned herself with a deposit slip even though it wasn't above 68 degrees all day, and I said in a refined voice, "My house burned down, and I've just been tramping through with the adjuster." She smiled, and I could tell all her teeth were capped because they had this thin black edge at her gum line. What's the point of having these perfectly shaped teeth when all anybody notices is that black edge? "Oh, I'm terribly sorry," she said and kept fanning. "The house on Valence Street," I said. There was a good chance she'd go riding through the four good blocks of Valence Street looking for a burned Victorian two-story and feel tragedy-stricken. Valence Street runs from the river twenty-five blocks, and if you're rich and don't believe in going more than two blocks away from St. Charles Avenue, you can think it's a high-cotton street, with those million-dollar houses at the avenue intersection. She thought she was talking to somebody like herself who was waiting for checks to buy a new life before nightfall, lease a car, rent a condominium, run through Canal Place and buy everything silk in my size. I bet she went riding up and down those four blocks, looking for blackened sills. "Now aren't you ashamed of yourself?" I said to her as she was leaving.

I had $237 in my checking account, which seemed like a reasonable amount for a checking account, and I took out $236 and felt flush. At the Shoney's across the street from the bank, I ate a day's worth of food at the salad bar, not because I was trying to get away with anything, but because I was starving and constipated and could take care of both problems at the same place.

I walked from Shoney's to the Hale Boggs Building to tell those people I didn't have a mail slot in my front door anymore because I didn't have a door, and they said, "Oh, now you don't have a house, well, as long as you are down and out we might as well tell you that your husband is dead, and you know it, and we know it, and now your Social Security is going to drop to $427 or $464 a month, you can choose, but, oh, by the way, you better rent a post office box and get back to us, thank you very much, next please." I walked out of there with a fistful of papers, no pen to write on them even if I wanted to, and I hollered behind myself, "See if I ever vote Democratic again!" I could hear the clerks laughing at me. They were far-left-wing fools who haven't heard that the sixties are over and it's time to get a real job; they happily voted for Walter Mondale and Michael Dukakis and Bill Clinton and think David Duke had nothing worth saying. This is basically Wilson and Zib's generation. Everybody thought they were going to get wiser with time, and a lot did, but some of those children born after the war have their heads up their asses. I was past Lee Circle going uptown when I decided that I wanted to walk back into the Hale Boggs Building and holler, "I was only joking, I wouldn't vote for a Republican if he was Jesus Christ," make them feel bad that I was one of their kind, but I was tired, and getting around is difficult with no car, and I am going to have to leave good answers and pride behind me.

Last night I sat in my dark house having two moon pies and a Barq's from E-Z Serve, trying to figure out what to do, because no one else was going to tell me. My eyes were good, and I thought I could see things I couldn't make out during the day, when stains of light came in. Still hanging on the wall across from where I sat was a painting Woodrow and I fought about for forty years. It was a picture of the ocean his uncle must have painted when he'd been out at sea two weeks and forgotten about color. It was waves and sky, waves and sky, like that stupid joke where somebody draws a straight line across a page and asks you what it is, and you say, "The *Titanic* after it sank." I always called the picture Woodrow's *Titanic* picture, and people would come into the house the first time and say, "Oh, what's that?" And I'd say, "Oh, that's a painting of the *Titanic*," and they'd go up close, thinking they'd missed something, and I'd say, "*After* it sank!" but we quit having people to our house after a while, and then all I did was fuss with Woodrow about it because the only color in the picture was Coke-bottle green, which did not go with orange and yellow upholstery. Woodrow would press his lips so tight I thought he was going to swallow them, and he'd say, "My uncle Randolph painted that when he was in the Pacific," and I'd say, "Your uncle Randolph painted that when he puked in the Pacific," and Woodrow'd say, "I was damn fond of Uncle Randolph," and I'd say, "You never been fond of anybody a day in your life," and Woodrow'd walk out of the room and say over his shoulder, "Touch that painting, and I'll throw everything of yours out the front door." Those were the nights I let him roll on top of me.

I pictured Woodrow in my mind, not when he was old and mean or young and cocky, but somewhere in between, when he was sad because he saw too much on television he wasn't going to have. The sadness made him soft around the edges in my mind, and I started to cry, lying on my back on that stinking sofa, tears running down toward my ears. I made myself stop. No one was there to see me, but I could never tell when I might find myself in the light, face to face with some-body with every right to make fun of me. I've cried a few times since I was thirteen years old, but never in public; once or twice I felt like doing it, but I was able to screw my face up until it hurt and the crying stopped. Zib can wail like a crazy person for nothing, and I've told her people will laugh at her; I've laughed at her myself, but she says genuine crying gets as much poison out of your body as your liver does; she thinks all the chemicals in your breakfast cereal and underarm de-odorant pile up behind your eyeballs and wait. "I can get out of a traffic ticket, Mama, just by crying; all you've got to do is make your face feel like it's crying, and the tears will come, I swear," to which I say to her, "Ever consider not driving like a maniac to begin with?" I screwed up my face and thought about Zib conning the Mississippi State Police, and my crying went away.

I wakened and had to pee so badly that I knew I wouldn't go back to sleep until I did something about it. I lay there try-ing to think of somewhere to pee in the house, but people are going to come in and have opinions about me, even if they're only the city demolition crew after I'm dead and my heirs have been contacted and they've said, "What the hell, tear it down to the ground, but first get that claw-foot bathtub out; it must be worth a hundred dollars." If I peed on the floor, it'd smell, and someone would know I did it. I walked to the back door on my tiptoes, making myself weigh less—that's a good one, I'll have to tell it to Gloretta. One of the back steps gave way under me, but I was holding on to the side of the house and I caught myself. Mealworm barked at me, and I whispered, "Shut up, you little ingrate," and then he sprung up and down so I could see his weenie bouncing around on the underside of him. That's what I like about dogs: they have no shame. I edged toward the bushes on the side of my property away from Angela's house, and I squatted and balanced against the fence, and I'd just started peeing when all the lights came on in Angela's backyard. The pee sprayed into my underpants, and I hollered, Shit, because they were the only underpants I had, and Angela came bounding down her back steps with more energy than she's shown since 1975 when she chased Zib up the block with a meat cleaver for fun. "I fucking knew it," she crowed.

I finished peeing like I was putting out a fire, pulled myself up and straightened myself out, walked toward her and said, "Okay, Angela, what'd I ever do to you?"

Dustin came stumbling out the door behind her, his eyes pig slits; I was sure he wouldn't remember a thing in the morning. Angela told him to go back to bed, and he said, "What for?" in a voice full of dreams.

"You're crapping in your yard," she said to me.

"Hey, I can have sex in my yard if I want."

"Not if my kid can see it."

"Like your kid hasn't seen a lot worse every Saturday night," I said, my hand on my hip; I felt like shaking my rear end side to side, but I didn't.

"You want to know what you done? *That's* what you done, you come in my house, tell Dustin I'm a whore and I ought to be in jail and God knows what else."

"You *were* in jail at the time," I said. I hoped the neighbors behind us on Cadiz Street could hear us.

Angela said she was going to call the police. I laughed out loud. "Yeah, right, they got a homicide a night in this city, they got enough crack cocaine on the streets to hop up the whole state of Iowa for a week, and they're going to come tearing over here because an old lady is peeing in her own backyard," I said.

"They know me at the Second District; you better not mess with me." Angela was down her steps, and I hoped Mealworm had left ass-bullets to squish between her toes.

"Give me my dog," I said. Angela crouched down and made the tutting sound you make when you want a cat to think you're something he can pounce on so he'll come to you. Mealworm came out from under her house and danced around a little, then backed off. "Fucking dog," Angela said, and she started after him, so he backed away on his skinny legs, and I said, "Jesus, just stand still and hold out your hand to him," and she stood up and held her hand two feet above his head, and I told her to squat down, and she said, "You told me to stand still." "I told you to stay still. Squat down and stay still." She squatted so fast that Mealworm bolted across the yard, and I started for the fence. "You come one step closer and I'll shoot you. Dustin, go get my rifle." Dustin hadn't moved a muscle since this whole fray started, but at the sound of his name his eyes opened, and he said, "You don't got a rifle, Angela."

"God, you are a stupid little bastard," she said, and then she tore behind Mealworm like an idiot in a greased-pig contest, and I was sure she was going to win by flattening him, and I hollered *Sit!* and the dog stopped where he was and sat down. "Why'nt you do that before?" Angela said as she scooped the dog up and came toward me. "Because I didn't think you needed my help with a two-pound dog," I said. I stuffed Mealworm under my arm and headed back into my house. I had no idea what time of the night it was, but I was getting out. I'd be better off on a bench in Danneel Park watching drug deals than I was living next door to Angela. I could pee behind the magnolia trees along the uptown edge of the park. Those trees are about thirty feet tall, and I think it's because so many generations of kids have come to the park and waited until their mamas were happy, sitting on a bench, talking to the other mamas, and then they've said they had to go to the bathroom. I don't know of a single child, even the colored ones since all that civil-rights mess, who has grown up in this part of New Orleans and not peed behind those trees.

A wriggling chihuahua can be as hard to carry as a half-dead Great Dane. I didn't have a leash for Mealworm, and I was carrying him toward the park, along Danneel Street, passing the cemetery, and he smelled the places he'd kicked up his feet, and he wanted to get down and be free the way Dustin must have let him. I told him to stop it, and he did a back flip like a goddamn cat and landed on his feet, then galloped to a place in the cemetery fence where chihuahuas, cats, rats, and mean high-school kids can sneak into the graveyard and dump whatever load they have. I saw the dog dancing over the graves, heading toward the mound at the back where all the chunks of bone have been churned up in the dirt. I looked around, and the street was empty, and I got down on my knees, then flat on my belly, and crawled under the fence. I didn't know how I'd get out with a chihuahua trying to fight his way out of my hands, but I wasn't about to leave without him. He'd go back to Angela's, and she'd stomp on him once and leave a grease spot on the sidewalk.

I caught up with him by the caretaker's shack. It was a pile of tin held together with spit and bubble gum, but I knew there was electricity and a phone line inside. I'd gone past it one night, walking the dog outside the fence, the phone had rung, and I'd almost had a heart attack.

I tried the door, and it wasn't locked. I wasn't surprised; the caretaker's shack is not the main attraction in a cemetery. I stepped inside, and nothing gave me the creeps. I figured anybody set on mischief was going to be white and goofy. Colored people are too spooked by death; I don't know how the archdiocese managed to hire a Negro to keep the place up. I was as well protected by the graves as I would have been by a yard full of starving Dobermans. I switched on the light and found a cot and a clock and a hot plate. I couldn't lie down where a colored person had been sleeping, and I couldn't eat off utensils that had been between big brown lips, but with a clock I could stay the night. The caretaker and his wife show up at about 5:30 in the morning. I'd seen them out there raking pine needles before daybreak. I hollered at him one time, "Why you come so early?" And he said, "We disturbing you?" nice and concerned, and I said, "Oh, no, I was just asking, I mean, you got to get on the bus in the dark and everything." He said, "Yeah, but we be finish in time to go home and eat dinner by two." I hollered, "Suit yourself," and he laughed. I thought the shack might be a good place to come in the afternoons. I could use the phone. Until then I'd wondered where I was going to sit and use the phone with a dog under my arm. Nobody ever talks to you

when you call. They have to call you back. I could see me
standing in the parking lot at the E-Z Serve waiting for the pay
phone to ring, expecting that at any minute the dog was going
to fly into the street. I imagined myself telling drippy-nosed
secretaries *I can be reached at the Valence Street Cemetery, 895-
8153, please have him call me here between 2:00 P.M. and 5:00 A.M.*
I put Angela's towel under me on the cot, set the alarm. It was
11:30. I shoved the dog up behind my butt next to the wall and
turned off the light. I had to tell myself over and over that the
floor was not going to give way, that no one was coming in.

Not only do they not let you on a streetcar with a dog, if they
find one with you, they throw you off and don't give back
your fare. I have Mealworm in a Harry's Ace Hardware shopping bag, and I've walked four blocks with him, swinging the
bag along so he'll get sleepy, but he picks the second my dollar
has gone into the fare box to wake up and start wiggling and
making noise. The conductor puts me off at the next stop,
Napoleon Avenue. If I was her color, she wouldn't do that.
Even when my kids were coming up, streetcars had two con-
ductors, both white and underpaid, one in front to drive, one
in back to collect your ten cents. Now they have these people
who belong to the union and try their best to ram expensive
cars that get stopped on the neutral ground. That's why we pay
a dollar and a quarter to ride, what with these people getting
paid twenty an hour to stay on a track that a blind man could
stay on, plus the lawsuits from all the hotheads who get broad-
sided on the tracks. The conductor is a skinny colored woman,
and she tries to take my elbow and help me down the steps,
and I jerk away from her. "You want to treat me like I'm an old
lady, you keep me on the streetcar," I say.

I step down onto the concrete pad at the stop, and Dustin runs across St. Charles through the moving traffic. He's winded and sweaty, and I figure he's running for the streetcar, which has the green light and is rolling, so I pound on the door. The driver keeps on going. They act like they have a schedule, like they have their pocket watches synchronized and have to hit each stop on the second; they'd have you believing that that's why they can take ten minutes to go two blocks. I know better. They can pick up on who their passengers are: if they're tourists, the conductor sails around the circuit fast enough to rock off the tracks, and if they're people late for work, the conductor rolls so slowly that doodlebugs on the track have time to get out of the way.

"Boy, I thought I was going to have to chase that streetcar all the way downtown," Dustin says.

"They come every five minutes this time of morning," I tell him.

He says he's not taking the streetcar, and I ask him where he thinks he's going. I don't have a watch, but I can tell by the kids from Sophie B. Wright hanging around the old KB's that it's about 8:30. The drugstore has a sign, THREE STUDENTS AT A TIME, and it opens at eight, but those kids have to have their barbecue chips for breakfast and they wait their turns. "I'm going with you," Dustin says. "You should've knocked or something. I saw you come out the cemetery, I saw you go in your house, but I must've been scratching on Angela when you come out, since I didn't see you until you were halfway up to St. Charles."

"You've got about ten minutes to get to school," I say. He's got on a white shirt and gray slacks, like all the colored boys who live across from the power station wear to school, and I wouldn't be surprised to learn Angela has him in the neighborhood public school, which has no white children except an albino from time to time.

Mealworm is wiggling in the bag like a baby in the eighth month of pregnancy. "They put you off the streetcar," Dustin says. "You're going to get put out of every place in the whole city with a dog."

"Well, you're not taking him back to that mother of yours. She'll drop him in the deep fryer one night and feed him to you for supper."

"Angela don't cook," he says and grins. "Anyway, I was coming to *help*."

"That's all I need, a boy eats as much as me." His eyes fill up. "You're not fat," I say, and the tears don't spill over. I tell him I'll phone him, I promise, I'll even hang up if Angela answers, and he trudges away. I follow him, and he turns on Milan. There's an all-colored school down that way. Angela should be shot. He turns and watches me as I head downtown, and I wave him toward school. If he's in third or fourth grade, he's been at that school four or five years, and no one's killed him yet, but I feel like I'm sending a boy off to that Gulf War, where he might not have gotten wounded, but he sure would have been going to father children with three eyes and no lungs.

It takes me an hour to walk downtown, swinging the dog in the bag until he ought to be seasick. It'd serve him right. We stop at McDonald's, but they won't let me walk up and put in an order, so I go inside, get a biscuit with bacon, cheese, and egg on it, and a Coke, and when I'm outside I offer a bit of the egg to Mealworm. He sniffs at it hopefully, then looks up at me from inside the bag like I'm a traitor. "Well, either you're dying, or you're damn picky," I say to him, and a man in a three-piece suit who's fast-walking past me toward the streetcar stops to stare.

"Give you something to talk about over the dinner table tonight," I say, and he keeps moving.

I figure I can solve all my problems if I wander around City Hall. But I read the directory on the ground level, and I'm too undone to think. Nothing is here. I'm looking for somebody to report stolen cars to, and the man in the information booth says I have to go out to Rosedale Street. I tell him, "I look like somebody that can go running all over town? I'm telling you my car got stolen, and you're telling me to go to some street I've never heard of." He's colored, but he doesn't try to find a way to throw me out of the building. Instead he picks up the phone and makes a call, and I stand there not paying attention, because I am worried this is going to be the moment when the dog decides to take a leap for freedom and go running into Loyola Avenue traffic. The man covers the phone and asks me my address, and I tell him, and then I add, "But it burned down; I can't live there anymore," and I hear him say into the phone, "Look, I'll get back to you, sorry about that," and then he asks a million questions; he thinks I'm a thief or a nutcase. I tell him never mind, and I hotfoot it out before he can go wake up a security guard.

I go into the post office up the street, and it is the first time I've seen white faces in hours. All the white people are the ones standing in line, nervous as long-tailed cats in a room full of rocking chairs; they're dressed up in gray wool suits, even the women, never mind that winter is not going to come to this city once again this year, and these people are sweating. They bounce on the balls of their feet, checking out whether the front of the line is moving, whether the clerks are wasting their important time. The clerks who work in the main post office got here by being the angriest ones in their neighborhood post offices, and the more they see these white people with their arms full of heavy-duty business envelopes, the more slowly they move. They hold their faces front, but they keep up a line of patter with each other about someone who has just left. A fat blond woman is in line ahead of me, and when Mealworm rustles in the bag I put my finger to my lips and let her look inside. "O-o-o, he is so cute," she says, while I'm looking off in the distance, and I say, "Sh-h-h," and she giggles, high pitched for so much blubber behind the sound.

When the clerk tells me it will cost me $21.50 for six months to rent a box, I reach in my bra and pull out a five and a twenty. I am not about to let her know I'm giving her money I intended to make last a full day. She has on earrings that cost that much. One nice thing about the post office, they don't add tax; I get back enough change to get lunch at Popeye's on Canal Street. I give the dog some chicken meat, no skin, and he goes for it like crazy, not stopping to sniff, and then he looks up at me from inside the bag with watery sad eyes, and I have to go back into Popeye's and ask for a small cup of ice water. He drinks too fast, spilling on the bottom of the bag, and the brown paper gets soggy and breaks, and I notice in time and pluck him out before he nosedives onto the sidewalk. "Well, you're just going to have to control yourself out in public," I say to him, stuffing him under my arm. I talk to him like he's a grown-up, the way I talked to Wilson and Zib, and as I walk down Carondelet Street toward the Hale Boggs Building, women straight out of business college, who've just gotten their first paychecks and blown them on makeup, take sidelong glances at me and walk straighter. About the fifth one I pass, I tell her, "Hey, your life isn't so far from hell that you couldn't slip right down into it before you knew what hit you." She gives me this wounded look, like she's done me a favor I haven't been grateful for.

It is late afternoon. I've been all over downtown, and I can rest easy tonight, now that I know that, if I can live long enough, a brown envelope with a green check for $464 will be sitting in a box in the main post office once a month. I pick up a copy of the *Times-Picayune* that someone has politely left on top of a trash bin, and I look through the classified ads, and the only houses for rent under $300 are in parts of town where no self-respecting white person could expect to wake up alive in her bed. I've lived here long enough to know addresses block by block. Take Valence Street, for example. You see an ad that says the 1600 block, and you know that after dark it's full of Bentley automobiles and artists that the rich people collect; you see an ad with the 2500 block, and you know that there'll be at least one crack murder before the year is out. It is ridiculous how much people want you to pay. Seventy-five dollars a week to live in one room on Canal Street, where old people go to sit around and smell each other's rot and wait to die. Our house note was $67, and we had three bedrooms. We bought when it was possible to get a place for $7,000, but times haven't changed that much. I'd rather sleep in a shack inside a cemetery than have to look at a landlord once a week and watch him grin with a big space between his two front teeth, knowing he can go out and buy diamond pinkie rings while I have no groceries.

It is going to be nightfall before I can get to the cemetery, but I start walking anyway. I get to Lee Circle and can't go another step. Streetcars are coming past every two minutes, and it must be rush hour because they have about a hundred people packed into each one. I could slip on in a crowd without the conductor noticing that I'm carrying a dog, but Mealworm is sure to be smashed to death, even if I stuff him under my bosom, and I don't want my dog's last breath to be full of stale perfume and mothballs.

I sit down on one of the benches and try not to fall asleep. A colored woman comes over and sits down next to me, and I can't do anything about it. Mealworm starts sniffing the air in her direction, and she smiles at him with her false teeth all showing. Colored people always want little dogs, and I tell him to settle down, and she says, straight at him, like he could understand, "I don't know why you sniffing at me; I ain't had no dog come within a hundred feet of me in years."

"I don't think *he's* been around another dog in his whole life," I say. I have left out of his life the part where he hung out with that bag of wrinkles that Angela calls a dog.

"Spoiled rotten," the woman says. *Sperled*.

"If you can call eating Popeye's chicken being spoiled."

"That'd spoil me good right about now," she says. *Sperl*.

Franchise food places are a few blocks down. Wendy's, Burger King, Popeye's. I never go into them late at night, because that's when the bums off Camp Street come crawling up the avenue, walking in those places and buying a cup of coffee so they can sit in a booth and whisper at you for money. With a car, it's easy to go up to Carrollton Avenue if I feel like having bad food. I tell the woman they don't let me in those places with a dog. "I had him in a Harry's bag this morning," I say, "but the little bastard got the bag all wet up, and I had to throw it away, and I haven't seen another one since."

"You buy, I'll fly," she says. I don't know what she's talking about. "I mean," she says after a while of me looking at her funny, "you give me the money, I'll go in." I shake my head no. I want her to go away, and I edge toward the other end of the bench. "Yeah, I hear you," she says. "Tell you what, I watch your dog, you go in."

"Right," I say, "you can get a hundred dollars for this dog."

"What I'm going to do, run a ad?"

I have to laugh. I think about it for a minute. "Okay, I stand outside, I give you the money, you go in, I watch you, fair deal?"

"I could get me something?" she says.

I nod. I was thinking I could get a hamburger and give her a bite, get a plastic knife and cut off a chunk so I wouldn't get her spit on my food, but I haven't talked to anybody all day who wasn't asking for my social security number. "But no double," I say, and I reach inside my bra and get a ten-dollar bill.

"Hoo-o-o-e-e-e," she says. You'd think it was a $10,000 bill. She's looking at my chest. I'll slip the rest into my shoe while she's in Wendy's. "Where you got that from?" she says.

"The bank."

"You not on the street? I thought you on the street." I look at her funny again. Colored people have expressions that mean something to them and nothing to anybody else, and they hardly ever try to speak normal English. "I mean, you got someplace to go?"

"None of your business," I say.

"That's what I figured," she says. "Look, baby, ain't nothing wrong with being on the street."

"I'm not 'on the street.'"

"I don't see you setting in your house watching the five o'clock news."

I give her this look that would drop a bull elephant from a hundred yards. "I hear you," she says.

For a colored woman, she has good manners. She goes through a dozen napkins, wiping mustard off her lip every time she takes another bite of her hamburger. She is a very careful biter with those false teeth. These people's skin is so dark that from a distance their teeth look white enough to be on a magazine cover, but then you get up close, and you can see the moss. Especially on the children. If I ever'd seen scum on Zib's or Wilson's teeth, I'd have brushed for them until they had no enamel left. This woman's teeth are like perfect rows of white corn, and I hide my mouth. I haven't brushed my teeth in so many days that my mouth feels like the inside of a smokehouse, all meaty and smoky and dry. I take a swig of Coke, slosh it around, let the bubbles wash away whatever they can. We're back on the bench by Lee Circle, and Mealworm is sitting between us, happy to stay because he might get something. The woman slips him a french fry. I tell her very nicely not to do that, he'll get the runs. "Good place for them," she says, pointing at the grass right around the statue of Robert E. Lee. My father was named after Robert E. Lee, and I think about telling her that, but I am not in the mood to fight the Civil War over again. I did enough of that with Wilson when David Duke ran for governor. Wilson would call me up on the phone, even though he hasn't lived in Louisiana in years; I could clock him for a few days running: it'd be the top of the CBS *Evening News,* and Wilson'd get fired up, like we were going to be hanging colored boys from every tree in the city if the man got elected, and I'd tell him, "Look, you don't live where it's only about forty percent white and a person has no rights whatsoever," and then Wilson would go out of his head for ten minutes, talking about hate. Nothing else, not quotas or welfare, just hate. I'd tell him, "Call back when you get something to say that makes sense," and I'd hang up on him. "Well, don't give him any more fries," I say to the woman, and I put some ice cubes in my hand and hold them out for the dog to lick. It's not their fault that coloreds don't know about healthy eating. They give their babies pickled pork and red beans until their belly buttons pop out, but that's all they have.

We went off daylight time weekend before last, though it doesn't make a difference when I have no watch. It's dark out by the time I've finished eating, but the woman is still taking polite little bites of her food like she's in Antoine's and is going to take a taxi to a hotel. I tell her in a complimentary way that she's a slow eater. "They done that in the Depression," she says. "My mama say, 'You chew a hundred times, you fill your stomach up with spit, at least,' so I remember that, I chew till I wear the paint off these false teeth. Sometime it work, sometime it don't."

My mother told me that, too, though not because we lacked food at my house. When I was eleven I started to get extra fat on me, and my mother told me no boy was going to look at me if I didn't trim down, and for a week I believed her and walked around half starved. Then I cut up during arithmetic, and that afternoon a boy named Harvey followed me home from school, and I invited him in, and with my mother watching I offered him a piece of cake that I'd convinced myself didn't taste good because we used oleo instead of butter and rationed sugar. He asked me why I wasn't having any, and I said, "Oh, I got to slim down some," and he said, "What for?" And that was the end of my chewing my food a hundred times.

"My mama told me the same thing," I tell the woman, surprising myself. I don't like to let colored people know they have anything in common with me, except the soaps. I've never understood why they watch the stories, when it's almost 100 percent white people. I never watch shows with stars like Eriq LaSalle. I don't get a thing out of two of them kissing each other.

She chews forever, behaving for her mama, though her mama is sure to have been dead at least ten years. She must be reading my mind, because she says, "I could tell that to Veronica, she'd just laugh in my face. You can't tell a child nothing these days." I ask her how old Veronica is. This woman has to be about my age, since, even though her Chinaman-yellow face hasn't many lines in it, her hair is gray. Veronica can be as old as fifty, in which case she has no business letting her mother sit on a bench and beg hamburgers off strangers. "Thirty-five," she says. "It took me to thirty-five to have her, and I was happy for about as long as it taken to get her home before she start making me crazy. I work for forty years wiping a old white lady behind to give that girl everything she want, I mean everything, and what she do? She up and get pregnant by the ugliest nigger in the city of New Orleans, somehow make the most beautiful baby in the city of New Orleans, I tell her she making a mistake, she go off to Chicago. With no forwarding address."

"Hey, my Wilson's in Chicago," I say. "Well, Evanston. He's a professor at the university." I figure her Veronica is selling drugs. "But he's useless as teats on a boar hog, too."

"Veronica got a teaching certificate. I figure if I want to try real hard, I can call the school board, track her down. But what I'm going to say? *Oh, Veronica, I apologize, you got me living on the street, I been duly punished for everything I ever done to you, how about you send me some money?* I rather die in a gutter."

A streetcar whines and rattles around the circle, and I wait for it to get past. I feel like saying *I hear you;* now it makes sense. "We buried my husband three weeks ago," I say. "And you know what my daughter does?"

"I thought you got a boy."

"I got *two*. Boy and a girl. Both worthless. You know what she does? We come back from the cemetery. Arlington," I say, even though this woman probably never had a husband to begin with. "Go to the motel. I lie down for a nap, I mean, I have driven all the way up to this place by myself, and here I'm burying my husband, and what's she do? She takes my car keys and goes running off to Washington, D.C., and she doesn't come back until the middle of the night, meanwhile leaving me stranded with no food or anything. I tell you, I threw my things in the car, got the hell out of there, even in the middle of the night, left those selfish fools to take care of themselves. Probably cost them a fortune to get back to the airport, and you know what? I'm glad."

"Sound like the boy didn't do nothing."

"Oh, he tried to act like the big, smart Ph.D., pull out this psychological bullshit, pardon my French. Like he was taking her side. He hates her guts, wouldn't piss on her if she was on fire, but when it comes to making Mama look like a bitch, he's her best friend. Hasn't called, either."

"You got a cell phone or what?" she says and grins.

"I told you, I'm not on the street."

"You could put me up?"

"No." I say no the way it means, *No, I wouldn't,* not, *No, I couldn't.*

She's quiet, like I've hurt her feelings. "You acting like I'm black and you're white," she says.

"Well, sure."

"You can't be pulling that shit on no street," she says, like she wants to protect me from something. I open my mouth to answer, and she says, "I know, you not on the street." I laugh. This woman is not stupid. Woodrow once told me that coloreds have excellent understanding because they don't clutter up their brains with thinking. The skinnier your nose is, the longer your ancestors've been around developing their brains,

Woodrow told me, and it made sense. He tried to tell that to
Wilson when he was in high school. Yeah, what about Jews,
then? he said. Jews don't think, they're machines, Woodrow
told him. Like those things I drop the pennies in at the bank,
they're born to count change. That's not thinking. I know that
girl Wilson's married to now is Jewish. And I know Wilson
told her our theory, too, because one time I was with her in
the drugstore, and she got a fistful of change, and she held it
out to me in her palm, and she said, "Watch," and she closed
her hand, closed her eyes, said, "Sixty-seven cents." "We *told*
Wilson that," I said, and she said, "I gave her seven dollars for a
$6.33 charge, Jerusha." She said it softly, like she was feeling
sorry for me, so I snapped at her, "Well, you could've done it if
you'd *tried*." She rolled her eyes at the clerk, who was colored
and had no idea what was going on, and I didn't talk much to
her the rest of the time she was down here.

I'm thinking about going back to the cemetery for the
night. Lee Circle is the 900 block, Valence is the 4800 block; I
don't have it in me to walk that far. But there is no way to pass
a night here. The streetcars make as much noise as 747 jets.
And though it seems like everybody has left downtown for
home, the traffic is steady. Part of me wishes I didn't have this
dog. For his sake. The wheels of the streetcar could slice him
even in two. Though I have never seen a dog or a cat run over
by a streetcar. They're so loud and steady that even a dumb animal can figure they're coming. "You need a good place?" the
woman says. I nod my head yes; I am too tired to be proud. I
ask her her name, and she tells me Murray. She asks me mine,
I tell her Ru. "I got a cousin in the country, name of Ru. Well,
her mama name her Jerusha, out the Bible, but nobody with
no sense going to call her that and walk away to tell about it.

She put me in the mind of you, come to think of it. Don't take nothing off nobody. She dead, though."

"Thanks a lot," I say, and she laughs.

A streetcar stops before the turn at the circle, and Dustin gets off. He's in silhouette, but I recognize him, the only round body under five feet with straight, white-boy hair that could be on the streets after dark. He's coming for me, eyes shining like he's won something. "I figured it out," he says, puffing like a smoker. He gets so close I can smell his sour sugar breath. "See, you were on the streetcar, so you were coming downtown, so all's I had to do was get on the streetcar and keep watching. I waited for you in the cemetery, and I'd've gone to my house to see if you called, but I didn't feel like seeing Angela."

"Your mama doesn't know where you are?" He shrugs. I look at Murray, who has worry in her eyes, even though she doesn't know what's going on. "You better get back on that streetcar before Angela calls the police on me," I tell him.

"The Second District don't come to our house," he says. "They said, 'Angela, you cried wolf for the last time, next time you defend yourself.'"

"I thought Angela had friends at the Second District."

He looks at his feet. "I think she's too ugly for them now. Angela used to be beautiful," he says to Murray. Though Angela *would* be pretty if she was colored, by their standards, all yellow, even if it's from her disease, and big-eyed with some waves in her hair now. I tell him again to go home, then I realize he'll need money, and I fish in my bra before I remember I hid my cash in my shoe. "You move your money in your shoe," Murray says. "I seen you watching me." She chuckles. "But don't be putting that boy on no streetcar this time of night. Here, go call your mama." She hands Dustin a dime and a quarter, and I snatch it away. "His mother is looking for a fight," I say.

"Angela gots company. She don't need me tonight. I seen him coming up to the house. I call her, all she'll do is holler. Sometimes I tap-dance on Bourbon Street, good as Marlon and Terrence." He looks at Murray like she knows every colored child in the city. Skinny colored boys dance for the tourists and tell them "I bet I know where you got your shoes." Then they say, "You got your shoes on your feet," and win a dollar off a drunken yahoo from Alabama. I'm surprised the *Times-Picayune* hasn't had a picture of Dustin doing that. He has on his school uniform, and I say, "Tomorrow you show up in school if I have to carry you."

I don't know where Murray sleeps, but she shows us a place next to the downtown library. The hedges are neat and thick for being on city property, and there's a space between them and the building where a person can hide and go to the bathroom and not be seen, "even in broad daylight," she says. She tells me she'll be right back, she's got something for us, and before I can get my towels smoothed out on the ground she's standing there holding a piece of clean red yarn about four feet long like it's the Holy Grail. "Well, thanks," I say.

"You tie it on the dog, tie him to your arm," she says. She tells me she'll find us in the morning, and then she's gone.

Dustin is asleep fast, on his back, arms and legs splayed like he has no fears. In my dreams, Woodrow is still alive, healthy as anything, and I am living in one of those old cages in the Audubon Zoo that smelled of bear farts and rotten popcorn. Wilson felt sorry for the animals in the old zoo, tried to refuse to go, trudged along with his eyes closed when I took Zib. Woodrow comes to see me, slips me a bologna sandwich through the bars, but all I have to drink is filthy water in a little trough at the side of the cage, and I get hiccups in my dream, my gullet full of sour bologna and dry bread. I wake up with a rumbling in my bowels and a chihuahua hanging from my wrist like a giant charm on a bracelet. I look around, hear Dustin breathing from the bottom of sleep, and with Mealworm in one hand so he doesn't choke to death, I back into a corner of the building and shit so long I want to die. Mealworm is sniffing the air like a long-lost friend has returned, and I get him away from that corner fast. It is turning cool in the night, and I ball up tight to try to go back to sleep. The public library is where Wilson first started putting on airs, flipping through the card catalog like a professor before he was eight, dragging me to books about cavemen.

17

Wilson

I AM HIDING IN MY HOUSE, AND I NEVER WILL BE ABLE TO BE alone in here again, knowing how easy it is to conceal oneself. In my sock feet, I can move without creaking a board, changing nooks and levels without Barbara's sensing my presence. Other people, clever ones, may have been living with us undetected for years. I watch her go about her day unselfconsciously, and I come as close as the distance created by the thickness of a door. I am not crazed; I will not do this for more than another day or two, but I have to know about her. I surprise myself, that I resort to stealth, to getting information without asking for it; as a scholar I generally do not choose this method. But I am mute when I am alone with her, though we seldom are alone together. Around me, Barbara goes about her business, assigning me chores or doing her own in front of me, and I pay no attention, concentrating instead on words that I cannot utter. Since I cannot ask her whether she is having an affair, I am watching her for evidence, and I am soaked with perspiration, though I have been hiding only a few hours and have spent most of that time in parts of the house that heat does not reach, closets and stairwells and dark corners of the basement.

She is in her office with its padded walls that once muffled primal screams. The door is open. I can hear the high-register beeps of a phone dialing. I have much to learn about espionage: I could memorize the seven-note tune of the number she has dialed, pick it out on another machine as if I were finding a popular song on the piano keys. But she has finished dialing, and I strain to hear what she is saying.

"I saw you with her yesterday." A long silence. "I don't understand." Another silence. "But you said . . ." I hear a small crash, dozens of pencils and pens hitting carpeting on a cement floor. Barbara keeps all of her writing implements in a coffee can that Connor covered in yellow-and-white checkered Con-Tact paper and decorated with tiny paint-pen figures in all the yellow squares. The coils of the phone wire knock it over when she paces, and usually she cries *Shit!* and continues to pace; it has happened half a dozen times when I have been on the phone with her, and I never have dared suggest a cordless phone. This time she says nothing about the crash. I hear her say, "You're a goddamn liar," and then I hear her dialing the number, waiting, dialing it again, waiting, dialing again. I am learning the sequence of beeps but have no way to retain the memory, and I lose it when she stops. She comes out of her office, slams the door. I plan to sneak out the cellar door when she goes upstairs, but she hesitates like a bloodhound, tiptoes around the basement until she is standing in front of me. "You stink of nerves," she says.

I am six inches taller than she is, but I look down, shrink until I see only her knees. "I'm not your mother," she says. I did not expect to be caught, and I have no explanation ready. Barbara tells me to look at her. This part of the basement, as large as half the first floor, is lit by one 75-watt naked bulb, and the shadows are garbled and scattered, but I see her tears. "I'm not crying over you," she says. "I think you are," I say, and she kicks me in the shin. She is in her stocking feet, and I am wearing wool slacks. The impact causes no pain, but I wince. I have learned from both my mother and my children that if I look as if I am in pain, they will stop sooner, my mother from satisfaction, my children from conscience. "That didn't hurt you," Barbara says. I take a step backward. "Jesus, Wilson."

Back upstairs, she treats me like a guest, offering me a choice of tea, putting cream in a small pitcher and sugar in a bowl before she places both on the kitchen table. She is using our wedding china, a floral Wedgwood pattern. When we married, we received eighteen place settings from Field's; no one in Highland Park gives as little as a dinner plate or a cup and saucer. Barbara exchanged six place settings for a sound system and a wok, the latter so she could feel somehow that she had kept with the spirit of the gifts. We have crystal and silverware, too, dusty and tarnished and underinsured. My parents sent us a Fry Daddy and said they were too busy to come to the wedding. When Barbara sits down opposite me, she uses a stubby fingernail to scrape at a congealed little puddle of ice cream that has been on the table so long I have begun to take it for granted. The table has a veneer of stickiness, as if it has been varnished in the humidity of New Orleans and never will dry. Barbara is working at the island of crystallized sugar and fat, spewing flakes, splitting a nail to the quick, undeterred, so she gives me time to think, and I go through my mental disciplines in search of a statement. What I need is a statement. Two clauses connected by *so*. I am ready all the time to synthesize thought; that is my job, the way I keep power over students, also the way I defend myself from colleagues who want to win debates by using abstract words at great speed. No statement comes, no tangle of ideas that needs straightening out comes, either. I cock my head to the side, look at her and wait. "You're making this difficult," she says.

My tea is too thin, too bitter; I add cream, and it is too cold. I stir it and make Escher patterns from the reflections on the slowly spinning surface. Barbara giggles nervously. "Say something, for Chrissakes."

I shrug, the way a boy shrugs when he knows that any answer he gives will bring a hard blow to the face.

"You picked one hell of a day to start all this," she says.

"The best defense is a good offense; you are devolving," I say because I cannot help it.

"I'm in love with someone else," she says.

I do not absorb what she is saying. Either I do not believe her, or I believe her too well. I am like a spider with its protective external skeleton; I can be destroyed, but not by conventional methods. I stare at her, though I should wince. "He's everything you're *not*." My pulse speeds up, sending blood everywhere in my body except my head and my genitals. I do not blink. "Do you hear me, Wilson?"

"Of course I hear you." I move my mouth as little as a ventriloquist, and if I were to look into a mirror I would see my father at my age, holding back the commitment of sound.

"He's Jewish. And he's rich. And you know what? He doesn't *think*."

I try to resist laughing, but a guffaw breaks out and sends tea out of my nose. "Do you hear what you are saying?" Pain shoots through my sinuses as if I have inhaled a snootful of chlorinated pool water, but I do not mind. I am giddy with relief. I cannot put it to words yet, but I know that Barbara is mired in some foolishness that I can pick apart and put back together and walk away from unharmed.

"Evidently not," she says.

I tick off my fingers. "Rich. Jewish. Brainless. Think about it, Barbara."

She shrugs.

"Does the name Bernie Greene ring a bell?" I say, and she hurls her cup of tea at me. The hot liquid flies out of the cup in an arc that travels in reverse, sending the cup in my direction and the tea spattering all over the table in front of her, burning her hand and spilling into her lap. It would be easy for me to catch the cup as it passes over my right shoulder, leaving a few cool drops on me, but I let it go. The cup hits the hardwood floor and separates into three neat pieces, easy to glue together and put at the back of the cabinet with the beveled glass doors that distort everything inside anyway. I am disappointed. I want chalk dust.

"Oh, shit," she says, a sob popping out involuntarily as she runs for the sink and thrusts her hands under the cold tap. She shakes the water at me.

"Look, when you met me, you said, and I quote, 'Gosh, Wilson, you're so different from anything I've ever known,'" I say in falsetto. "You wanted Jewish? You wanted rich? You wanted mindless? You should have stayed in Highland Park and found someone on the Board of Trade. Is that what you have now? Someone on the Board of Trade? Send me a fucking postcard."

"I didn't say I had anyone." She is crying full force now, and her features are contorted and puffy. She puts her hand in front of her face, and I am grateful. Her fingers are short, and her nails are scrappy. I like her hands.

"You said you were in love with someone else." My voice is lower, gentler. It is those hands.

"But maybe he doesn't love me back."

My instinct is to console her, advise her. But she has given me power over her, so instead I say, "Surely you do not expect sympathy."

"He says he loves me," she says hotly.

"That is a fucking mantra, Barbara. A man rocks back and forth on top of you, and he chants *I love you* so he will clear his goddamn head. Are you fucking him?"

"Jesus, you can sound clinical even when you're using four-letter words, you know that?"

"Are you fucking him?"

"None of your business."

"I take that to mean you are not."

"Maybe I am, maybe I'm not."

I tell her it is my business, that at the millennium all that counts is what the Centers for Disease Control have to say. "It'd be your business if you were sleeping with me," she says.

"Hey, the last time I wanted to make love to you, I came home and found a *note*."

"The best defense is a good offense, Wilson," she says in singsong.

I walk out of the room because I have to go to the bathroom, and in my posture I feel my father's lack of spirit. Barbara follows me to the bathroom and pounds on the door at the wrong time. My bowels clamp shut. "I'm waiting," she says. I say nothing. I get up and zip my pants, close the lid and sit on it. "I know what you're doing," she says.

"No, you do not."

"You're just sitting there." My eyes go toward the keyhole, through which I can see a pinpoint of light. All that locks that door is a hook. This house was built in 1905. New houses are designed better for meanness, with brass-plated doorknobs that lock by turning a button. I may be able to get a paper out of that idea.

With one swift motion, I unhook the door and throw it open, expecting I will hit Barbara in the face. But she is standing across the hallway with her arms folded. "I know you pretty well, Wilson Bailey," she says. "Trouble is, lately I don't know you at all."

18

Zib

WHAT I NOTICE ABOUT UNCLE GEORGE'S HOUSE IS THE DUST.
I haven't set foot inside this house since my grandmother Bailey died. Maybe she left it this way. As a child I wouldn't have paid attention to anything that didn't move. But I give Uncle George full credit for the way his house is now. A feather duster would leave this room spotless. I see no crumbs. No grease. No fingerprints. A shiny footprint path worn onto the linoleum rug. "Wipe them feet," he says when I walk in the door. Like I've seen him ten minutes ago.

I've come here because my mother's had so much to say about Louisiana law. Louisiana law is a queer and ever-changing set of rules. It's designed for people who drink too much and marry too little. Anybody who passes the bar here is equipped to do nothing but stay and fight with his cousins. My mother hasn't written a will. To my knowledge. But she's been a fanatic about inheritance law. She's full of analyses she's bought wholeheartedly from the *Times-Picayune*. She could draft a fully binding statement about her final wishes without paying anybody. I'm guessing she's heard about some part of the Constitution that gives her a piece of Uncle George's house. Mama wouldn't mind walking in here and announcing she's come to claim what's rightfully hers. *You'd better never walk through this house naked from now on, George,* she'd say.

I tell him I'm Elizabeth Bailey. He studies me for clues. "Your niece," I tell him. "My name's George Bailey," he says.

"Yes," I say. "My daddy was Woodrow. Your brother." Wilson may be right. Since I was born, Wilson's taken advantage of his one year of extra experience on earth. I'll never catch up with him. I remember a math puzzle about the hare and the tortoise. With a certain lead that tortoise would always stay ahead of the hare. I think it had to do with powers of numbers. I *know* that all I understood was the drawing on the chalkboard of the two figures veering off into infinity. From that I learned that Wilson will forever know more than I do. Even when he dies and I'm still alive. If he saw Uncle George when he was nine and I was eight, he'll always have Uncle George figured out more completely than I do. Wilson thinks Uncle George is retarded. When I was eight he seemed fine to me. He could say *fuck* and *shit.* So he was a fully formed adult.

"Woodrow died," he says. Like he might report that Woodrow took a flight out yesterday. But his accent and pitch are the same as my father's. A quick shock of grief goes through me. I'm glad Wilson's immersed himself in the Midwest with its flat vowels and inflections. He's inherited these same vocal cords. But he plays them like a violin instead of a fiddle.

I ask him if he remembers my mother. I try to picture her at the age she'd have been the last time he saw her. She'd have been a few years older than I am now. Mama has let nature take care of the color of her hair. Though without help it's still gone through a spectrum of color. From honey to almost black. Then streaking with gray to full gray. Now close to silver when it's clean. Mama sees herself as a billboard *against* the hair salon next door to her house. She and the owners and clients have moved together through their forties, fifties, and sixties. She's let the rest of them chop a decade off their looks with dyes and hennas. She's walked around advertising what a woman of a certain age is supposed to look like. Uncle George furrows his brow. Like he's making a mental picture of my family tree. Tracing along Woodrow's leafy branch. Which lies alongside his dry, dead, termite-pocked one. "Jerusha. Ru. She probably had hair the color of mine last time you saw her," I say. "But more brown in her eyes. Pale, pale eyes. But not like mine. She's still got her eyes, but her hair got older." He chuckles. Telling him a joke is as easy as saying *poo-poo* to a four-year-old and waiting for giggles.

"That's a mean woman," he says.

"You wouldn't let her park in your driveway. You made her mad. We had to walk ten blocks to the parades. Before we could practically walk."

"She was mad?"

"My family didn't get anything from when your mama died," I say. "I guess she thought you could've shared. One week out of the year, anyway." Somewhere in the back of my mind is a memory, unformed and floating. That she's had other reasons for her dislike of Uncle George. But it's like those recovered memories. The ones psychiatrists once were wadding up and tamping down into patients' brains so they could tug them out again. Like magicians who stuff yards and yards of scarves into their cuffs. Then they pull them out of thin air to rounds of applause. It's easy to imagine George making passes at other men's wives. Even his brother's. I can be like a gullible psychiatric patient. One who takes a chip of memory, an orgasm in sleep, and pretends her father gave it to her.

George bursts into tears. "My mama died."

I squat in front of him. I fold my hands on one knee. I don't know what I'm supposed to say. But I saw Jack Nicholson sit like this in *Five Easy Pieces*. The posture feels right. "It's been a while," I say.

"But I miss her," he blubbers. I wonder if this is how Pop looked in his last days. To hear Mama tell it, he did his complete life cycle. He became as helpless and irritating as a newborn. "Where's your mama?" he says.

I tell him that's why I'm here. I'm looking for her. I live in Florida. I'm checking every place I can think of where she might be.

"I been to Florida. You know what? There wasn't one palm tree." I'm certain that the Baileys never ventured past the panhandle. I explain that gulf-coastal Florida is about the same as New Orleans. He says, "We got palm trees. Over on Carrollton Avenue. They freeze, yeah, but we get new ones. You saw the pope when he come to New Orleans? They put up whole new palm trees for him. One day there wasn't any, next day there was a whole *line* of them. Like that house up on the avenue, one day it's got no flowers, next day all the beds're full of tulips. Who they think they're fooling? You can't fool the pope, you know." I tell him I'm looking for my mother. "You want a Coca-Cola?" he says. He stands up so fast that I rock back to avoid a nose-to-nose collision. I've been squatting less than two minutes. But my joints are stiff. I have to grab the seat of his chair to steady myself. It's warm and damp. I wipe my fingers on my skirt.

A cat is lying in a box near the kitchen door. With two kittens kneading blindly at her teats. I start to bend over to look. George says, "Two done died." I avert my eyes. I don't like to see doomed animals. I never replayed the video of *Mondo Cane* Wilson gave me. I knew that one moment a steer would be looking at the camera, and the next moment I'd see a cross section of its neck where its head had been. Wilson was a vegetarian for a while. He got attached to the chicken we had for dinner one night. I never went to such an extreme. It was easier to stay away from videos like *Mondo Cane* and channels like APL.

The kitchen is a shrine. Nothing's been touched since my grandmother died. Except maybe the refrigerator handle. It reminds me of the apartment in the Quarter I borrowed from a friend. I was nineteen. She went into the hospital to have an ovarian cyst removed. She got complications. Told me I could use her place until she came out. I moved in with suddenness and gratitude. I touched nothing for the three weeks I stayed. She came home to find her juice glass with dry, hard pulp on the bottom still in the sink. I'd thrown a sheet over her sofa and slept there. So her bed was unmade the way it had been the morning she kicked out at five A.M. to check into the hospital. Right down to the smallest wrinkle. She said nothing afterward. Since she didn't thank me, I didn't thank her.

I sidle over to the spring-green vinyl countertop next to the sink. When George's head is turned I push the Mixmaster back an inch. It leaves a clean inch-wide arc on the counter. And soft dust on my fingertips. I see my prints on the white glass bowl. I blow gently on the spot until they disappear in a tiny storm. I leave streaks of gray-brown on the white. George takes out a frosty twelve-ounce can of Coke. Sets it on the counter. Pulls the Mixmaster back where it was. Removes an aluminum ice tray. He manages to put his fingers on four cubes while he's struggling to pull back the release handle. "It's not hot out. I don't need ice," I say. I imagine the garbage scent of a poorly washed drinking glass. I tip back the canned Coke and drink.

Uncle George comes up to me. Meets me at eye level. His spine has crunched him down to my height. Carbonation is still fizzing on my lips. He leans over and kisses me on the mouth. Hard. So hard I back up and he's still attached to me. A tingle of electricity comes and goes in my abdomen. So quickly I can believe it didn't happen. He grabs my breast. Fills his hand with it. Squeezes until it hurts. I'm pressed against the counter. I let out sounds of strangulation. But he doesn't back off. I feel his old-man penis toughen like an overcooked giz- zard. My hand sweeps across the counter. Knocking the Mix- master onto the floor. The bowl breaks into shards and splin- ters. George sends out a primitive howl. He drops to his knees. He narrowly misses a four-inch shaft of glass. "Oh, Jesus, I'm sorry," I say. Like I've destroyed a two-hundred-year-old piece of porcelain.

"Go on home," he says miserably.

"I need to know if you've seen my mother."

"I told her to go home, too," he says. I get the pop of adrenaline that comes of false alarms. "When?" He rolls his eyes upward. He's concentrating on his own skewed measure of time. "A long time ago. She teased me, too."

I don't look at the cat as I leave. I don't look at Uncle George, either.

19

Jerusha

I WAKE UP BECAUSE MY FEET ARE COLD, AND I SIT UP, SEE MY shoes lying next to me, and it doesn't take a Ph.D. to figure out that colored woman left us where she could get my money in the night. So nice of her to leave my shoes; I guess they aren't her size. Dustin is still sleeping, and I tip away, out into the early daylight.

I move over to one of the steps near the library door so I can warm up some and figure out what I'm going to do with no money until the federal government comes through, probably after I'm dead. I was going to put Dustin on the streetcar, find a cheap motel on Tulane Avenue and check in for a night, take a bath, wash out my clothes, use the toilet. Mealworm squats on the grass, makes hard little poops, whines with the effort. For that I'd usually give him one more day, then haul him over to the vet on Freret Street. I don't have a nickel.

I'm looking around, being safe, though there is nothing anybody can do to me, and up walks that colored woman. Murray, though she doesn't deserve a name. "You've got a lot of nerve," I say.

"You doing okay?"

"You take every cent I have, what makes you think I'm doing okay?" She looks at me like she has no idea what I'm talking about. I tell her I woke up with my shoes off and my money missing. I better not run her off; she has about two hundred dollars, and she might feel like sharing it with me without admitting where she got it. Negroes are terrific liars. "You ain't put your money back in your bra?" she says. "Nobody stupid enough to leave money in a shoe; shoot, you fall asleep, that the first place they going to look."

"You don't have my money?"

"You think I take money, then come right back and wave it at you? Shit, if I got a roll, I be sitting up right now in Betsy's, throwing down on six waffles. Besides, I been going to the Mount Calvaree Baptist Church my whole life. I go *hungry* before I steal from somebody, especially somebody poor as me."

I believe her. There's nobody more honest than a churchy colored person. Especially a churchy white person. I ask her what she does for breakfast. Nothing, she says, like breakfast is the same as high tea, a fancy snack that some people go through their whole lives without ever eating. She starts ticking off all the places I can go tonight for a free meal, and I tell her I don't take charity. "So what you going to eat, that dog?" she says, and Mealworm looks up at her hopefully. I think about the old *Looney Tunes* where Elmer Fudd looks at Bugs Bunny and pictures him on a platter, and I laugh. "You get humble after a while," Murray says, and she gives me four cigarettes. I tell her I'll look for her later, that I'm going to have money before nightfall. "Maybe you white, maybe you can, but you know, you old. I try to find me work after that old woman up and die and cut off my pension, nobody want to look at no old face. No matter you work all your life, they don't want no heart attacks in their kitchen, no."

"I'm not going to work," I say, not wanting her to think I'm willing to do maid work, though that's what I did for Woodrow for free. "I just need enough to get me through to my social security check."

"You lucky at that. The old cow say every month she putting in for Social Security, you think she telling the truth? I'm sitting up there, thinking she so mean she going to outlive me, never mind she got no mind left to speak of. Her nephew tell me, 'You retire, Murray, we give you a check every month,' then she fall down the steps, they say the girl took my place push her, I come to the funeral, that damn nephew say, 'Sorry, Murray, we probate the will, that the end of you.' Sometime I go past his office, I feel like walking in, show him, big-shot lawyer, what he done to a woman who look after his auntie when nobody else studying about her, but I know he going to say, *Get out, can't you see I'm busy, Murray,* so I just sit around. Something have to happen after a while."

I pat her hand before I think about it. I've never done that in my life, especially to a colored person. Her skin feels the same as mine, dry and tired. "You watch," I say, and I pull my hand back before she can notice.

The bushes next to the library building rustle, and Dustin lumbers out like Lon Chaney. "Lord, I forgot about that boy," Murray says, her hand over her heart. I crook my finger at him, and he comes at us like a sleepwalker, only his eyes aren't as far open as a sleepwalker's. I ask Murray what time it is. "After seven," she says, looking at the sky. "You can figure by the sun, up to a point, then you got the traffic. The most cars be about 8:45. But not many at that. This city got a sorry excuse for a rush hour. You learn after a while. Unless you feel like running in City Hall every time you think time important. Which don't be often."

I smooth the wrinkles out of Dustin's shirt with my hand. Good thing they invented permanent press before they started making public-school children wear uniforms. I know half those children wear those uniforms all week, night and day, peeing in the bed and air-drying on the way to school. "You've got about an hour and a half to get to school, mister, so you better start walking now," I say to him.

"I can take the streetcar," he says, like he's thinking about going back to bed for a while. I tell him the streetcar's a dollar and a quarter, and I don't have a dollar and a quarter, I got robbed. He fishes in his pants pocket, and he has to arch his back way to the other side because the pants are so tight that his hand won't fit in the pocket otherwise, and out comes a dollar fluttering between two fingertips. I see no bulges in his pants. "You have my money in there?" I say, and I pat at him carefully. All I need is for Angela to come along and see my hand two inches from this boy's private parts. I feel coins and nothing else. I ask him how much money he has. "About two dollars," he says.

"Why didn't you tell me?"

"You didn't ask."

"I hear you, little man," Murray says, chuckling, and I shoot her a dirty look.

Dustin is fat, but his brain needs food. "Give me your money," I tell him. "You're going to get something at Burger King."

He stuffs the dollar bill into his pocket and clutches at the side of his pants. "Uh-uh," he says.

"Uh-*huh*," I say.

"That's all the money I got. I get breakfast at school anyway. If I *can*. I mean, I've got to get there on time, and the little arm hand on Angela's clock's all loose. It just swings there."

"What a white boy doing getting free lunch?" Murray says.

Dustin shrugs. "All my friends get free lunch."

Murray looks like she's going up and down the streets of New Orleans in her mind, trying to think of a public school full of poor white children. I haven't had a child in public school for more than twenty years, but I read the *Times-Picayune* enough to know that the only little white children in public schools are the ones whose left-wing mamas and daddies, of which they have both, get a wild hair up their asses and put them in the gifted programs in those schools where the parents have to camp out for two weeks in their L.L. Bean tents on the sidewalk to hold a place in line. "His idiot mother put him in Crocker," I say.

"You all right, little man," Murray says, and I get him away from her fast. He's on the streetcar before I remember that he's been with me for more than twelve hours and hasn't peed.

I'm hungry, so I walk up St. Charles Avenue, and when I get to the part with the mansions along it I start ringing front doorbells. It's early, so no colored maids answer the doors, just rich ladies who, without their makeup, make you wonder how they snared rich men. I ask them if they want to buy my dog. They never open the door more than a crack, and I want to say, *Hey, you see a weapon on me?* but I don't. I tell them my house burned down, that my husband's dead, that I have no place to stay, that I'm waiting for my check, and they narrow the crack in the door to less than an inch, and I say, "Yeah, I don't blame you, I wouldn't believe me, either," and they close the door all the way.

I make it almost to Valence Street. I ought to try the one of Gloretta's daughters who lives a block farther up. Getting help from people I know isn't charity, because I can tell them I'm good for it, and besides, I'm giving them my dog as proof I'll be back. He may be constipated, but he's a purebred.

I don't know Gloretta's girl's last name, but I know what block of Perrier Street she lives on, and I walk up and down until I see a house that looks like I've seen it before. I dropped Gloretta there once, but it was after dinnertime, and nothing in this city looks the same in daylight as it does at night. A house that looks like a million dollars at night with a porch light can look like a haunted house in the daytime. And vice versa. I ring the bell, and a colored maid answers. I ask her, "Is Cheryl home?" nice and polite like I've dropped in for coffee.

"Cheryl who?" she says with no respect. "I don't know Cheryl's last name, her *married* name," I say right away, because it sounds more personal, and it's true. "Nobody name of Cheryl live here," she says. I tell her I'm a friend of Cheryl's mother, Gloretta, that Gloretta is in the hospital, and she brightens up, happy to hear tales. "Her mama have like a stroke?" I nod. "You talking about Mrs. Bell over there." She points to a house across the street that is the same Victorian, only a different color. "Housekeeper say her mama got no sense left; it's a crying shame." I tell her thank you like a rich lady would, with no gratitude, but I smell too bad to fool her, and she doesn't frost up, says, "That a fine little dog you got there."

Colored people love little dogs, and I ask her if she wants to buy him, even though she'd feed him garlic water for fleas and never get him shots. "Oh, no, honey, what I'm going to do with a dog? I got seven children, only two of them grown."

"He's too much for me at my age; I have to find him a home."

"I hear you," she says, and I know how much of what I've said she believes. Negroes in this country have so much understanding because they've already pulled every trick in the book by the time they're grown. That isn't necessarily bad.

I ring Cheryl's bell, and she comes to the door herself. She has on a jacket like she's about to go out, and she smells of good soap and fresh makeup. "Oh, my God, Mrs. Bailey," she says, like she's expecting me, the way people in a prison town expect an escaped killer. She starts to take off her jacket, thinks about it, shrugs it back on, tells me she has errands and has to be somewhere for ten, but "your daughter's looking for you."

"Zib," I say.

"Yes, Zib." Cheryl is the same age as Zib, but for a long time she has acted like Zib has a disease that she'd catch if she ever came too close to her or uttered her name. Gloretta and I had a fight about that one time. "One's no better than the other," I said, and Gloretta said back, "Yes, but you got to admit," and I said, "I got to admit nothing, at least Zib's earned a living. Cheryl never did anything in her life that took effort except shake her boobies at a rich boy." "Cheryl does volunteer work," Gloretta said, and I said, "Yeah, she wants to help every poor person in town except *you*." "I don't need any help," Gloretta said, and I left it at that.

"I don't want to talk to Zib," I tell her, but she gets this can't-blame-you look on her face, and I say, "She's as big an ingrate as you."

Cheryl gives out this big phony horse laugh, throws back her hair that is full of honey-colored streaks and cut so perfectly they must have used a magnifying glass. "I have to hand it to you, Mrs. Bailey, you don't ever change."

"True," I say proudly, hoping she'll get the hint.

I ask her where Zib is, and she says she doesn't know, but she's probably in New Orleans as far as she can guess. I ask her what for. "I told you," she says, like I'm a fool, "she's probably come looking for you." She starts jingling her keys around, tells me she has to get to the thrift shop, but she only has a four-hour shift, would I like to come back later?

"I just want to know if you want to buy my dog." I hold Mealworm up in the palms of my two hands, and he gets a showy posture, like he's picked out a fine place for himself to live in. I want to slug him.

She puts her keys down, takes off her jacket, tells me to take a seat in the living room, "No, wait, how about the kitchen?" and goes off to make a phone call. I follow her into what I guess you call the library in that kind of house, though all the book spines match and look like they've never been cracked. "I'm not trying to call your daughter, if that's what you're thinking," she says with her hand only half covering the mouthpiece. "Yeh, I can't make it today. Can you manage without me? True, true. Thanks *so* much." I notice that Cheryl sounds like she's spent her entire life in Natchez, Mississippi, where they have this thick, rich drawl that sounds so much more dignified than the way most people in New Orleans talk. Only the debutante types call the city *Nyew Aw-yunz*. And people like Cheryl.

"So," I say, seating myself at the kitchen table and putting Mealworm down on the floor. He stands there, since the house has no smells in it, but Cheryl starts ticking at him like he's a cat that she wants to come to her. She and Angela have something in common. I tell her he's house-trained, not as a way of selling him, but as a way of letting her know I can read her mind.

"I have no idea how to find your daughter," she says, straightening up, but keeping an eye on the dog.

"I'm sure you don't," I say. I'm hoping she'll offer me something to eat, but she's the kind who made sure she wouldn't learn how to turn on the stove when she moved into this house. "Look, I'm having a little trouble here. All I want to do is get this dog settled so I can get around. Tell you what, you don't have to keep him forever. How about you give me a hundred dollars for a couple of days; I'll give it back to you when I come get the dog."

"Your house burned down."

"So?"

She offers me something to eat. I'm tempted to tell her no, because she's feeling sorry for me in a way that makes her feel good about herself. I ask for a cup of coffee. It'll fill me up. She looks around the kitchen like she's just been put in charge of the cockpit of a B–52 bomber. "How about a cup of tea?" she says. "I could make you a nice cup of tea."

I don't like to drink anything I can see through. I've had a total of three cups of tea in my entire life, and only when I had a sore throat and filled it with so much bee honey that I could eat it with a fork. It's fancy these days to put honey in everything instead of sugar, so I say, "That would be wonderful if you have honey." Of course, she says, surprised as hell.

She asks me where I'm staying, while she goes through cabinets looking for tea bags. She fills the kettle with tap water, though she has a springwater dispenser sitting where I can see it, with a five-gallon bottle almost full. "Guess you're not having any," I say, looking straight at the water dispenser. "You prefer bottled?" she says. "Never touch the stuff," I say. I read in *The Star* that sometimes springwater companies fill their bottles straight from the city tap or take it from wells that are full of benzene, but I'm not about to tell Cheryl that.

She goes into the refrigerator and takes out a china plate loaded with sweet rolls. The icing on top is white and hard, and all it would take to make them good would be to wrap them in aluminum foil and stick them in the toaster oven for five minutes at 300 degrees. But she puts the plate in front of me, and I don't say anything, because I know she's dying to say, *Oh, it's been so long since I've done a thing in the kitchen, you'll just have to forgive me.* I eat one, softening it with the hot tea in my mouth, eat another, take a third. She sits with her arms folded on the table watching me, saying nothing, and I don't care what she thinks. "I have an idea," she says too brightly. "Hmm," I say, my mouth busy with tea and hard, sweet bread.

"You can call Wilson." She says his name right out. There's no shame in knowing Wilson. Wilson runs out of money on the twentieth of the month, but Wilson has a Ph.D. "A Ph.D. automatically puts a person in the upper-middle class," he once told me.

"Calling Wilson's as bad as calling Zib," I say. She gives me this apples-and-oranges look. "They're just alike," I say. "Not from your point of view, but they're just alike." She's interested. She sits around the Junior League thrift shop, waiting for raggedy people to come in and look for things that don't have perspiration stains, and she gossips about anybody. *Oh, did you hear? He may be a distinguished professor, but he has the exact same mental illness as his sister, who works as a checkout girl at the Winn-Dixie.*

"I told you, they're just like you. And everybody you went to school with. They don't know how to say thank you for anything. We go up to Arlington. . . ." I say that because Cheryl types are impressed with prestige; I've never gotten over how people like her ran to shop in that Wal-Mart that Donald and Ivana Trump were in years ago, then ran around bragging about it: *Got the same sheets as little Donnie Trump, imagine!* "We go up to Arlington, bury Woodrow with military honors, we come back to our rooms . . ." Let her imagine a country inn. "And they leave me stranded."

"Now I'm sure Wilson wouldn't do such a thing," Cheryl says.

"Well, he's worse than Zib. Gives a reason for it. At least Zib doesn't think."

Cheryl chuckles with uptown-lady pleasure, showing only the bottoms of her front teeth. She must have caps. "Northwestern, right?" she says, and I have no idea what she's talking about. "The university, right?" Now I know what she's talking about, but I don't let on. "Outside Chicago." She furrows up her brow, like she's digging for the only scrap of information that's left in her brain. "Oh, Evanston, right; I almost went there."

"You almost went to LSU," I say. She probably tells her friends that her daddy was an executive at Maison Blanche. Her daddy ran the elevator in the Maison Blanche building. Cheryl went to UNO and lived at home and rode the Elysian Fields bus to college. She met her husband by hanging out at the University Center at Tulane. Gloretta denies it, but Cheryl pretended she went to Newcomb and belonged to Kappa Kappa Gamma, quoting Shakespeare and wearing tank tops with no bra.

"I considered Northwestern," she says, all huffy.

"Okay," I say. She asks me if he lives in Evanston. "I'm not telling you," I say. She picks up the wall phone that she hasn't replaced with a portable for some reason and starts dialing, and I hear her say, "Evanston, Illinois" then, "Wilson Bailey, Dr. Wilson Bailey," trying to impress the directory assistance operator, and I roll my eyes back in my head. Her hand flaps around like she's blind; she's been so smart that she's forgotten to get a pencil and paper, and I smile at her, so she nods at the computer voice on the phone, lets it repeat its nasal little routine until she has the number memorized. She hangs up and runs into the pantry like she's going to wet her pants, then comes right back with a pencil and paper, writing as she goes. "I read somewhere that the higher your intelligence, the more numbers in a row you can remember," I say.

"I have instant dialing on my phones," Cheryl says, like I should know better than to think that anybody depends on the human brain now that we have computers. When she starts to dial, she has to look at the sheet of paper twice, and I walk out of the room. Her house is so large that the furniture is spaced far apart, so sound travels well, and if I leave the kitchen I can hear her without her realizing it. "Hello, I'm trying to reach Wilson Bailey." Pause. "Cheryl Bell in New Orleans." Long pause. "No, she's fine." I'm tempted to pick up the extension, though it's too late to find out how hopeful my daughter-in-law sounded when she heard a stranger was calling from New Orleans. Cheryl says she has to go look for a pencil, even though she just had one. That wife is too cheap to have Wilson pay to call Cheryl back. That's how Jews have so much money; they hang on to it like somebody is going to round them all up and take everything away from them, though in this day and age that makes no sense if you think about it.

"Hey, Wilson!" Cheryl is saying in her phony Southern-lady accent, and I pick up Mealworm and take him out into her backyard so he can say he's been here. Everything is neat, even the bougainvillea only comes out so far over the little fish pond before it's clipped. Mealworm walks up to the pond carefully, knowing if he falls in he's a gone pecan; a couple of Cheryl's goldfish are as big as his head. He barks at a fish, then backs up fast. He is one useless dog; I don't know why I keep him.

I don't hear her come out the sliding glass door, and she's almost on top of me before I notice her. "He's coming down, and he's not exactly happy about it," Cheryl says.

"That's his problem."

"You could call him up, have him wire you some money, get you set up. For that matter, *I* could give you some money."

"I told you I'd sell you my dog. Or you could hold him for whatever you call it. Collateral."

"I know you don't want to do that." She's talking like I'm a retarded child.

"You don't know jack shit," I say, and I pick up Mealworm, head inside the house, get to the front door. Cheryl is scurrying behind me like I'm about to make her forfeit her chance at winning the *Times-Picayune* Loving Cup. "Where're you staying?" she calls after me as I go down the steps.

"With friends next to the downtown public library," I tell her.

"At the hotel that used to be the Warwick?"

"Right," I say.

20

Wilson

BARBARA SAID NOTHING WHEN I TOLD HER THIS MORNING THAT I was coming down here. Nothing. I apologized, and she did not let me catch her eye. She walked out of her office, up to the second floor, scooped all the laundry from the hamper, tromped to the basement, loaded the washer, stood in front of it through the full cycle, arms folded across her chest. "I hope you know I resent going down there," I said. She stared at the machine, smiled as if the click from rinse to spin marked a personal triumph. "I will phone twice a day."

"If I'm not here, leave a message," she said, and plucked the first load, the whites, from the dryer, folded my undershirts sleeve cuff to sleeve cuff, pressing in a crease that ran off-center where my sternum would be. My mother folds undershirts the way they come in the package, I had told Barbara once. "If you plan to sell them, I'll fold them that way; otherwise, what's the point?" I had laughed nervously, knowing I had come perilously close to being told to fold my own laundry. I do not have the manual dexterity, and I like uniformity, even in closed drawers. Barbara folded every shirt unevenly, but exactly the same, and the pile looked good. She dropped the whites neatly into my open overnight bag. My mother probably was not going to see that packing job and fuss about the careless women I marry, but I still did not look forward to seeing her. "I don't care anymore if you bring her back or not," Barbara said when she walked in with all my permanent-press shirts dangling by the open collars from her index finger, one shirt inside the other. "I will try not to," I said, and she flounced out of the room.

I am in New Orleans by eleven at night, $450 poorer. The cabdriver has told me what a fine neighborhood I am visiting. "I drive cab, but I try to make nothing but the airport run, you know, otherwise people get in your cab, take you into the projects, rob you blind."

"Is that what you are supposed to tell tourists?" I say.

"Well, we suppose to warn people, you know."

I forgot that people like Cheryl are another of the reasons I do not live in the South, and try never to visit here. Cheryl is in her nightclothes when I ring the bell, and she speaks in whispers in case I fail to notice that most people are asleep at this hour. "She got away," she says when she opens the door.

"What?" I say. I expect to find my mother waiting for me, so sick of a full day of Cheryl and powerlessness that she is willing to promise to behave if I will take her to Chicago.

"Just walked out, like that." She snaps her fingers. "Hours ago. I'd have phoned you, but what good would it've done?"

"Christ," I say. I am still standing on her front steps. "If you ran an ad that you found someone's dog, at least you would have tied it up in the yard."

"I don't think you want me tying your mother up," she says, and I catch the same pretentious sugar-drawl that I thought I picked up when she phoned this morning.

"You could have given her something to eat, bought her some clothes; you know I would have paid you back."

"You don't have to pay me back." It sounds as if Cheryl has in fact given my mother a day's worth of survival, and I am relieved. "Besides, all she had was a couple of stale Danishes."

I imagine myself grabbing Cheryl and slamming her up against the beveled glass in her front door. I know I once punched her in the abdomen when we were children, and it is almost as if I have lifelong permission to give in to impulse where she is concerned. What holds me back is fear of a loud noise that will resound in a quiet house. Her whispering protects her even more than my daily struggle for decorum.

I ask her where my mother is, and she asks me if I want to come inside. "I don't like being so visible on the street," she says, pulling her Chinese silk robe tightly around herself. I have not seen one person come by on foot since I arrived, and only one car, a sleek black Lexus, has passed. I tell her I have to go look for my mother. But I also want to keep her out here until some black person, who has come off an honest three-to-eleven shift, walks by, to see what she will do. Cheryl's father was an elevator operator, eight hours a day, cheap flat wages, until he was replaced by electronic gadgetry and took up beer, and I know he used to walk past the best houses on Valence Street to get home at night because he did not have a vehicle. Cheryl's husband surely does not know that.

I step up so that I am almost in her face. Trash remembers trash. "*Where* is my mother?"

She does not take a step back, the way she would if she had been raised among exclusively good boys and girls. She flings her hair to the side. "She said something about staying with friends near the main library." I tell her that is the business district, that no one lives down there, and she shrugs. "I'm just telling you what she said. Oh, I remember, I said, 'You mean the old Warwick,' and she said, 'Right.'"

I take another step up. She is two stairs higher than I am, but we are eye to eye. "Think, Cheryl Higgins. If you were staying at a hotel with obviously terribly generous friends, would you come dragging all the way uptown to ask someone you have not seen in twenty years if she will buy your damn dog for fifty dollars?" She opens her mouth to speak, and I interrupt her. "And don't tell me, *Well, hotels do not allow pets,* because I am resisting every impulse to throttle you right now."

"It's Cheryl Bell," she says, her right hand having drawn her robe closed all the way to the throat, a gesture she must have seen on television. I back down the steps, still facing her, trying to decide how I am going to get away from here without asking for a ride or the loan of a phone. "You know, you could've said thank you," she says in a stage whisper.

"Where I grew up, we were not schooled in the niceties," I say, and then I turn and jog toward the streetcar stop, my overnight bag bouncing so it tears the muscles in my upper arm more with every step. I break into a full-out run, because just jogging seems too dignified, and whenever I come to this city, the thin layer of polish that I have brushed all over myself does not chip away slowly; it dissolves in the mean wet air. I look like a man whom the police would stop.

My mother is living on the streets, and looking for a homeless person is like looking for a dog that has run away. When I was small, we had a puppy named Susie who was confined to the backyard. Because no one ever walked her, she had left no marks on the earth any distance from our house. After days of burrowing under a side fence with all the tenacity of a prison lifer, she escaped, and once she broke out into a happy, free run, she left no trail behind herself. "You want to find a dog, you got to go out before sunrise, catch it while it's turning over garbage cans," Mother said the first time Susie ran away. I thought that meant that we would form a search party first thing the next morning, but when I went into my parents' room in the predawn hours, my mother smacked me hard, instinctively, on the arm. "You know to never wake me," she said as an apology, and with the sort of welt on my arm that makes a person impervious to further injury, I slipped out of the house, tiptoed around the streets, even though I was only eight, whispering the sibilants of Susie's name, and I found her three blocks over, almost to the traffic hazards of Napoleon Avenue, pawing through a brown paper sack of garbage. She was content to follow me home, but after she pulled the same trick three more times in as many months, I came home from school one day to find her gone. "Your pop's taken her to the SPCA," Mother said. I wailed that they were going to kill her in three days, begged to be taken down to rescue her, and Mother said, "Don't worry, your father gave them five dollars to take care of her." I could have sworn she was smiling an ironic sort of smile when she said that, and I wakened for several nights after screaming from dreams of dogs being mowed down by gunfire, until my father came into my room. "I want Susie," I shrilled. "Want in one hand and shit in the other, and see which one fills up first," he said, then padded back into his room.

Even in Chicago, homeless people disappear in the daylight hours; only in the night, no matter if it is dead of winter, do they come out on the streets and lie down and disabuse everyone of hopes that these ragged people have a place to go. I can find my mother if I go out searching now, and when the streetcar passes the Columns Hotel, I get off only long enough to check in, throw my bag on a bed in my room, and get back on the streetcar headed downtown.

One other passenger is on the streetcar, a boy who appears to be about ten. He is riding at the back on the seat where one

conductor used to ride when there were two, and he is looking out the back window at the tracks. I ask the conductor
what he is going to do about a child riding his streetcar in the
middle of the night. "Shoot, the mayor put in a curfew, I know
that boy ain't going to be old enough to pass curfew for another ten years, but I got a schedule to keep, you know? I can't
be getting off and calling no police. He stay on all the way to
downtown, they pick him up like a shot. You got to give him
credit, that boy got raw nerve."

We are moving along fast; with no one waiting at the
stops, the conductor rockets past them. I stagger back to where
the boy is sitting. "What are you doing, out at this time of
night?" I say. "I don't talk to strangers," he says, keeping his eyes
focused past the window glass. "Good idea," I say, and he looks
at me. "What're *you* doing out this time of night?" he says in
spite of himself. I tell him I am from out of town.

"Sometimes I dance, you know. I got to have music,
though. If you're from out of town, you ought to see me
dance. Me and my friends. People *pay* us."

"You are white," I whisper, though the conductor cannot
hear me. Barbara and I saw skinny black boys with bottle caps
stuck into their tennis shoes tapping and break-dancing on
Bourbon Street when we went to Galatoire's on a visit before
Connor was born. Barbara went up to one and handed him a
ten-dollar bill and said, "I'll give you this if you'll go home and
stop setting yourself back like that." He took it and material-
ized a few blocks down minutes later.

"I got a lot of black friends. I'm good as them. They're not
born dancing, you know: they learn. I can shake my booty and
not even think about it. I like the Beatles better, though. I tell
my friends the Beatles got all their ideas from Little Richard,
and you know what they say? 'Who's Little Richard?' And I

say, 'Like on that commercial that used to be on TV.'" He lets out a Little Richard scream that is as pure and dead-on as it can be. The conductor turns his head, sees distance between me and the boy and no blood, and keeps rolling.

I laugh and tell him my name is Wilson Bailey. "Oops," he says, giggles, then falls silent. One stop before mine, he presses the button and jumps down off the streetcar, breaking into a run when he touches pavement.

In the dark and silence of the abandoned city at night, I revert to instinct. I go toward the library because I have the fact of it, but an extra sense draws me to its perimeters, rather than to nearby buildings. There are many places for a stray person to hide down here, especially around the corner near the hospitals, but I am looking for my mother, the one to whom I was imprinted at birth, like it or not, the one whose chromosomes I pretend have mutated to make me different from her. I walk up the path to the library, crossing open space, a frightening thing to do at night, though danger lurks only in the places I cannot see. I hear nothing but the hum of night power in the city, the cry of an ambulance as it reaches the ramp at Charity and abruptly becomes silent. "Mother?" I whisper. Nothing. I walk along the edge of the building, remembering the times Zib would steal something of mine and hide it, then trail me through the house, "You're ice cold, warmer, you're hot, boiling hot, oops, cold again," until I realized that half the time she was lying. "Mother?" I say a little more loudly. "Mama?" I hear rustling in the bushes. "It is Wilson," I say boldly, in case a different woman is hiding in there, having hoped to hear someone call for Mama for quite a while, now coming out of a rock-hard sleep, trying to be sure she is not dreaming. Out from under a shrub squeaks my mother's dog, or one identical to him, and when I hear, "Goddamn you, Mealworm," I know I have hit pay dirt.

"It is Wilson," I say again, not moving, as if she is naked behind the bushes.

"Aw, Jesus," Mother says, and she stands up, brushes herself off. In the halogen lights, everything is reduced to black and white, to degrees of shadow, and I am surprised how old my mother looks. She eats too much processed meat and cheese and keeps her skin puffed up with fat, and she does not seem to have lost any weight, but her face is tired, as if it has given up and let gravity take over. She rolls her hair once a week instead of going to the hairdresser, because she worked herself into a feud over a Spiegel catalog that was delivered there by mistake ten years ago. She wraps her pouf of hair in toilet paper every night, from one washing to the next, never mind that Jackie Kennedy has not lived in the White House for decades. Now her hair is still in a bouffant, but it has been mashed and mussed so it looks like dead gray cotton candy on a humid day, full of wisps and pocks.

She folds her arms across her bosom and says, "Grab him," and I look around, see the dog skittering across free space. He stops to lift his leg, and I bend over and nab him. He turns his head 180 degrees and nips at my hand. I quickly put both hands around his belly, offer him sideways to my mother as if he is a snake. Mother clucks at me, "You're still scared of hurting yourself." My mother never has gotten over the fact that I am not John Wayne. I find myself avoiding all pain, even the strain of opening a mayonnaise jar, because I am proving something to her, whether she is around or not.

I tell her I have a hotel room. She smiles at me, but I have no illusions. "Last time we stayed in a hotel room, your sister robbed me blind. What fun have you got in store this time?"

"I have no earthly idea where Zib is," I say.

"She's probably in New Orleans, don't give me that."

"Unlike you, Mother, she left no clues."

"You want me to find Zib, if she's here I'll find her. Just go through the yellow pages under hotels, call them up until you find the one that charges the most for a room: I guarantee you can phone the place, ask for Elizabeth Bailey, and they'll say, 'One moment, please, I'll ring her room.'" She looks at me with something that is close to affection. "You, on the other hand, I bet I can guess where you're staying. Let's see, two choices. You staying by the airport?" I shake my head no. "Okay, I know that stinking Cheryl called you up. You went to her house, right?" I nod. We are standing out here in the dark, and she is playing twenty questions, but I let her keep it up, certain she will scurry away otherwise. "So. You've got a Ph.D. It took you five minutes, tops, to get ready to kill Cheryl for being a fool." I nod some more, enjoying being so well known by another human being. "And you checked into the first place you came across. Which would be that *Pretty Baby* hotel on St. Charles."

"It *is* on St. Charles," I say, slipping into her game despite myself.

"Where they made *Pretty Baby* with Brooke Shields, remember? She stood up in the bathtub, naked." *Nekkid.* "And she was getting little boobies, and it was this big deal? They built condos next door, where they did all the outside scenes, but inside the hotel I think you can see where they had the piano and everything, though I've never been inside, I can just imagine."

"The Columns," I say.

"Yeah, the one with the columns. The Columns, that's right. Am I right? Didn't I tell you? Gloretta said one time they don't have locks on the room doors. You're not very careful about where you sleep, are you?"

At that I begin laughing. So hard that I cannot speak, can barely breathe. I point at the bushes. "People don't come looking to rob you in the bushes," she says. "They come looking to rob you where you're paying a lot of money to stay in a hotel room." She casts her eyes aside, which means she has caught herself in a small error of fact, one that destroys her argument but that she knows no one else will catch, so she forges ahead with her argument, anyway.

"You were robbed, Mother?" I say.

"None of your business," she says.

I want to give her something. Money, a pat on the arm. I extend my hand toward her, and she wraps her arms tightly around the dog, recoiling. "Don't talk down to me, Wilson."

"You need to come back with me to Chicago," I say. I thought about this on the plane. The best I can do for her is to stay a while, find her somewhere to live, figure out ways to get her some money. But I do not have the time. I have two exams to write, classes full of panicky, achieving types who secretly would love me to fall far short of telling them all there is to know on a subject and then test them comprehensively, so they could call their attorney fathers and say they have been cheated. I should not bring Mother back to my house when Barbara is full of disgust and silence and the holidays are coming in a matter of weeks and opening my family to the bruising that a marriage of a Jew and anyone else takes. But leaving her here means she will die from lost teeth and snapped bones and open sores in slow, nasty ways that make the expected wasting from emphysema and lung cancer look like a blissful death. Part of me wishes the pain on her; that is why I never have told her to stop smoking cigarettes. I ignore that part of myself.

"I hate Chicago," she says.

"So I am supposed to leave you here?"

"You'd pay for my plane ticket, right?"

I nod.

"So give me the cash instead."

I tell her I do not have the cash.

"Woodrow Wilson Bailey, Junior, I know very well you have never run a credit card up over forty dollars in your entire adult life. You have cash."

I feel a low-grade terror about standing here, neatly dressed, talking about money, imagining urban desperados in every distant shadow. "It is all on my credit card," I whisper.

My mother is impressed; for a full minute she says nothing. "I can't believe you give a rat's ass," she says, clearly pleased, and I almost want to take it all back.

"I hate Chicago," she reminds me.

"I have not thought past Christmas."

"Two days in your house and I feel like I've been sucked into the cast of *Fiddler on the Roof.*"

"This is better?" I say, waving my hand around, knowing that anyone listening will agree and take no offense.

"Yeah, this is better," she says, meaning it, then shrugs. She is acquiescing.

I start to tell her that we will have to sneak the dog onto the streetcar, then sneak him into the hotel, and she stops me cold. "You meet me here in the morning," she says.

"Are you out of your mind?"

"Don't you talk to me like that, Wilson, or I'll knock you into the middle of next week." I think I hear a bit of playfulness in her voice, but I have been wrong before and quickly sorry.

Every muscle in my abdomen tightens, and I silently curse Zib. "I've got somebody I've got to deal with first," she says. "I have a life, you know; I'm not some houseplant you can carry on a plane and put in the corner of your living room and forget about it."

I have no choice. I tell her to watch out for herself, that I will be back at eight, right here, and I walk away. I feel more curiosity than dread, wondering how I will be if I come back tomorrow and find her gone. Or dead. The somebody she has to deal with might not enjoy her lack of subtlety. "Hey, Wilson," she calls after me. "You got a pencil and paper? I could use a pencil and paper." I breathe a sigh of relief, but not so loudly that she can hear.

The Columns not only does not have locks on the doors, it does not have phones in the rooms. I go downstairs, borrow the yellow pages, ask to make a few calls. I try the Inter-Continental, the Westin, the Windsor Court. "Elizabeth Bailey, one moment, please," the Chalmette voice says. The phone rings once, twice, ten times, and voice mail comes on. I hang up smiling, knowing enough. I phone my house on my credit card. I am about to hang up after the sixth ring when Barbara answers. "You are there," I say happily.

"Do you have any idea what time it is?"

"I am so glad you are there."

"Okay, Wilson, okay," she says, and I let her go back to sleep before she can waken fully.

21

Zib

I DON'T KNOW WHAT I EXPECT TO FIND AT MY DOOR. SOME-body's knocking at midnight. It doesn't excuse me to say I've had a long day. First driving to New Orleans. Then seeing Angela. Which was the kind of strain I don't feel until it's over. Like running up a flight of stairs in a panic. I don't get winded until I get to the top. Going to Uncle George was different. Dealing with men who have no sense is a skill I've had to use recently and often. So regret and annoyance are very familiar. I've been in a dead sleep since eleven. When I hear the knocking, I have no idea where I am. I go to the door. I'm safe because I'm not wearing contact lenses in the dark. I have that power that comes of believing I can go back to sleep if I don't like what's going on.

"I should've guessed," Angela says. She walks in past me. She flicks on the light switch. Like she's been staying in this room for days herself. She has on a halter top that bares her midriff and a miniskirt. Her hair is swept up and wild. Her lipstick is a dark plum color. She looks healthy. She's a woman a man might take to bed without being afraid of a deadly disease. "I bet you got one of those refrigerators with all kinds of shit in it, right?"

"I'm asleep."

"Hey, people who *live* here don't sleep, much less everybody else."

I stumble to the bed. Slip between the covers. Fold my arms across my face to block the light. Angela sits down on the foot of the bed and bounces. Even after I tell her to cut it out, to go away. She crawls across, finds my ribs, tickles me. Now I'm wide awake, giggling and swatting. She pulls the covers off me in one great sweep. "Somebody with this much energy ought to go out and get a goddamn job," I say to her. She laughs.

"You have fucking curled up and died, and you're not much past forty," she says. "One time, you'd've given anything in the world to be sitting on the edge of the Quarter, with no curfew or nothing. And a valid driver's license. Not that anybody'd card you now, you're about a goddamn hundred years old. I swear, Zib, I got the liver of an old wino, and I look better than you. We walk down the street, somebody'll ask me, *What you doing out with your mama?*"

I sit up in the bed. I can see myself in the mirror across the room. Though without contact lenses I see only streaks of color. A lot of hair. Two smears of dark eyebrows. No detail as small as a nostril or wrinkle. "You're not going to pull that one on me," I say. She takes my hand. Drags me over to the mirror. Now I can see as much as any passing stranger on the night street might. "Makeup," I say. "It's the makeup." I look from her image to mine. Remember her yellow eyes of this afternoon. Lined with kohl and blurred by my myopia, they're as mesmerizing as they were when she was sixteen and flicking boys away like they were beach flies. "You give me ten minutes," I say. I'm furious.

We cut over to Bienville Street. I skip to keep up with Angela. She's walking on three-inch heels at a remarkable clip. "Where's your kid?" I say. I'm almost out of breath.

"He's ten," she says. "Give me a break."

She goes directly to this bar. Like she knows every land-mark along the way. It's on Bourbon Street. Five blocks down. We pass T-shirt shops and strip joints. They're all so similar that I don't know how an owner can have any pride. "I love this goddamn place," she says when we walk in.

"We're the only women in here," I whisper.

"We're the only women in here," Angela says out loud. No one pays attention. On the bar, one man is dancing to heavy-bass music. The rest stare at him. With as much interest as they'd give to a sixty-second commercial on television. He's a small man. With no extra body fat. Swarthy and covered in oil. Wearing what looks like a white diaper. His movements are feminine. I'm thrown off by the dark hair on his legs. And the liquid motion of his steps. Angela doesn't take her eyes off him. I lean over to her. I say in her ear, "He's repulsive."

"I feel sorry for him," she says.

"You've never felt sorry for anybody in your life."

"Shhh," she says, annoyed.

I lean back in my chair. I wish I were back at the hotel. The recorded music starts to play over. The dancer doesn't drop either a beat or a stitch of clothing. I close my eyes. I'll rest until Angela's ready to go. I'm close to dozing. I'm slipping down into that best part of sleep. When everything around me twists into new stories. Angela taps me on my arm. I open my eyes. A bartender asks me what I want to drink. His eyes are so blue that I can tell he's wearing tinted lenses. "Jesus, Angela, I'm already falling asleep."

"You got to get something," she hisses.

I order a Coke. Though the idea of jarring myself awake isn't appealing. The bartender glares at me. Then at Angela. "Give me Scotch and water," she says.

"Don't," I say to the bartender. But he's used to people like me. He pays no attention. "Hey," I call after him. He looks over his shoulder. Peers around the dancer. Who's now in a G-string and dripping perspiration on the bar. If a drop of his poison sweat lands in my Coke, I'll pay for it and leave it untouched. "This woman's got Hepatitis C. It's killed half her liver. She looks like a jack-o'-lantern in broad daylight. She drinks that, she'll fall over dead on your floor." He shoots a pleading look at Angela. She says, "I come in here all the time. *Usually* the friend I'm with'll drink something besides a goddamn Coke. This isn't McDonald's, you know. They care if you come in and don't order anything." I ask the bartender how much a Coke is. He tells me two-fifty. I give Angela a triumphant look. "Hell, I could use a drink anyway," she says. "It's not like I've never done it before."

She puts away that Scotch and two more. I sip the Coke slowly. I hope its speediness will wax and wane at the same time. I'll be left no more conscious than I was when I came in. The dancer is now down to no clothes. He's building himself a slow erection. So slow that his penis stiffens the way an air mattress does when you try to blow it up by mouth. It's impossible to see the change unless you don't look for a while. "Give me a dollar," Angela says huskily. I don't have much cash. But I'm curious. Angela reaches up. Strokes his balls for about three seconds. Hands him the dollar bill. His erection wilts. But the room comes to life. Two men get up from their seats. Like they may consider following Angela's lead. "Wash your hand," I whisper to her. She pours a tablespoon of her drink onto her fingers. "Alcohol kills anything," she says.

"Except you, obviously," I say.

By the time Angela's ready to leave, she's slurring and tripping over her words. She's a cheap drunk. At least for somebody who used to put away a fifth of bourbon in half an evening. And find her way home. The bartender tells us how much we owe. I ask him if he takes food stamps. Angela gives me a withering look. Then bursts out laughing. She stands up and weaves around. I pay the check with my credit card. When we're out on the street I tell her she needs to go lie down. She shakes her head no. Her head bobs around. Then she laces her arm through mine and leads me to the bad end of Decatur. She's leaning on me heavily. "You're horny now, right?" she says. "Not really," I say. "Well, maybe a little." I want to go along. I feel so sleepy that I could fuck happily if pressed. "Wait till you see this," she says. *Shee this.* She pushes me through a narrow doorway. Into a shop.

It's easy to tell what kind of place this is. A glass case full of bold jewelry and a rack of Carnival satin underthings don't jack up the store. This is a porno shop. With little baskets of condoms. On the counter where peppermints would be in a restaurant. "I'm going back," I say loudly. I turn toward the door.

Angela takes my arm. I pull away. Her right hand is still wet. With hepatitis-laced alcohol and deadly virus sweat. Surprisingly, Angela lets go. She's not as strong and mean as she was when we were children. Then she could cut a wide, powerful swath across a playground. "Wait," she rasps. She beckons me into a corner. Her back is to a pegboard. On it dusty dildos are displayed. Like giant pink Christmas-tree icicles in a drugstore. I can't help studying them. I hear only half of what she's saying. *Meet men . . . so horny . . . make you look like you got a cunt full of alum.*

I may not have AIDS after all. Why else do I think of arguments to give Angela? I imagine this place is full of gimpy, pock-faced men. I want to say to Angela that men who come here will make us sick if we sleep with them. Though the half dozen customers could pass for healthy Winn-Dixie bag boys.

Angela has a bloodstream full of yellow toxins. Which won't destroy her unless she has a lot more nights like this one. And there's a good chance that I'm clean. The math kicks in. I see Angela standing in front of me. Nothing's oozing from the natural holes in her body. If she's well, then my chances are even greater of having no microscopic secrets. "Fucking somebody in here, even fucking those things . . ." I point to the dildos on the rack behind her. They're huge and erect and lined with swollen blue veins. "You want to commit suicide?"

"Fast or slow?" Angela says. I laugh. "Look," she says, "I can get off just looking. Try just looking." At that she crooks her finger at me. Seductively, if I didn't know better. I follow her into the back room. Sleepwalking. I can wake up any time I want to.

Every wall is covered with racks of magazines and videos. I see a magazine with a man sucking off another man. On the cover. A color close-up. I walk over to it like its headline promises immortal life.

Angela and I are alone in this room. Like in a crazed race for orgasm. A circle jerk for girls. We move from one magazine to the next. Taking nothing personally, not tracking each other. Unless it's the day of my father's funeral and I'm out of my mind, I take sex personally. I need to know how mean a man is before I want to touch him. He has to be a good man. Perfect if only for the moment. But these pages—covered with shades of tumescent pink and swatches of body hair—fill me up. So intensely that I want to slip my finger under my skirt. And rub my clit like it's on fire. I know my face is bright red, my ears white and bloodless. A woman's hard-on. I don't care that Angela's in the room. "Jesus!" I say when I catch myself at what I'm feeling. I turn to find Angela in the middle of the room. She's teetering and as pale as an orange person can be. "I feel like shit," she says. She grabs my arm with her filthy hand. I don't pull away.

Angela has to lean on me all the way back to the hotel. She wobbles and sways like a drunk. She pukes once on a side street. I don't look at the puddle. Angela says, "There's blood in it, I know there's blood in it." I'm too scared to look. We keep on going. Moving away from the possibility with each step. "You needed to get the alcohol out of your system." I say it to reassure myself.

"Right."

We reach the front entrance of the hotel. I'm about to signal a taxi for Angela. I want her to disappear. And take my dread with her. "I got to stay," she says. *Shtay.*

"You still kick?" I say. I remember the times we shared a single bed. We didn't live in houses like the ones Wilson manages to provide for his children. Each with a bedroom with twin beds. Matching sheets. Matching comforters. I know I asked my mother for a double tester once. I tried to negotiate down to twin beds. Said I was willing to settle for a trundle. "I got enough kids in my house at night," she said. "You get an extra bed, you're as good as *inviting* them, like putting out food for your neighbor's cat."

"Nobody complains," Angela says. She smiles without letting go of a sorry weakness I've never seen in her eyes before.

She lies down on the side of the bed that's made up. Folds her hands in a tight knot across her belly. I tell her she ought to call her kid. "He's not supposed to answer," she whispers. "He answers, I'll kill him."

I awaken after ten in the drape-darkened room. Angela is still on her back. Uncovered. Hands across her diaphragm. Breathing fitfully and deeply. Like she's far down in nightmares.

My eyes adjust to using the little light that filters into the room from outside. I see dried white spittle around the edges of her mouth. I sit up next to her. I can smell foul scat-breath. Not the raisin-sweet stench that usually lingers after too much liquor. Silently I let myself into the bathroom. I use every little bottle of oil, cologne, and conditioner the hotel's placed on the sink for me. Not because I have my father's poor-man greed for anything free. Because I want to get clean. I keep the water running. Its constant sound covers any bumps and knocks I make. I respect Angela's sleep. Even though she's contemptuous of it herself. I treat everybody that way. I tiptoed around Mama's house every morning for years after she slapped Wilson hard for waking her. He had a bruise across his arm that nobody mentioned to him the entire week it lasted.

The maid knocks on the door. I run to open it before she can let herself in with the key. She's a black woman who looks so tired that she doesn't complain about anything. I promise her we'll be out of the room by one o'clock or she can skip it. Angela doesn't deserve someone cleaning up around her lazing body. I flick on a lamp at the desk. I make a list of things I might do today. I figure I'll go down to the auto pound. If I can't find Mama, at least I can have her car waiting when she comes back to the house. I'll phone the hairdresser next door to the house. I can wheedle somebody into looking in on Angela's boy. Mama thinks the women who work there are pure evil. Probably not because of the Spiegel catalog they once took by accident. Probably because so many customers arrive in chauffeur-driven Cadillacs from Jewish neighborhoods across Claiborne. "You look at all those brown-haired old things," Mama once said. "You can put Joan Collins's hair on them, they're still going to look like they're at death's door. A waste of money, but they've got nothing better to do with it." Women who spend the whole day currying and petting old ladies have to be kind on the inside. They wouldn't want to know a ten-year-old boy is cowering alone two houses down.

I'll try the Salvation Army. Volunteers of America. Where else? I pull out the yellow pages. I can't figure out what to look under. I go all the way through the index until I find Social Service Organizations. I run my finger down the line. AIDS Hotline. I hit Anti-Defamation League and laugh quietly. I'm on page 998 of the book. It slips off my lap. Hits the floor with a loud, dull thud. I look guiltily over at Angela. She doesn't stir. Adrenaline rushes through all my arteries. I go over to the bed and call her name out. She doesn't react. I turn on all the overhead lights. No reaction. I shake her. Tell her to cut the crap. I mean it. By now Angela would be trying to hide a smirk. But her face doesn't move. I scream her name. Then I let out a piercing shriek that brings no one. I run out into the hallway. I cry out, "She's dying, oh, God, she's dying." Only now are they certain there's no man with a knife in my room, there's a rubbernecker's fantasy. Half of housekeeping comes bumbling toward my door in a matter of seconds.

22

Jerusha

I READ ANN LANDERS AND DEAR ABBY. I KNOW WHAT THEY SAY I'm supposed to do, and I see the wisdom of it. It also helps that Abby and Ann are from around here, and they're Jewish, so they're going to tell me to do things the way that would keep Barbara in particular very happy. I'm living in Barbara's house in spite of what she might want, and I know I should make myself stay in my room, keep my counsel, and do needlepoint and smell like violets. But Thanksgiving is in three days, and the house is full of my grandchildren who I'm afraid are going to grow up spoiled and helpless if Wilson and Barbara don't do something. Yesterday I kept quiet with the oldest one of the four, a girl named Jessica that I've only seen three times, ever. "My mom says you're white trash but it's not hereditary so I don't have to worry," she told Wilson. I wanted to talk to her the way my grandmother talked to me, to say, *Look, missy, you talk like that again, I'll jerk a lung out of you.* Wilson just smiled and said, "Your mother is still angry at me." Jessica's ten years old and wears jeans that cost sixty dollars, as she'll be the first to tell you, and I say to her, "Did your daddy send you that kind of money?" and she says, "My granny in Connecticut sends me stuff." She pretends she's not accusing me or looking down on me, but I know better. I tell her she's wearing my week's groceries on her backside, not accusing, either, just telling facts, and she looks at me like she has no idea what I'm talking about. She and her brother Eric live in Colorado now; they visit Wilson for Thanksgiving, Christmas, Easter, and the Fourth of July, and Wilson's sauntered around the house for days like Jim Anderson on *Father Knows Best,* hands in his pockets, never hollering, crinkling his eyes when he smiles. I want to say to him, *Look what happened to Billy Gray and Lauren Chapin, not to mention Robert Young, you walk around here putting up with all this mouthy behavior, you'll have four kids on crack cocaine and giving all their money to Reverend Moon.* But I don't. It's not just that I know I'm a beggar who can't be choosy; I also know these are blood relatives, and I probably love them.

I have to share a room with Jessica for four more days. She throws everything on the floor, and she doesn't clean up without having me point at every pair of soiled underpants, Crayola marker, and Butterfinger wrapper. Barbara says nothing to Jessica, says to me, "Hey, there's a limit to what you can do in four weeks out of the year," and I say, "Maybe there's *not?*" and she sulks. Barbara is looking for fights with all the wrong people. Changing me is impossible; changing Jessica would be a favor to Jessica.

When Dustin crosses my mind, it's usually at mealtime. Wilson's children eat like rich children whose mamas have never told them about starving people. With half of eastern Europe all torn up from war lately, American mamas can show their kids pictures of families that look like their own, remind them about wastefulness. But Wilson marries women who have safety nets, and Wilson has bone-thin children who will toss a plate of food in the garbage if a smidgen of mashed potato drops onto a chunk of meat. Dustin stores his fat for the winter. I put him on the streetcar for school the day I came here with Wilson. He warned me Wilson was looking for me, and if it wasn't for my dog, Wilson'd never have found me. "You probably *need* a house," Dustin said to me when I left. He won't come after me, but that doesn't mean he went back to Angela, either. I told Murray that if she saw Dustin on the street to call me collect; she wouldn't have to put thirty-five cents in the pay phone for a collect call. "I see that boy, I'll go upside his head," she said. "I hear you," I said, knowing she didn't mean it, and she was going to hug me. I edged away from her because I'd do that with anybody.

I have Veronica's phone number. All Murray gave me was the girl's name, and I've been a good detective. Especially given that I don't live here and don't know one part of Chicago from the next. I started with the Chicago white pages, which are big enough to list every man, woman, and dog in Louisiana, and there she was. Veronica Nobles. Not even V. Nobles. A woman who's not scared of anything. I like that.

I've never been nervous about making a phone call, not even when Woodrow was sick and I was calling to find out how soon he was going to die. But I've put off calling this girl, though I've had her number on a scrap of paper on my dresser for days. Twice this house has been empty of children, and I've picked up the receiver, put it down. This afternoon Barbara has taken all four children to see Santa Claus near where her parents live, which surprises me, because everybody there is Jewish. "I think Santa flies right over Highland Park," I said to Jessica; I thought she would laugh, the way older kids like to have secrets with grownups that they keep from the little ones. But Jessica put her finger to her lips, looked me straight in the eye, said, "Shhh." Jessica and Eric are being raised Episcopalian; Wilson married the first time for seeing the perfected image of himself in their mother. Marrying Barbara is his way of going to the other extreme, taking a woman who's nothing like him and nothing like what he wants to be. In two days Barbara is going to be in that lopsided kitchen of hers all day, baking and pretending to be a television mother to match Wilson's version of a television father, and the children will all be there, and if I'm going to phone Veronica Nobles, now is my best chance.

I ring the number, not knowing what I'm going to say, and what sounds like a white woman answers. "Oh, maybe I got the wrong number," I say. She asks me whom I'm trying to reach. *Whom.* Nobody colored from New Orleans ever said *whom,* not even the mayor. Nobody *white* from New Orleans ever said *whom.* Except Wilson, of course. I tell her Veronica Nobles. "This is she." *She.* "Veronica Nobles that used to live in New Orleans?" "Yes," she says, curious. "Are you black?" I say, using the correct word, since this is important, and I'd better not mess up. Generally, whatever word I learned to use coming up is the one I stick with; that way people figure there's no point in trying to tell me different. If I say Negro, they let me by when I say Indian. If you go around calling colored people black, everybody is going to expect you to call Indians Native Americans and cripples physically challenged, and after a while you can go nuts keeping up. It has nothing to do with how I feel about people who don't have the privileges I've got.

"Who is this?" Veronica says. She's miffed.

"A friend of your mother's. Your mother Murray Nobles?"

"Yeh." Mention her mama, and she eases up on acting like Wilson acts.

"Yeh? Just yeh?"

"Where's Mother?" she says, and I can't tell if she wonders whether her mama is alive or wonders whether her mama is standing right next to the phone.

"*Mother* is living under the interstate ramp and begging people for food, that's where *Mother* is." I'm sure Murray doesn't like being called Mother any more than me.

She's silent for a full minute, and while the time goes by very slowly I wonder if this is a toll call, crossing area codes and everything. I don't want Wilson to wave a phone bill at me and tell me I have a lot of nerve. "This a toll call?" I say.

"Lady, I don't know where you are. I don't even know *who* you are."

I apologize. I tell her I'm in Evanston, hating myself for maybe sounding snobbish, because Wilson likes to wave around the fact of living in Evanston, like it's Oxford in England or something. Though walking around the streets here, strangers automatically look at you like you're more intelligent than they would if they saw you on any street in New Orleans.

"How do you know my mama?" Easing up even more. She'll drop some verbs if I keep at her long enough. I'll like her a lot better. It'd be like Wilson calling me Mama.

"I gave her a hamburger. She was sitting on a bench on Lee Circle, starving to death, and I bought her dinner. You know she's starving to death?"

"Do I sound like the sort of person who'd let her own mother starve to death?" she says. Loud. I want to say, "Yeah, you sound like one of those black people who vote Republican." I feel sorry for colored people who vote Republican; it's like they've joined a club that only lets them in because the law says it has to, and nobody knows the members are laughing at them.

"You ran off and left her with no money. An old woman with no money is not going to be buying cornish hens at Langenstein's."

She's crying, though all I hear are muffled whooshy sounds. When I was a girl, I couldn't picture colored people crying; I was even surprised that they bled red blood. I never saw one in private, and back then people only bled and cried in private. The television news has gotten me used to seeing brown arms and heads and bellies blown open, and brown faces wet from crying. Colored women are on the New Orleans news every day now, grief-stricken because their boy's been killed. Either they're teary-eyed and stunned or screaming and wailing so loud you want to holler at the cameraman to go home. I don't say anything for a long time. I can explain one phone call to Wilson. "I didn't call to make you feel bad," I say.

"I know," she says, so softly I can barely hear her.

I hear a little voice in the background, and Veronica says, "Hush, baby."

"Your mama says you have a beautiful child," I say. I feel a little bit like a phony saying it, because I don't know what a pretty colored person looks like, except Clifton Davis.

"Aw-w-w," she says, sobbing into the phone.

"What're you crying about, Mommy?" says this perfect little voice that, unlike my grandchildren's, has none of that flatness you get if you stay in the Midwest too long. Connor calls Coke pop. *Pahp.* It sounds awful. I ask Veronica how old her child is. "Four," she tells me, snuffling up a storm. "Hah, my grandson's five and he can't talk like that," I say. Murray would get a kick out of hearing that.

"She's a little woman," Veronica says, not proud and bragging, just sad. She's probably so lonesome that she's hugging the child half to death right now. It's not a good thing to do, but it's not my place to correct her. Barbara's trained me to swallow my ideas. She doesn't threaten to put me on the street, she doesn't look like she'll complain to Wilson, she just gives me this look that says, "You tell me one thing, I'll do the opposite."

I hear the groaning of the garage door at the alley at the back of the yard, and I tell Veronica I have to hang up. "Wait!" she says, like I'm holding her mother for ransom. I tell her I have a full minute; that's how long it takes one of those children to come buzzing through the house and catch me at what I'm doing: they throw doors open, think nothing of finding a rubbery old lady in her bra and underpants.

Veronica fires questions. She's a schoolteacher who doesn't mess around: seven times eight, ummm, *next*. I tell her everything I know, about Lee Circle and free dinners, but I say I don't want to tell her my name. She's got what she needs, but she says, "Why not?" She's got a point: the only thing I need to hold back is opinions. "Well, it's Ru, Ru Bailey," I say.

"Mommy?" the little girl says.

"Sh, sh, sh, I have a lot of figuring to do," Veronica says. "Thank you, Ru Bailey," she says to me.

"Don't spoil that child," I say and hang up.

I'm wiping my hands on my skirt like I've just fired a gun when Barbara and the children walk into the kitchen stomping snow off their feet and brushing it off their coats; the little one is doing a funny up-and-down dance, and I stop myself from asking her if she needs the bathroom. Barbara doesn't pay attention. "I have to call my mother," Barbara says. She's in her coat and boots, and she puts the receiver to her pink, icy ear, then holds it away and looks at it like it's burned her, shrugs, then dials, hitting two buttons, a trick I've gotten used to. She and Wilson have speed dialing, and I've sneaked a look at their in-ink list of most-called numbers. Number one is Barbara's mother, number two is Wilson's office; it goes all the way to ten, and I'm not on it. "Even if you don't come through the ravines, you're not going to be able to get here to see the kids for days," I hear her saying. Pause. "It's still going to be falling,

Mom." *Mahm*. People around here are country; they think nothing of going twenty miles to visit, sleeping over when they get stuck. You don't do that in the South unless you're under nineteen years old, not even if a hurricane's coming. The Greenes will wind up here tonight, and they'll act like sleeping on the sofa is perfectly fine, though they're people who get squeamy when the housekeeper doesn't get in twice a week and change their sheets for them. I don't want to see these people. I've been here for weeks and the only time I've seen them was the Friday dinner right after I arrived. Marge said to me, "Sorry about Woodrow, I guess it was all for the best," and I smiled and said, "No, it *wasn't*," and I've managed to have a headache every Friday night since then.

The children go insane when the Greenes walk in. Marge is carrying a plastic bag of Hershey's kisses that cost her a little more than two dollars, but Jessica snatches it and they run from the room to divvy it up like it's a sack of money. Marge hands her fur coat to Wilson, turns to me and says, "Barbara won't touch it; she'd throw red paint on it if she didn't know me personally." She laughs, and I like her for a second.

Connor runs into the room, a ring of chocolate around his mouth, and Marge backs up. She's wearing a white wool dress, something she should have thought about when she bought the candy. Mealworm gallops right behind him, and Connor waves an unwrapped chocolate above his own head, which is so high I'd have thought Mealworm would have given up on any hopes of getting it. "You can't give him that, he'll mess on your mommy's floor," Marge says sweetly. "Before or after he keels over dead from chocolate poisoning?" I say, and pluck the candy from Connor's hand. He lets out a screech that at that age Wilson would have held back, even if somebody'd put a hot poker through his belly. Connor hollers, "Jessica only gave me eight!" and all the grown-ups look at me like I've stolen candy from a baby. "You going to poison my dog?" I say and I hold the piece of chocolate as high over his head as he held it over Mealworm's. "Yes!" he screams. "Well," I say. "I only got eight!" he says, louder now. "Are you going to kill my dog?" "No." I give him the candy. "Mother," Wilson says. I pick up poor Mealworm, who's shaking all over, but if I'm honest I know he does that because he's a chihuahua, not because he has any sense. His brain and skull are the size of a walnut in its shell. "Don't worry," I say to Mealworm in a grown-up voice. Talking baby talk to dogs is as foolish as talking baby talk to babies. "I would suggest putting him outside," Wilson says, like he thinks I've written him off anyway so he might as well suck up to the Greenes. "The Greenes aren't even driving home in their heated car on a night like this; I don't think a poor, hairless dog from the Deep South would last five minutes out there," I say to Wilson. He just shrugs, says, "Mother still is adjusting to the climate," to the Greenes, and offers drinks all around. I ask for a Pimm's Cup; I'm not going to give these people one more reason to laugh at me behind my back.

Barbara sends Wilson halfway to the airport to get delicatessen food, though it's snowing like crazy. I see Bernie Greene slip a hundred-dollar bill to Wilson, and I see Wilson take it like it's his due, and I would give anything to run up and press my own hundred on him, but Wilson took me out of New Orleans so fast that I never made arrangements to have my checks forwarded. Besides, when I got on the plane for Chicago I wasn't thinking about much beyond the given minute, as long as I had a round-trip ticket and a carrying crate for Mealworm. I owed Murray for the four cigarettes, and I sat by that library the rest of the night waiting for a way to repay her when I had no money, watching Dustin, finding the words to send him back to his house, making no other plans. I have as many as three checks piled up in my post office box, and I get through the days here by figuring I'm earning something sitting still, taking whatever Barbara and Wilson buy for me. They tell me to write what I need on the grocery list that hangs on the corkboard in the kitchen, like I'm going to tell people what brand of deodorant I use. I don't write anything, and Barbara buys extra of what she uses and sticks it in my bathroom, and I have to give her credit, because I'd have thought she'd have gotten me either the cheapest or the most expensive stuff, both being ways of looking down on me. Wilson buys me cigarettes every week with no messages, except that he gets those long Virginia Slims that are so low in tar. I only smoke in the backyard, since Barbara took me aside the night I got here and said, "Wilson's absolutely paranoid about cigarette smoke since his father died, you know," and I wanted to say *I hear you* because it's exactly the right words, but it's the wrong person. The next day I was in the yard trying to pull hot smoke through my mouth while my nose was taking in icy air, and Connor came outside to watch. "I want to see you burn the house down," he said after a while.

"Then where'd you live?" I said.

"In a tent," he said, delighted.

Wilson asks me to ride along with him, the way somebody might ask a child who knocks over lamps; he's probably thinking that the Greenes will say he's a saint, or whatever it is that Jewish people say. We ride along, say nothing; the radio plays classical music, which Wilson ought to remember bothers me because it doesn't have words to help me keep track, and I'm not nervous about the snow. I've never been in snow before except the three times it's fallen in New Orleans and the one time Woodrow took us across the Rockies in June, but already I'm getting a sense of the stuff, and I can tell that it's dry and sticking and solid to drive on where there's salt on the streets. "I'm going to pay you back, you know," I say after a while.

"Do not worry about it, Mother." He lowers the volume on the radio a little bit.

"No, look, I'm going to write down everything you pay for, keep track, pay you back when I get home, get on my feet."

"You are my mother," he says. "Do you want to bill me for the eighteen years I lived with you, plus all I have borrowed?"

"Don't think it never crossed my mind," I say, and he laughs. "That man gave you a hundred dollars."

"That is like a dollar to anyone else. You become accustomed to it."

I remember feeling like a dollar was a hundred dollars only a few weeks ago. "I guess you can get used to anything," I say, and I see Wilson stiffen up; that means he thinks he's going to get hit, and I say, "Don't worry, you don't have to get used to me."

"I never became un-used to you, Mother," he says quietly. I carry the cold cuts out of the store, hold the bag on my lap in the car, carry it back to the house from the garage, do my part.

We're going to eat in the kitchen at a big old round wood table that's sticky whenever you touch it, and Barbara has set out paper cups and plates and napkins, but in the middle of the table is the bread from the deli, wrapped up in a pressed linen napkin. Wilson says the Greenes have been acting a little religious since that messiah in New York died of old age, which is all backwards in my opinion, though I haven't told him that. I try to give Wilson a look, so he'll know I feel sorry for him, being the odd man out, but he doesn't let me catch his eye, and when Bernie starts to pray I clear my throat. He stops and looks at me, and I whisper, "I'm not Jewish." They all smile like I've hit on some private joke, so I say, "Well, Wilson's not Jewish, either," and they give each other meaningful looks and burst out laughing. This time I make sure to catch his eye. "You Jewish, Wilson?" I say. He looks down at his plate and says, "Sort of."

"Sort of, nothing," Bernie says. "The Nazis come marching through here, there's a paper with your name on it, says you're about as Jewish as you need to be to get carted off to the ovens."

"Thanks a lot, Bernie," Wilson says good-naturedly. I'm so angry I can't see two feet in front of me, and I go running upstairs to my room. I hear Wilson say, "Thanks a lot, Bernie" again, and he tears up the steps behind me. I shut the door behind me, but he catches it before it clicks and comes in right after me.

I tell him he should get out. "I am not Jewish, but you are pushing me almost to wish I were," he says.

"I don't have anything against Jews, I don't mind having my son marrying one, I don't even mind all that business of waving their hands over a loaf of bread in front of me and talking in jibberish, but what're you doing, Wilson? You come from a good Christian family."

"You never set foot in a church more than about twice in my entire life, and only then for weddings and funerals."

"That's beside the point."

Wilson's watching himself in the mirror, not self-conscious, but curious about how he's looking here, and his face calms down, and he says, "Look, if you must know, it was an accident. I told Barbara, all right, we will raise Connor Jewish, so she went to the reform rabbi, and she said she wanted Connor to be Jewish. So he said, 'Well, your husband ought to come to classes,' so I went to classes, very docilely, all the way through her pregnancy. Mother, it is not a bad religion, it is a sort of non-religion. Anyway, Connor was four days old, and we were going to have him circumcized, so the assistant rabbi came to the hospital room, I thought for some preliminaries, and he began praying, and before I knew it I was Jewish. He had seen me at classes, and he thought I was converting, so he was saving me travel time or something. Jewish, as easy as that. Listen, you can wave your hands over me and say I am a robin redbreast, but that does not make me one." He's still looking at himself in the mirror, and he smiles.

"It's true what Bernie says, you know."

"Society learns from its mistakes," he says, with the voice of an Organic Evolution teacher who knows these things. "We are not going to have another Holocaust."

"At least not in *Illinois,*" I say.

Wilson likes how patient he looks in the mirror; he's giving himself sympathy. "Look, Mother, this is not a big deal."

"I don't want to stand around and pray," I say, not saying that I especially don't want to stand around and pray to a God who's always trying to get even. I hope they can't hear me downstairs, and they probably can't. Everything gets lost in this house. "I was trying to be polite because Barbara's about to explode. Though I can see why." I'm imagining Marge giving Barbara a sack of candy and sending her off to another room. "Marge was rude about Woodrow, you know."

"This is my home, Mother."

"Then you never should've brought me here. I didn't like using the bushes for a bathroom, but it beat this. At least when you're on the street, everybody else out there doesn't act like they're better than you."

"I guess there are no Jews on the streets," Wilson says, not sounding like his self-controlled self.

"Probably *not,*" I say, giving it back, but he doesn't flinch. "But there're a lot of black people out there."

"Black?"

"Yes, black. That's what they want to be called, you know."

"Right now they want to be called African Americans."

I slap him across the face. He sees himself getting it in the mirror, sees the red mark come up out of the white of his skin, sees the hurt expression on his face. "I think you should say that you are sorry, Mother," he says, still watching himself in the mirror.

"Son, I was trying," I say. "Please give me credit, I was trying." He backs out of the room, closes the door behind himself. Gently, so I can barely hear the click of the latch. I say, "Sorry," in a low voice. Neither one of us will really know if he heard me.

23

Zib

EACH DAY ANGELA GETS A YEAR OLDER. LEAVES ME BEHIND. I sense now that she's almost seventy years old. It's time for her to die. It's all right for her to die. She's been in a hepatic coma for three weeks. Lying in Charity Hospital, where she's guaranteed to go out in a body bag. Even the medical school doesn't want her when she's finished bloating up and turning bloodless and waxy. Like a rutabaga, Mama'd say if she saw her. My mother used to say that nobody in Charity Hospital was worth saving. Which didn't offend me. Because Mama didn't think of herself as good salvage, either. She didn't put it on paper, but she wasn't interested in drastic measures. "I get like this, take me out in the backyard and shoot me," she said when Pop got sick. We were in his hospital room. Pop said, "Give me something to live for, Ru." Without opening his eyes.

Today's Thanksgiving. Even at Charity it's time for calming down about everything that makes you angry. I sit there on that ward. Sometimes six hours at a stretch. There's so much kindness around me. I wonder if it'll travel through the air and infect me. Like tuberculosis. It's four o'clock. I'm back at Angela's house for an hour before I go to work. At Winn-Dixie on Tchoupitoulas. I feel right about calling Wilson. Up to the moment Barbara answers. I can hear her disgust through the receiver. I tell her it's Zib. She says, "Oh, God." Like I've been calling every hour on the hour for days. Instead of having been out of touch for a month. "Well, I'm happy to talk to you, too." I say it with a cheerful voice. She says, "Sorry. It's insane up here with my parents and your mother and Wilson's kids, and I have a splitting headache, and the button hasn't even popped up on the turkey yet."

"My mother?" I say. She slipped her in with the crowd. But Mama's name stuck out like a fat girl in a beauty contest.

"Yeah, your mother," she says.

"Let me talk to Wilson," I say. She says she'll put him on. Goes off for a full two minutes. I consider hanging up. I don't have money to waste on long-distance calls. Finally I hear puffs of conversation coming toward the phone. Then Wilson. "Zib?"

"What'd she say, 'Your sister's on the phone'?"

"As a matter of fact, she was kind enough to whisper it into my ear."

"So Mama *is* there."

"Where are you?"

"Oh, God," I say. "Angela's going to die. She's really going to die, Wilson."

He asks me again where I am. I'm choking back tears so hard I can barely talk. "Here." He has tried to find me for weeks, he says. I smile. "I guess Mama really is there."

"I do not want to pawn her off on you," he says. All bristly. Like he could have been trying to find me just to see if I was all right. His tone makes me want to cry again. I haven't had more than five hours of sleep in as long as I can remember. I can cry at everything now. A gurney in the hall with a skin-over-bones old woman who gives me a full-denture smile. A nurse with a cross-eyed turkey pin on her lapel. The absolute toughness of Dustin. Who asked the clerk at the dry cleaners to come with him to school for grandparents day.

"What is the matter with you?" Wilson says softly.

"Angela's going to die. Any day now. She's going to die."

"You hate Angela with every fiber of your being."

"You motherfucker," I say. I hang up. But he doesn't know where to call me back. I dial his phone again. He picks up on the first ring.

"No kidding, I mean this in the kindest way possible. What are you so unhinged by?"

Dustin is in the front room. He's watching *It's a Wonderful Life*. He's making silly comments to the air. "Oh, God, Wilson. This is *hard*," I wail. "So hard."

I hear somebody come into the room where Wilson is on the phone. He covers the receiver. All I hear is his voice saying, "I will tell you later." I ask him who that is. He says Barbara. I tell him not to tell Mama I'm on the phone. I can't cope. "Though she'd probably say exactly what you're saying," I say. I still feel like crying.

"All right, start from the beginning," he says. He's using that quiet voice. The one that used to make me slug him in the stomach. Now it calms me down.

"I came here looking for Mama," I say. I walk the portable phone into the bathroom. To get a long piece of toilet paper to blow my nose. "So Angela gets sick. I mean *instantly*. The minute I come to town. Though it's no accident. And no coincidence. She's going to die. She's never coming out of this coma. She looks about a hundred years old. And she has this kid."

"Holy shit," Wilson says. This is the first time I've ever heard him say *shit* without sounding like he's quoting somebody else.

"This kid is incredible. But, God, I can't handle this. It's killing me. I mean, he's no trouble or anything. You don't even have to make sure anybody's watching him. He goes off like a street dog. And he always has a little money. You don't even really have to worry if he's getting food. But I can't exactly *leave*, you know?" Wilson's quiet for a while. Then he asks if I want him to call me right back on his nickel. The dollar or two isn't worth owing my brother. He could easily walk away from the phone, having called me back, and feel like he's been generous.

I tell him I can afford it all right. Not to worry. I can hear the pellets of curiosity rattling around in his head. They're challenging him to find a clever way to learn where I'm getting money. "Winn-Dixie isn't like a university," I say. "You can transfer from one to another. If they want you badly enough. Nothing lost." It's a lie. I had to yell and scream and threaten a lawsuit over the phone. And send everything about my life documented and notarized before Mr. Scamardo let me stay here. He told me I could have my job back if I ran out of dying people. He has problems with personnel turnover. He's in a market where everybody's transient. I want to think I'm only a statistic. "You coming back for your furniture?" Mr. Scamardo said. I couldn't tell what answer he wanted. Maybe he wanted me to come there one more time to say good-bye. Or maybe he wanted me to leave my things in Florida so I'd come back when I ran out of dead people. "I don't have any furniture," I said. "Well, I'll buy you dinner if you're around anytime soon," he said.

"I was not prying into your personal business," Wilson says.

"Pry away."

"Well, where are you, for starts?"

I tell him I'm at Angela's. I give him the phone number. He knows the address. We knew the street number of every house on our block when we were small. Wilson was always trying to figure out how a block with five houses could be numbered 2001, 2023, 2025, 2039, 2041. Every block on the street, on every parallel street, too, had the same set of final digits. *I* wondered what the address of the cemetery was. A mailbox hung on the gate. Though I never saw mail in it. Finally I asked Wilson. He said, Look it up in the phone book. And there it was. Number 2000. With a phone number and everything. That's when I got a healthy respect for the magic of telephone books.

Wilson weighs his words carefully. As always. He's had the habit since long before he started living among geniuses who are mean as hyenas. "So what exactly is going on with Angela?" he finally says. What he means is, "What's with you with Angela?" So I tell him all about Angela herself. The hepatitis. The three Scotch-and-waters. The way she's all ballooned in that bed in Charity. Dripped full of clear sugar water. Each day filling fewer plastic bags with thick brown piss.

"You sit there for hours," he says flatly.

"Look, I don't know why. I know you want to know why. And I can't tell you."

"I have to say I am impressed." I feel good. Then he says, "Father was lying in his own bed, in his own house, urinating in the commode, not wanting to die, and I did not see you moving back to New Orleans. Not even for five minutes." He says it gently. With no venom. And I start crying so loudly that Dustin comes running into the room. A tiny smile of alarm is on his face. "It's okay, she's okay, this's my brother," I say, choking.

"You scared me to death," he says matter-of-factly. He turns and goes back to his television set. I've had the house hooked up with cable. You'd think I've given Dustin a million-dollar stock portfolio. He takes it that seriously.

I can't stop crying. I breathe in. Images of Pop come to mind. The pitiable images of him. In his bank uniform with sweat stains on a hot afternoon. In the backyard on Sundays trying to toss a football at a reluctant Wilson. All the air rushes out of me in a wracking sob. I see nothing in my mind's eye until I try to inhale again. "You ought to talk to Mother," Wilson says.

"Where was she?" I say. I use up all the control I have over my voice.

"You have to appreciate the irony in this," Wilson says. "She was camping outside the downtown library." I tell him that's not funny. Having one pitiful parent is more than I can stand. "You have permission to laugh," Wilson says. "Mother thinks it is hilarious. She has gone around Evanston telling everyone that she evened up the score with the library for turning me into an egghead. She was using the bushes for a toilet, for God's sake."

"Jesus, she's not a woman you're exactly going to feel sorry for," I say. I laugh in spite of myself.

"I am glad you called," he says. Not in a hanging-up way.

"Well, I feel better. Though for the life of me I don't know why. Wilson, I'm scared shitless."

"That is Angela in the bed, not you."

"Oh, I'm not scared of dying anymore," I say. There's something about being on a ward at Charity for hours on end. I see no drama in Angela. Only her steady breathing. That craggy line on the monitor. The numbers going up and down. I distract myself with what happens to everybody else. I've seen three deaths down there. One was very quiet. The way I expect Angela's will be. A black woman so old that she looked old. All alone. Found in the early morning by a nurse. Removed in silence. With no curtain drawn. The other two screamed for hours. Vigorous and alive. Then lapsed into mumbling silence, calming me. Then screams, this time from the women at their bedsides, erupted once again. I'm unafraid of death. Nobody seems to die from dying.

"Animals do not fear death; they just fear the pain that accompanies it," Wilson says.

"Oh, have you interviewed several?" I say, then giggle.

"I just do not think animals grapple with the notion of nothingness," Wilson says. Deadpan. Then he giggles, too.

"Clearly they've never worked checkout at Winn-Dixie," I say. Now we're laughing together. Loving each other.

"Do you want to talk to Mother?" he says.

"Leave it to you to ruin a perfectly good conversation," I say. I'm still laughing.

"May I tell her where you are? She is so nervous about running up bills here that I guarantee she will not call you."

"Don't. I'll know what she's thinking."

Dustin phones me at the Winn-Dixie at one in the morning. I'm running around. Trying to get the checkout candy racks refilled by spoiled private-school kids who think it's cool to have a job.

"They say to come down," he says. His voice trembles hard. I can hear it over the din in the store. "I said can I come down, they said all right." He lets out a polite little cough.

"Oh, Jesus," I say. I stop myself from panicking in front of three kids waiting for me so they can punch out.

"Come *on*, Zib," Dustin says.

It will take another hour to get the store closed. If I go now I'll have to leave it in the hands of children. Children willful enough to go running down the aisles throwing open boxes of corn flakes all over one another. Then quitting and laughing about it. Or children so preoccupied with secret longings that they simply and honestly forget to lock the door. I tell Dustin I'll be home in an hour and a half. Tops. "You know that's going to be too late," he says quietly.

"Oh, no, it's not," I say. I screw up my face to keep from crying because these kids would enjoy it too much. One girl says, "Anything I can do, Miss Elizabeth?" But the rest are suppressing a laugh. "Punch out, punch out," I say. They recoil as a unit. Punch their cards quickly and mechanically. Like they're doing a remake of a Charlie Chaplin film.

"Hey, Zib, this's the first thing I ever asked for," Dustin says softly. Almost apologetically.

"Look," I say, "you call a cab. Get that twenty I've got on top of Angela's dresser. I'll meet you down there. I promise."

He begins to snuffle. "I can't do that," he says. He's right. Charity Hospital is as big as two city blocks. The only reason I've been able to find Angela is that I was with her when the EMTs brought her in. I followed her to the bed she's in now. I noticed landmarks along the way. "No cab companies come for little kids," Dustin says.

"Wait," I say to the girl who offered to help. She cuts her eyes at her friends. Like she's gambled and lost. I ask her if she can do me a personal favor. "What," she says. Like I have to come up with the right answer or it's too bad. I haven't inspired loyalty in these kids. But I'm supposed to hate them. And they're supposed to hate me. "Look, I have to close. And I need to get my kid down to Charity Hospital. You've got a car, right?"

She puts her hands on her hips. Like she's been waiting for this moment. "I've got a car. Like, I've *even* got a license. And you know what it says on the back of the license?" She fishes in her wallet. Which I know is full of fake ID cards that she and her friends make on their personal computers. She flashes a driver's license in front of my face. "It says, like, if you're under seventeen years of age, you're not supposed to be out driving after eleven. And guess what?" She waves her hand toward her two friends. They're standing in the doorway to the office. Transfixed and thrilled to the marrow. "It's about one o'clock in the morning, and you know what? The Winn-Dixie is putting a half dozen sixteen-year-old kids out on the street every night, just waiting to get pulled over by the police. I think if we're like killed, you're probably responsible. Besides, I have no idea on earth where Charity Hospital is."

"Get out," I say. They all back out. They wait until they think they're out of earshot. Then they high-five one another and break out in nervous fits of laughter.

The phone's gone dead in my hand. When I ring back the house nobody answers. "Shit," I say and slam down the receiver.

I get the store closed in an hour and a half. I do everything myself at high speed. At Angela's house, the lights are out. And my mother's car is gone. The police found it two weeks ago. The three Lafitte Project boys who stole it made the mistake of speeding in a school zone on Rampart Street. I've kept it parked out front in case Mama came by. Dustin's only limitation is his pipsqueak voice. He can drive a car. He can find his way through the maze of corridors of Charity Hospital. He just can't phone United Cab and get anybody to take him seriously. He's obviously tried before.

I don't waste time going into the house. I keep going, speed down Claiborne Avenue. I dare the police to pull me over. I'd like to flaunt the importance that comes from emergencies. Fifty-two in a thirty-five zone. Nobody is on the street here at Martin Luther King. Where I've read about three fatal accidents. And I don't even live here. I take the downside of the overpass at sixty. Ingmar Bergman's Death isn't looking for me tonight. I always park next to the nursing school building. There's one meter that's had its head sawed off. It took me three days of feeding quarters to other meters before I discovered it. But I pull up and find Mama's station wagon parked in my spot. Neatly. Parallel to the curb. The car is large and sincere. Not like when Mama was tearing down the Virginia highway in it, daring anybody to get in her way. I circle around for no more than a minute, break a few small laws. I get as far as the public library. Decide to play it safe. Go over to the dollar-an-hour garage at Tulane.

Dustin is sitting on a folding chair in the hallway when I run up. His hands are folded in his lap. He's staring straight ahead. His eyes are so wide I can't see the lids. I tiptoe up to him. My heart's pounding. I whisper his name. He doesn't turn. Doesn't blink. Finally he says, "I told them you'd be here by three. They said they'd wait until three. I don't think it's three yet." I kneel down in front of him. I take his chin in my hand the way I've seen good people do in movies. My hand's shaking. "Wait?" I say.

He nods. Way up and down. Probably so he can get my hand off his chin. "It's not your fault that you didn't get here on time. *I* barely got here on time. Though the nurse said she was waiting for me." Now he looks me in the eye. "You think she was waiting for me?"

"*Tonight* she was waiting for you," I say. He starts to cry. I stand up. Step back. Like he's a man who, for once, has the right to cry. But he stops fast.

I'm standing in front of him. Not thinking. Not feeling. Not knowing for an absolute fact that Angela is dead. A woman walks up to me. She's wearing a laminated badge. At her waist where I can't read it. She has that look that nuns have. Of plainness so extreme that you look for a smidgen of beauty and still find none. She puts her hand on my shoulder. It's cold through my shirt. I let her lead me away from Dustin. He's still sitting with his knees together and feet on the floor. Only now he's bent over slightly. His face in his hands. Not crying. Just avoiding.

I want a polite word. A politically correct word. Though Angela would think nothing of saying, *So, she crumped yet?* "Is it over?" I say finally. I think I've found a phrase that covers every medical, emotional, and religious possibility. Unless somebody feels like quibbling with me about how smoothly a good person can move over the cusp from life to afterlife. The woman nods. I don't feel sadness. Just the memorableness of the moment. She asks me if I want to see her. "I'm not sure," I say. I've never seen a dead person before. Except every relative of Angela's who got painted up and laid out at Lamana-Panno-Fallo. And the three old ladies who died on the ward, at night at a distance. "It looks like she's sleeping," the woman says. So I follow her onto the ward. The curtain's drawn around Angela's bed. "Oh, shit," I say under my breath. The woman's step doesn't falter. So either she's not a nun or she's spent enough time at Charity to be realistic. I walk slowly. With one hand extended in front of me. Like I'm moving through pitch dark. She opens the curtain at the foot of the bed and slips in ahead of me. I can look first over her shoulder. Angela from here looks no different from the way she did before. Except that the tubes and wires are gone. I feel a peace in her dead presence that I never did in her living one. "What'm I supposed to do with her?" I whisper to the woman. I tiptoe toward the head of Angela's bed. I've read about near-death experiences. Part of me believes that Angela is still floating around over this tiny space. Watching. Curious and smirking. I sound very responsible. I suppose Angela is getting a good laugh. There on the ceiling.

Looking down at her own body the way they do in those magazine articles. I'm close to her face and not frightened. All nicely rounded and drained of anger. Angela looks exactly like she did when she was ten years old, telling me what to do. I shake my fist at the ceiling. I think I can see where her spirit is hovering. I say, "Goddamn you, Angela, quit making fun of me." I laugh nervously. The woman backs off a little. Like she's being thoughtful. I turn to her. In a matter-of-fact voice I say, "Her only relative's a ten-year-old boy." The woman nods. "I'm just her neighbor. Well, her former neighbor. I mean from when she was growing up. Her best friend from when she was growing up. I'm not even Catholic." The woman looks relieved. She doesn't have to strain to minister in the middle of the night. She asks me whether Angela has insurance. I look over at Angela and let out a little snicker for her benefit. "How're you supposed to get life insurance when you're (a) destitute, and (b) dying?" I say. I feel like I'm Angela now.

"Well, there are things we can do here, though I think she had Hepatitis C, so that may have complications."

"You mean cadaver lessons versus potter's field," I say. I'm on a roll.

"Would you like to step out into the hall?" she says. She's giving me meaningful head tosses to the left. Toward the part of the ward where a few women are sitting with dying relatives.

"Sorry," I say. I'm back to being Zib again.

I can see Dustin down the hall from here. Once again he's sitting up. Brave and still. Like he's waiting for his turn at the dentist. I tell the woman I have to find out what Dustin wants. "I thought you said he's ten years old," she says.

"Which means *he's* going to remember this," I say. I imagine the Technicolor, inflated-to-bursting images Dustin's going to carry in his head until he dies.

She pulls me over. Her icy hand takes my arm instead of just my sleeve. "He doesn't have any good choices, you know." She's whispering with pity in her voice. I feel like saying, *He can have whatever he wants. He wants a fur-lined casket and six limousines, five of them empty, I'll go to the credit union.* I look at him. What I notice are his shoes. Size five black Nikes. Dustin wears size three. But Angela found those Nikes for him at Thrift City next to the bowling alley for $3.50. Dustin treats them like silk slippers. He's adjusted his gait ever so slightly so his heels don't come out with each step. "He's not stupid," I say to the woman. I walk toward him. She hesitates. Like staying put will buy her indulgences. Then she follows me. Mincing along, three paces behind.

"Angela didn't plan for this," he says. Before I can open my mouth to speak.

"*I* thought she'd live forever," I say. I kneel down. I give him a tentative little smile. It occurs to me that the woman is grimacing behind me. I hope Dustin can see her, see that she's a fool.

"Angela?" I hear her say.

"That's my mother's name," he says evenly. He's dry-eyed and a little dazed. Children don't react much to death because they so thoroughly don't believe in it.

"Um, Dustin," the woman says. She has the high treble of a social worker. "Um, you know, this is a sad time. It's all right to be sad."

"I'll be sad if I'm sad," he says patiently. The woman looks down at the floor. The toe of her shoe scuffs halfheartedly at a flattened piece of gray chewing gum. It's been waxed over a hundred times. It's as easy to extract as the trick quarter embedded in the cement outside that bar on Chartres Street.

"Look, Dustin," I say gently. "I'll put it to you straight. When a person dies, you have to do *something*. The hospital'll handle it. If we don't. But I'll help you out. If you want. You know? I mean, there's a graveyard for people with no money." I don't say that last week a man walking his dog around the potter's field found a human foot sticking out of the dirt. "Or you can maybe give her body to science. Or, if you want flowers and stuff. All the limos and everything. Like they have across the street from your house. Well, I could probably lend you the money. You know, payable in twenty years or something." My mouth is clacking dry.

He takes a deep breath. "You know how your mama had Mr. Bailey in a box? Like she could take him where she wanted. For a kid my age, I think that'd be good." He turns to look up at the woman. "I would like her in a box, please," he says. As nice as you could want. Like he's in Gambino's asking for a dozen glazed doughnuts.

24

Wilson

SHE WOULD NOT ADMIT IT, BUT MY MOTHER HAS BEEN AT WAR with the Greenes since we sat down to dinner, waging battles comparable to the skirmishes of the American Revolution, when the British stood up straight and proper and clean in their bright uniforms, fighting truthful battles according to convention, while the Americans were scruffy and dirty and made strategies up as they went along. "Oh, I should have offered to make the oyster dressing we always had at Thanksgiving. Remember how I made that oyster dressing, Wilson?" Mother says as Barbara serves up a modified kosher meal. I whisper to her that the Greenes have decided that oysters are not allowed. She behaves as if this is news to her, and possibly it is; I myself would not have categorized mollusks with crustaceans. I also know that some people know little more than that pork products are off limits. But I see subliminal signs of frustration in my mother, and I know she would find a way to get even if she could. "Why?" Mother says.

"Dietary laws date back thousands of years," Marge says in a tone she would be wise to save for very small children.

"Don't you think it's a little silly, living by rules that were made up a couple of thousand years ago when nothing was clean, and now everything is? I mean, if there's cholera in the oysters, they'll tell you, you know," Mother says. Barbara starts to explain to her why Jews observe such laws, and that is a stretch for Barbara, who agrees with my mother on this topic and knows her own mother *used* to agree. I wave my hand at Barbara from my end of the table, shake my head no so she will remember with whom she is dealing, but she ignores me. Mother interrupts. "I apologize," she says to Marge, then she eats in silence. A month ago she was rationing out her money for a meal a day at McDonald's. Into the silence that is interrupted only by noises of tongues and palates and mouthfuls of thick food, I say, "We have a lot to be thankful for, kids."

"Yeah, right," Jessica says. Bernie pushes his chair back and stands up so fast that I would not be surprised if he hit her, though she is not his grandchild. He is two seats down from me, and I grab his arm. "Get out, Jessica," I say.

"I was just kidding," she says.

"You know what the trouble with you kids is?" Marge says. I see a scowl of annoyance on Barbara's face, and I breathe in. "The trouble with you kids," Marge says, "is that you never lived through the Great Depression."

"Marge, your idea of the Great Depression was watching the maids handing bread out the back door to beggars," Mother says, and oddly enough I can tell that she is trying to be conciliatory.

Marge puts down her fork, scans her audience quickly. "Well, Jerusha, as I recall, you told us years ago that the only hunger you felt growing up was the week or two your mother put you on a diet. And we did *not* have a maid." She takes a sip of wine, playing fair, smiling triumphantly.

"Maybe I lied," Mother says, and she continues to eat.

"Grownups aren't supposed to lie," Connor says.

"Get real," Jessica says and looks around.

"Well, they're not," Bernie says.

Mother puts her fork down noisily, avoids hitting china or crystal, but splatters cranberry sauce on the tablecloth; my mother is experienced in doing only harm that fades—bruises and welts and memories. To my surprise, she looks sad. She turns to Connor, who is probably wondering when he will get an opportunity to slam a fork down on a table. "You want to hear a lie, Connor? What'd your daddy tell you I came up here for? Because my house burned down and I need to visit until they could build me a new one, right?"

"He said you were lonesome," Connor says, his eyes wide and unbelieving. He is the third child of four, and he never has spoken before at a family gathering without interrupting someone.

"Lonesome!" Mother says.

"What did you want me to tell a five-year-old child?" I say.

"Connor, you ever see people living downtown in cardboard boxes?" Mother says. He gives her a look of noncomprehension, and Jessica pipes up, "That was on *60 Minutes* last week, Connor. Oh, right, your mother doesn't let you watch television. Well, *I* know about homeless people, Gammy."

"Oh, hush up, Jessica," Mother says, and I have a freeze-frame of memory, of our kitchen table on Valence Street: *Oh, shut up, Zib.* "Well, Connor, I *wasn't* lonesome. And I didn't have a cardboard box. But I was living on the street. I slept in the bushes."

"Where'd you go to the bathroom?" Connor says, and Barbara slams the palm of her hand against her forehead, kicking her eyes half up into her head.

"In the bushes, Connor, in the bushes," Mother says.

"Cool!" Connor says, and Jessica reaches over Eric and slugs Connor hard on the arm.

Bernie, who is a ravenous eater, especially when someone else is providing, has put down his fork. His face is pale under his year-round golfer's tan, and I wonder whether he is having a heart attack. "That is god-awful, Jerusha," he says, his voice full of more sympathy than I imagine my mother could take even if it were spread over a lifetime.

Mother looks at Bernie, but I know she is talking to me. "It's not god-awful. I didn't mind it one little bit. I'd still be there, thank you very much, if *somebody* hadn't decided that he was supposed to take care of the entire world and come running down there waving plane tickets at me and acting like I was going to die any second if I didn't come up here." I see her giving me a glance to be certain I am listening. "I tell you what, Bernie: I looked at the *Sun-Times* this morning, and it's sixty-four degrees in New Orleans today. I could've sat on the foot of that statue of George Washington by the library all day and gotten a suntan that'd make *you* look like a bottom-feeding fish."

David has said nothing today that did not involve accepting food and drink. He wears his depression as a shield. Being glum saves him the trouble of having to be politic, because it saves him, too, from having to speak. I imagine that his food goes down hard, his punishment for a dry mouth, and because he is my friend I do not press him at these gatherings. No one presses him. Rather, his parents divide up his air time between themselves. "I don't know why I come to these things," David says.

Barbara begins to cry tearlessly, and the dining room becomes silent except for her sobs. No one is looking directly at her, no one else notices that, though she means it, she does not feel it. I look over at David, who is sitting next to her, and he shrugs, as if she is a piece of electronic equipment that he never is going to figure out. Mother has resumed eating, though she is taking great pains to ensure that her fork makes no noise against the plate as she picks up food. I catch Marge's eye, and she points at me. I shake my head no, point at David, and Barbara sees me, throws down her napkin, and storms out to the kitchen. Marge mouths to me, *This is* your *responsibility,* scurries behind Barbara as if she were our runaway child in a department store. No one speaks, and we can hear Barbara in the kitchen. "This is *my* house. I want them all out of *my* house." Her voice is dry and clear.

Children react to an adult's histrionics the same way they react to a snowstorm: either they are so awestruck they fall into silence, or they are so stimulated they lose control. My children lose control, push back their chairs, clamber down and run off to other rooms, find reasons to squabble, then run back to the table, take a handful of food, shove it into their mouths, go off again, and leave trails of greasy turkey skin, crumbs, and smashed green beans. Their noise makes Barbara louder, and Bernie puts his hands to his face, blocking out everything. Mother continues to eat, does not look up; David eats while staring at the empty chair across from himself, expertly finding food without looking. The meal is over; I am fooling no one by sitting anchored in my place, waiting for them all to come to their senses and have dessert.

The phone rings, and when I choose to ignore it and it continues ringing, my mother surprises me by pushing slowly away from the table and shuffling off to answer. Before I can catch Bernie's eye to give him a conciliatory *Women!* look, I hear Connor scream. I take the stairs three at a time, find him standing in the doorway with his $125 model steam locomotive clutched so tightly in his hand that the pistons never will rotate again. "What is your problem?" I say.

"I don't want Eric to touch my train city," he shrills, and I look past him, see Eric sitting silently next to the controls, waiting expectantly, willing to abide by my decision.

"Eric never did anything wrong to your train set," I say. "Look, Connor, he is only going to be here three more days."

At that Connor shrieks as if threatened with a knife, and I pry the train engine from his hand before it becomes a nugget of scrap metal. He fights me back, and I can imagine the little wheels bending so that they never again will sit right on the roadbed. I grab his wrist, shake it over the rug, and he holds tighter. "Let the godforsaken train go," I cry, and Connor screams back, "I hate you," and I slam him so hard against the wall that the locomotive flies from his hand, lands on the wood floor, and crumples in on itself. I can hear Barbara downstairs, shouting at her mother, "How can that woman complain that Wilson wants to save everybody? It doesn't cross his mind to save *me*."

The thud brings them all upstairs. "You should've done that four years ago," my mother says, ignoring Barbara, folding her arms across her bosom and not moving.

"No, I should not have," I say, and then I begin to cry, put my head on Connor's tiny shoulder and sob so hard and wetly that I almost cannot breathe. Connor stands stock-still, his arms at his sides, and only when Eric walks over and silently pats me on the head does Connor move; he places his hand tentatively on my back, then strokes me so lightly I can barely feel his touch. I look up and see Barbara shrug; she heads downstairs, tugging Marge behind her.

"I got a phone call a few minutes ago," Mother says. "I'll be leaving soon." She turns and walks away. She gave me those beatings the way some people give black pepper to dogs to make them mean, and I am no more heroic and steely than I was at birth.

No tending is done before bedtime. David has slipped out hours before dusk, but nine people still are in the house, snow-bound, and our orbits do not intersect, as if each of us is a guest waiting for the host to become organized. Food hardens under a patina of grease on the plates, on the table, the turkey carcass sprawls on the sideboard with enough meat for another meal, dries out and turns gamy, a Boston cream pie sits in the warm kitchen air, still shiny under a perfect spiderweb of white sugar on the chocolate, filling with salmonella. The children are shoeless, their fingers sticky, and no one speaks to them. I walk from room to room for hours, catching no one's eye, finding one child after another dropped in place as if felled by poisonous gases, and at ten o'clock I crawl into my side of the queen-size bed with my clothes on.

I awaken hanging off the edge, a tiny foot positioned neatly against my left kidney so I will experience intense pain if I do not heft my body in whatever direction the foot wants it to go. I reach behind my back and gently grab the ankle to which that fierce little foot is attached and with a single swift movement turn Morgan ninety degrees clockwise, so her head lies in the valley between the bed pillows. She is face-down, but she will not suffocate. I father children with amazing breathing systems that protect them from choking and smothering and even from whining, though not from burping and snorting. I can hear Eric sawing twigs on the throw rug at the foot of the bed, his eight-year-old epiglottis flapping delicately.

I roll over and see Barbara, and her expression holds no gratitude, though my having moved Morgan's foot out of my kidney also has moved the child's head out of the warm cave between Barbara's breasts and her belly, a place where I have found refuge a time or two, closing my eyes and breathing in her late-night muskiness. "I heard what you said in the kitchen last night," I say.

"I don't care whether you heard me," Barbara says groggily. She swings her backside down like solid ballast so that she lies on her back, and she folds her arms across her chest, stares at the ceiling.

"I know you better than to believe that," I say.

"I don't care what you believe."

"I know you better than that, too."

She turns her head toward me. "Trouble is, you *don't.*" I want to cover my ears, as if I am in a frightening movie and can protect myself from the bad part. "You know the day I told you I was in love with someone else? And your only reaction was to go jump on a plane and look for your *mother?* Well, I could have had him."

My blood freezes, turns to sludge, cuts off sensation to my hands and feet as if they are asleep. "Could have," I whisper. "You *could* have?"

"I don't know," she says miserably. "Maybe *did* have."

"For a woman who did not censor herself last night, you certainly are being cryptic."

"He wouldn't make love to me."

I feel no relief; she went so far as to picture herself with someone else, not in a daydream, but in his presence, her eyes on his body, her hands reaching out. "He said it was because I was married. I didn't say I'd leave you. Maybe I should've said I'd leave you."

"You did not sleep with him?" My mouth is dry, my senses free enough for an olfactory hallucination of Safeguard soap fresh on her skin.

"No, but I could have. I know I could have."

"It helps that you did not," I say, cocking my head to the side, trying to make her smile.

"Maybe so," she says. "Maybe so, but I don't believe that yet."

Morgan flops over onto her back, and her arm lands on my diaphragm with surprising force. I lift her like a bag of wet sand and toss her gently to the foot of the bed. Her eyes do not open, but she crawls back toward me, butts me with her head. I push and tuck her slowly until she is all the way onto Barbara's side of the bed, her toes, her elbows, loose strands of hair. "Please do not ask me to help you sort it out," I say. Barbara does not say anything, and I am afraid I will doze off the way a man does when he has had children so long that he settles for what sleep he can get. "If you want my attention, you have succeeded," I say to keep myself awake. She does not flinch. "Look, I love you," I say. Barbara looks in Morgan's direction, as if seeking permission. "Sometimes I hate you, Wilson," she says quietly, and sits up in the bed as if she is leaving. I take her wrist, which I still can encircle with my thumb and index finger, hold her back, say nothing, lie here until I feel no resistance from her, let go, and she lies back down. I watch her muscles loosen, hear the catch leave her breathing.

"Mother says she is leaving soon," I whisper. Barbara looks at me to be sure I am serious, and her eyes smile. I break into a grin that bares my lower teeth, and she leans across Morgan, plants a tentative bad-breath kiss on the corner of my mouth.

"I was turning into her," I say. "I think you woke up one morning and found a big old hairy Jerusha Bailey staring at you."

"What I find in my bed never surprises me anymore," she says, and leans over across Morgan and kisses me with her mouth open and her tongue probing for a split second, leaving me with a pang of regret. I look down at Morgan, who sleeps so deeply that she can be moved from place to place, subjected to the roar of a vacuum cleaner, and does not waken, but who will spring to life at the sound of a first sip of hot coffee three rooms away. Without Eric on the floor, I might draw Barbara to me, but Eric has such tender sensibilities that I try never to risk anything in his presence, certainly not lovemaking, usually not even angry thoughts. "Maybe you should grow a beard," Barbara says.

"What?"

"You know, cover your chin. I can see her chin on you. I really don't want to look at a bully's face every morning. She's a bully, that's what, a weak old angry woman who beats up on everybody. You don't owe her anything."

I feel no need to share with Barbara my feeling that maybe my mother is not so bad, either as we perceive her or as she once was; even if she conceded that that was possible, she could argue effectively that change of any sort does not eradicate old damage. This is not the time for such a discussion. "I could send her money," I say.

"You don't owe her anything," she says again.

"Sending her money would make her miserable. Does that help?"

She gives me a qualified smile. "Nope."

"I have been a little crazy since my father died, you know."

"So get over this dead-father shit," she says, but I cannot laugh this time.

My father handed over his paycheck every two weeks. Then he waited for his food and turned off even sixty-watt bulbs and waited to die. When the time came, after almost fifty years of waiting, he was not ready. "I do not want to scream the way he did," I say. "He did *not* go peacefully. You are supposed to go peacefully, unless you are pinned under a truck."

"You talk to people. You probably talk to more other people in a day than he did his entire life. At least you used to.

You're not going to scream, Wilson. I'll be standing right over this bed, healthy as a horse, and *I'll* see to it that you don't scream."

The phone is on my side of the bed, and I have the right to refuse to answer it, but when it rings Barbara is too curious, so I pick up. I hear only silence, then one good soggy sniff-back of mucus. "Oh, Wilson," she says. "I've been so business-like." She sniffles again.

"Zib?" I whisper, and Barbara groans, turns over to face the opposite wall.

"I swear, I haven't cried—well, maybe once, for about two seconds, but Jesus, Wilson."

"Oh, Lord, she died," I say.

Barbara sits up, jostling Morgan, who squirms the way she does before she wakens and shrieks as if she is being born all over again. "Who?" Barbara says.

"No one," I say, and Morgan sits up, too, opens her mouth to fuss, and I motion Barbara to get her out. "Hey!" Barbara says, and I say I am sorry, and she asks me again who died, making me pay the price for her cooperation; I say Angela—a name will hold her for a while. She picks up Morgan like a baby monkey and marches out of the room.

"No one," Zib snuffles. "That's about right. What a waste."

"She was not stupid," I say. "She could have *done* something."

"Well, actually, she did," Zib says, with a you-walked-right-into-it tone.

"Wait, wait," I say.

"Wait what?"

"You are about to jerk me around, Zib. And I only woke up five minutes ago."

"My best friend just died, Wilson." She is trying to sound wounded.

"Am I wrong?"

"Look, I just had this terrific idea. I mean, I wanted to tell you she died and everything—I'd have called you anyway—but I've been sitting here for, what, three hours, and I'm trying to think this through like a sane person, though I haven't had any sleep in as long as I can remember, and I got this idea. How about I trade you Dustin for Mama?"

I begin to laugh so hard I kick my heels up and make the bed covers dance, and Eric sits up on the floor, looks around, sees nothing but me, and lies down again, satisfied.

"It's not *that* funny," Zib says. She is about to burst out laughing, too.

"Hey, I tell you what, I will throw in my José Canseco and three frogs," I say, and laugh again.

"Aw, shut up, Wilson," Zib says, giggling and sniffling.

I catch my breath, ask her what she plans to do now. "I didn't expect her to die," she says.

"Did they not give you a prognosis?"

"If they did, I didn't pay attention. They bring so many little teenage doctors through there playing guess-the-diagnosis that after a while I'd hide in the hallway when I saw them coming or they'd have started looking down my throat and telling me I had six weeks to live."

"Do you have AIDS, by the way?"

"Not funny, Wilson." She pauses for a second. "Matter of fact, I probably don't. I got a blood test. Negative, but you never know. I'll do it again in a couple of months. But the guy was an intellectual. Intellectuals don't get AIDS."

"Tell that to the arts community in New York City," I say.

"I mean straight intellectuals."

"I am sure you do not have it," I say, and I mean it. But I also do not want to give Zib permission to decide she is dying so she can run off to work out her days at the Kathmandu Winn-Dixie.

"Look, you've got four kids. What's one more? I mean, this is the easiest child ever born on earth. It's like Angela said to God, 'Hey, don't send me more than I can handle,' so he sent her all she could handle, which was zero. This kid probably changed his own diapers."

"So you keep him."

"I don't know how," she wails, and if she were in the room right now, I would fantasize about shaking her by the throat so that her brains rattled into place, like coins in the exact-change machine on the bus.

"For Chrissakes, this is not a puppy you picked up at the SPCA on a whim. You cannot pass him around until you find someone with a big yard. And you cannot take him back to have him put to sleep when you change your mind."

"I'm here helping out Angela. She was supposed to get *better*, Wilson."

Eric sits up on the floor again, gets up and crawls into bed with me. He lies neatly on Barbara's side, until I motion to him to come close, and he wriggles up under my arm and freezes in position, breathes shallowly, as if he is playing a dead body in a television close-up.

"I cannot take him," I whisper, covering the receiver so Eric cannot hear me. "I have come too close to failing the family I have already. I go slapping the name Bailey on anything that moves; that is not enough. But do not leave. I will send you money, I will let him come up here on vacations or something, but please do not leave."

"I'm not like you." I hear regret in her voice.

"I do not know what to tell you, Zib," I say and hang up.

25

Jerusha

SINCE I TOLD WILSON I WAS LEAVING, HE'S LOOKED AT ME LIKE I'm a cat that's sat in his kitchen, drunk his milk, and kept one eye on the door in case somebody opened it wide enough. I could tell him the truth, that grown children have no business taking care of their parents, and vice-versa, but he's been around the Greenes too long. They spend every nickel in their pockets on you, tell everybody they're doing it, then go home and fuss because they're put-upon. Wilson would say, *Oh Mother, I owe it to you; I will take care of you for the rest of your natural life,* and then he'd crawl into bed every night with his wife and listen while she said, *Jesus, you wouldn't believe what that old bitch did today.* I'd watch them, catch her cutting her eyes at him, and I'd have to see how far I could go before they couldn't stand being nice. Or I'd become one of those whipped-down old women who baby-sit and wash out the pots, full of gratefulness and empty of everything else. Murray lasted with Veronica two days before she knew she was in danger of turning into a hollow fool. "Baby, she had no *idea,*" she said to me on the phone. Yesterday, Thanksgiving, she was in a New Orleans hotel room where it cost seventy-five cents to call out locally, a dollar-fifty a minute to call anywhere else. "See, I done assume she so mad at me, she know I'm on the street, she don't give a shit, but the girl run off to Chicago, figure I'm set for life, what with that pension. She send me a birthday card that June, I don't answer, she figure I'm still mad. Honey, we setting up in the Royal Orleans, she buy me everything in one of them little shops, none of this dry rot like I used to get at Krauss. I mean, I got me a bra from Victoria Secret. A forty double-D, I ask her, 'Who going to want to look at some droopy old cow in purple lace,' the girl in the shop hear me, she treat me like a queen, tell me, 'Hey, you not dried up yet, not by a long shot,' and here I am, no teeth you can call my own, hairs growing out my chin, she telling me some man going to want to look at this. Girl, they treat you fine when you got money, don't you let nobody tell you no different."

"Uh-huh," I said. "And what's Veronica want?"

She chuckled. "Nothing. Excepting my heart and soul. She say we going to Chicago tomorrow, she got a two-bedroom apartment. She figure I pick up the baby after school, I save her on day care, do a little ironing, save her on the laundry. I say, 'Lincoln done free the slaves,' and she all hurt, but no way I'm a go to Chicago."

"They don't ask me to do anything," I whispered. Barbara and Marge were hollering in the kitchen, ten feet from me, but I took no chances. "But they *still* own me."

"I hear you."

"You happy?"

"Shoot, woman, I been eating garbage for a year and a half, sleeping on the cement, now I'm setting up in a snooty hotel in the Quarters, I can order prime rib at midnight I feel like it, you want to tell me one good reason I *ain't* happy?"

"Because of tomorrow."

"What you trying to do?" Murray said, like she'd known me long enough to talk to me that way.

"I'm not trying to do anything," I said.

"Well, you sure throwing ice-cold water on my good holi-day." She said nothing for a dollar's worth of long distance. When she spoke again, her voice was sad. "Lord, I love that grandbaby. I took her a picture. Veronica got bad taste in men, but she sure know how to pick one going to make a beautiful child."

I asked her whether she'd seen Dustin. "You know, I been looking for him. Not by the library, no, but on the street. Danc-ing. We been out in the Quarters last night, leave the baby with a sitter, a college-girl *white* sitter, and go up to some boys out there tapping so hard they money fly out they pockets, and I say, 'You know a white boy name of Dustin?' They say yeah, but Dustin been staying away, no accounting for what he up to. They busy, though, them boys make good change money; maybe I ought to go putting me some bottle caps on my shoes." She laughed.

"You know, you're all right," I said.

"I think you turning out all right, too. That's why I call."

Barbara was mewling in the kitchen, Jessica and Connor were flap-mouthing all over the house, Bernie was sitting at the table holding his breath until I thought he'd pop. I kept on eat-ing, tried to pay no attention, but then I went into the back family room downstairs so that I could get out to the yard for a smoke, and there was Mealworm, leaning up against the skirt of the sofa like he was trying to blend into it. And in the middle of Barbara's nineteenth-century throw rug—which had no busi-ness being in a room where everybody went to begin with, but where Marge insisted she keep it so every visitor could see what a generous mother she was, passing on an heirloom while she was still alive—there in the middle of the rug was a little pile of chihuahua cannonballs, stacked in a pyramid like they belonged on a model of a Civil War battlefield, stinking to high heaven. Seeing me, Mealworm whimpered, and I knew I had to get out of Chicago before I started messing up in spite of myself, then leaning against the furniture and whimpering. I left the dog shit where it was. Barbara won't notice it for a week.

Yesterday afternoon I told Wilson I was leaving, and this morning when he gets out of bed I tell him that I've called the airline, that I can get on the nonstop tonight, that all it'll cost will be a $25 surcharge on my open-return ticket plus freight for Mealworm. When we left New Orleans, Wilson bought me a round-trip ticket; I told him I wasn't boarding any plane unless he did, and he bought it to shut me up, rather than have the ticket agent call security and tell them that this looked like a kidnapping to him.

He doesn't argue with me about leaving tonight. We are sitting at the breakfast table, and Marge is asking Barbara for CoffeeMate not cream and Equal not honey and Diet Mazola not butter every time the poor woman sits down. "It's a long trip to the airport," Marge says. "Maybe you should wait until he's taking Jessica and Eric." "No problem," Wilson says. He takes care of his mother, who asks nothing unreasonable. "Where'll you go when you get there at ten o'clock at night?" Barbara says. "She will manage," Wilson says.

Connor pitches a hissy because he wants to ride with us to the airport. The three others are waiting to see what they can negotiate if Connor wins. "If you tell him yes, the rest are going to want to come, too," I say.

"Will you be quiet in the car while I talk to Gammy?" Wilson says to Connor.

"You ever see a five-year-old boy come within two miles of an airport and keep his mouth shut?" I say pleasantly.

"I can just *look*," Connor says, hitching up his shoulders.

"I'm riding in front," Jessica says.

"No, me," Morgan says.

"Jesus," I say, and I put Mealworm down on the floor. He's wobbly on his little legs, having taken his travel pill an hour ago, and I think about picking him up again, but we're going to be standing here for a while, and I take off my coat, too.

"Look," says Wilson, so tired I wouldn't blame him if he hollered. "Look, you four all stay here, I will take you down to the beach and let you climb on the rocks first thing tomorrow. I will be all yours."

"Big deal," Jessica says, and I fold my hands up inside my sweater.

"I am going to count to *one*, and if all of you haven't gotten out of this hallway, your daddy's going to come home and find you dead," Barbara says, looking sideways at her father, daring him to move a muscle.

The children scatter and I burst out laughing, and Wilson picks up my valise, which has enough strong clothes in it to last me until it gets too hot to breathe in New Orleans. I put my coat back on, and before I leave I scoot into the back room, pick up the dog poop with a tissue, and flush it down the toilet in the powder room.

We pass the sign ENTERING SKOKIE, and after having driven in silence for ten minutes Wilson takes in a deep breath and says, "Mother, I have something to tell you." Wilson's about to confess something. When he was small, he confessed a lot, until he figured out that it didn't win him anything, and then he quit confessing, instead spent a lot of time wishing and straining and praying that I wasn't going to find out. "Zib is in New Orleans."

"Stop the car," I say. He keeps on driving. "For Chrissakes, Wilson, you did this on purpose."

"I have been trying for two days to get up the nerve to tell you. There was no opportunity."

"If you're screwing around on your wife, *that's* when you need an opportunity to tell."

"If I am screwing around on my wife, I am not going to tell you."

"Hell, Wilson, I don't care." He catches a yellow light and sails through it. I'm not going to have a lot of time before I get to the airport at this rate. "But I want you to tell me what I'm supposed to do about the fact that I'm getting on a plane in an hour and a half, I've got my dog drugged into a coma, and you pick now to tell me she's home."

"She is not *home*. She is in New Orleans. New Orleans is a big city. You can stay away from anyone you want to."

"New Orleans is the smallest town on earth. I get off that plane, I guarantee you within an hour somebody who knows Zib is going to see me."

"Zib is willing to take you in, if you must know." He has a tiny smile on his face; he's not telling me the whole truth.

"Wait. She lives there?"

"Well, in a manner of speaking." Wilson comes up on a yellow light and stops for the red, and I hear a car behind us skid. "As long as I am at it, Angela died."

I consider that possibility. "Don't give me that. Angela's going to live forever. Angela probably took out a million-dollar life insurance policy and faked her own death."

Wilson pulls over into a McDonald's parking lot. "I am not kidding, Mother. She spent about a month in a hepatic coma. You cannot fake that."

"What about the boy?" I say.

"That is why Zib is there."

"Oh, shit," I say. "Well, all right."

After he's unloaded my valise in the departures drop-off lane, Wilson hands me two hundred dollars in cash. "This will carry you until you are settled," he says. "Especially if you go stay with Zib." I tell him I have about three good checks waiting for me at the post office. "Well, stay in a hotel tonight."

"With a dog?" I say.

"There are places. Just *ask*."

"I'm allergic to asking," I say, and he laughs.

"I am only letting you go because you were going insane in my house," he says solemnly and looks around like one of the guards on the ramp will come up and shoot him for taking more than a minute to tell his old mother good-bye.

"I wasn't going insane in your house; *you* were going insane in your house, and you know it."

"You are not exactly the first person to tell me that."

"You let yourself get used too goddamn much," I tell him. It is freezing, but I don't mind. Mealworm's in his carrying case on the ground in front of me, and I turn the carrier so the wind won't come through his little window.

"Barbara thinks she uses me too *little*."

"Barbara needs to get rid of Marge and Bernie. Nobody owes them anything. Their daughter wouldn't lose control of herself if they'd done right by her."

"Oh, Mother, please," he says.

"Look, son, I'm just telling you, take care of yourself. I mean, take care of *yourself*." He hugs me, and for the first time since he's been an adult I'm not bothered by it, probably because I'm so cold out here. When I walk into the airport, I don't look back.

A half dozen blind people have checked in for my flight. They don't have their dogs, but they're all getting by with white canes, and most of them have come out onto the concourse by themselves. One blind woman winds up in the seat next to me on the plane. I edge around in my seat so I'm facing her, and I clear my throat, and she looks me straight in the eye, even though both of her eyes have a thick egg-white patch in the middle of the blue. "You have a dog?" I say, and then, so she won't think I'm blind and start talking shop, I tell her, "I mean, I can see; I'm just asking."

"Yeh," she says, bristly. "He can't fly in the passenger section." I tell her I know, that I have a dog on board, too, and I imagine a half dozen German shepherds breaking loose in the baggage compartment and making an in-flight snack out of Mealworm. "There must be six or seven of you on this plane," I say.

"What's that supposed to mean?" she says, and I consider sitting back in my seat and not moving for two hours so she'll think I've disappeared.

"You can't see," I say.

"You mean I'm blind." I tell her I'm sure a fancier term has been invented by now. "Visually impaired," she says. "Personally I can't stand euphemisms. I'm blind. Period, paragraph." She smiles, and I chuckle a little so she knows I'm smiling, too.

I don't need to read a magazine or wish for a cigarette. I can watch this woman the whole time without her knowing it. She sticks her finger in her Coke cup until it's full. She even whips out a little computer and pushes keys that aren't on a typewriter, and a piece of what I guess is a poem about leaves comes up on the screen, and I read the poem and notice that she has a gray mud puddle and brown leaves and fire-red pyracantha, and I want to ask her where she learned about color, but I keep my mouth shut and watch until we dip over Lake Pontchartrain on our final descent. She returns her seat and tray table to their original upright positions and stows her computer under the seat in front of her, and the only giveaway is that she holds her head up straight, like it's too heavy and will wobble off the stem of her neck. Now that I can see the city skyline off the left side of the plane, I think about what I'll do when I land. I ask her where she's staying in New Orleans with a dog, and she tells me the Hyatt, that's where the convention is; they have a little patch of grass out back for dogs, and I ask her what she's paying. I can get in a taxi with her and the rest and pretend Mealworm is a genius, and she tells me eighty-five dollars a night, like that is some fabulous bargain. I settle back for the landing, try to figure out what those blind people will do at baggage claim, and wonder what I'll say to Zib tonight when I pull up in front of Angela's in a taxi.

Zib

Ten-year-old children don't kill themselves. Or go on psychotic rampages. As far as I know. But I'm not taking any chances. Ever since I brought Dustin home this morning, he's been acting like the maître d' at a fancy restaurant. Like the guy who makes sure you see his molars when he smiles. And Dustin smiles a lot for somebody with no reason to. "We'll go home in my car. Take the streetcar back down. I'll drive my mother's car back home," I told him when we walked out of Charity. "Well, I'd never drive in broad daylight," he said. And smiled. It's midafternoon. I've paced through this house for two hours. Moved fast so I can keep from thinking. And from noticing Angela's things. Dustin shadows me for the length of a room. "What you need is a nap." He says it in his sweet maître d' voice. I gently grab the front of his T-shirt. "That woman at the hospital was a first-class asshole." I say. "But she *was* right."

"When I'm sad, I'll know it." He remembers the only re-mark the woman made to him.

"Christ, I don't know what to do with you," I say. I want him to dissolve into tears. Then I can cry, too. A crinkle of worry crosses his face. "You don't have to do anything with me. Really." He grins idiotically. I say, "Well, I'll do *something* with you." I pace. I pick up Angela's things as I go. I put them in plastic bags. Take them out. Put them back where she left them. I pat the dog until his jowls clack. He's not looking sad. Except that he's naturally sad-looking.

The grinds and moans of Pro Skater come from Dustin's room. Then silence. I tiptoe to his doorway. He's asleep. With Tony Hawk in midair on the screen. I tiptoe out again. In the kitchen I pull out the phone book. To see my options. If they're to be found at all, they're in the sixteen blue pages. There are 272 pages of business listings to the sixteen for government. I don't have to wonder how Republicans feel about such a system. Possibilities for help are so thin. I try to remember what I was looking for in the phone book that morning in the hotel with Angela. It was the yellow pages that fell on the floor. They made a sound so enormous that the people in the room below would have cursed me. But the sound had no impact on Angela. I hold the white pages tightly. I go in Dustin's room. He's still as death. I back out. I hear an ear-splitting scream from his room. Though I'm holding the phone book tightly. He's sprawled across his bed. On his back. His arms are loose at his sides. "I *can* hold my breath!" he screams. He's holding his breath at the bottom of a dream. In reality he's inhaling deeply. Getting ready to scream again. "Seven minutes, it's a world record!" He starts to sob. I reach out to touch him.

My fingers brush his cheek so gently that I'm sure he can't feel them. His fist comes up. Makes contact with my jaw. Then flops down loose on the bed. "Damn you, Dustin," I say. I want to slug him the way my mother slugged me when my only assault on her was a sassy word. But I know better. His eyes open. He looks bewildered. But he swims up fast from sleep. From holding his breath and proving himself. He says, "I didn't mean to fall asleep."

I have to work tonight. From six until closing. I bring him with me. I am not about to leave him in the house with just the dog. He's groggy and fighting sleep. And he's behaving so beautifully. If I were he, I'd break out in a full-metal rage. He sits on the bench next to the pay phone. With a box of sixty-four Crayolas and a roll of cash-register tape. He rations both out to himself so carefully. I want to go over, scribble down the crayons, unroll the paper, shout *There's more where that came from!* He makes Christmas decorations. He's inspired by the load of Scotch pines outside the store. It sends its clean smell through the door every time a customer leaves. Dustin alternates among violet red, magenta, maroon, brick red, and red violet. He's giving his plain red a rest. He has less luck with the number of shades of green. Jungle, forest, pine. He asks permission to use olive for Christmas. "I'll buy you a box of eight with all regular colors, ease up," I say. "Wear that regular green down to a nub." He smiles. Shakes his head no. His strokes on the paper become lighter. His drawings are quite fine. A bag boy or two has come past and said, "Hey, little man, you've got major talent." Dustin has pressed his lips together with pleasure.

I don't notice that my mother's walked into the store. Not until she's right up on me. Often I see women come into the store, and I think they're my mother. Though they never are. I think this is another optical illusion. Big breasts and a gray bouffant and a dare-me attitude. Though this woman looks less like my mother than others I've seen. I stand stock still in front of her. "You can hug me if you want." She says it more quietly than I've ever heard her speak in public. I put my arms around her. I wonder how it will feel. She's so sturdy that I find myself holding tight. She gives me a few fluttery pats on the back. "I'm glad to see you," I say. Like she's a former employee who swore she'd never shop here after I fired her.

"Glad to hear that," she says. Like she's that employee who's decided this place is not so bad after all.

It's a slow time at the store. The night after Thanksgiving. Everybody's indoors and sated. Leftovers are fresh. Only the express line ticks away like crazy. People grasp milk cartons and whiskey bottles. They pay cash and scurry out because somebody's home waiting for them. I look past Mama. I spot her whale-belly car in the parking lot. I tell her I didn't know she was coming. "Well, that makes us even. I didn't know you were here until I was on my way to the airport."

"Wilson, Wilson, Wilson," I say good-naturedly. "Wilson, Wilson, Wilson," Mama says back, deadpan. I laugh. I throw my arms around her neck and hug her tight. "Hey," she says, embarrassed and almost pleased. I let go.

Dustin tiptoes up to us and stands next to me. Mama takes one look at him. "Oh, Lord, look at this child, sitting up in a supermarket in the middle of the night," she says. She looks around for somebody to blame. I tell her his mother died this morning. She says, "I know that. Where's the manager?" I tell her no manager in his right mind works past eight o'clock. I'm the one in charge. "Well, this is terrible," she says.

"I don't mind," Dustin says.

"That's what Wilson says all the time, 'I don't mind,' and look where it's got him," Mama says.

"She bought me sixty-four crayons and everything, I'm not upset. It's interesting sitting over there. Nothing good's on television tonight, anyway. They've only got reruns during vacation, you know."

I ask her how she got here. "You mean the car? Easiest thing I've done since Woodrow died. I know where the boy keeps his house key. I let myself in, found the car key, went to the nearest Winn-Dixie. Oh, shit, you feed that dog of yours,

Dustin? I threw Mealworm in the backyard. He's come this far, I don't want him getting eaten by that duffel bag you call a dog."

Dustin giggles on cue. "Zib works in a grocery store, Mrs. Bailey. We even get lamb-and-rice dog food. We don't run out of nothing."

"Anything," Mama says. "We don't run out of anything."

"Hey, ease up," I say. Dustin's grammar is his legacy from his mother.

"If I hadn't corrected Wilson all the time, where do you think he'd be right now?" she says.

"Working as an assistant manager in a Winn-Dixie," I say.

"Come on, Dustin, we're going home," Mama says. Dustin looks to me for permission.

"I'll be okay," I tell him. He doesn't move. Waits for something else. "I think we're all going to be living together," I whisper in his ear.

"Well, maybe Letterman'll be good tonight," he says. He trudges off toward the exit with my mother. He doesn't miss a step when he passes the bench and grabs his crayons and paper. He wasn't taking out more than one crayon at a time. In case he had to make a fast getaway.

Acknowledgments

REALLY, MY WORLD IS DEFINED BY SMOKE, IF NOT BY MIRRORS. My smoky-voiced agent, my fire-fighting husband. My delightfully incorrigible tobacco-fiend publisher and editors. My children who at least never touch a cigarette. And then all my good friends who defy categorization: the never-wills, the used-to's, the sometimers, the other-substance aficionados. I thank you all. Muriel Nellis. Ed Muchmore. Jack Shoemaker, Trish Hoard, and Carole McCurdy. Esme and Andrew and The Big Wern. Cherri Ainsworth, Jennifer Blalock, Rolph Blythe, Connie Buchanan, Beth Butler, Muffett Dingilian, Lynda Friedmann, Kathryn Harrison, Keltie Hawkins, John Hughes, Wendy Lestina, Nancy Maron, Drew McInvale, Heather McLeod, John McLeod, Joe Nellis, Elaine Polack, Werner Riefling, Jane Roberts, Talia Ross, Stephen Ruwe, Jane Vandenburgh, Margaret Wade, Chris Wiltz. Yes, mirrors, too, now that I think about it.